CINEMA INTERVAL

OTHER BOOKS BY TRINH T. MINH-HA

Drawn from African Dwellings.
In collaboration with Jean-Paul Bourdier, 1996.

Framer Framed. 1992.

When the Moon Waxes Red: Representation, Gender & Cultural Politics. 1991.

Woman, Native, Other: Writing Postcoloniality and Feminism. 1989.

En minuscules. Book of poems, 1987.

African Spaces: Designs for Living in Upper Volta.
In collaboration with Jean-Paul Bourdier, 1985.

Un Art sans oeuvre. 1981.

TRINH T. MINH-HA

CINEMA INTERVAL

ROUTLEDGE

NEW YORK LONDON

Published in 1999 by
Routledge
29 West 35th Street
New York, NY 10001

Published in Great Britain by
Routledge
11 New Fetter Lane
London EC4P 4EE

10 9 8 7 6 5 4 3 2 1

Library of Congress Cataloging-in-Publication Data

Trinh T. Minh-Ha (Thi Minh-Ha), 1952–
Cinema interval / Trinh T. Minh-ha.
p. cm.
Includes screenplays for A tale of love and Shoot for the contents.
ISBN 0-415-92200-3 (hbk.). — ISBN 0-415-92201-1 (pbk.)
1. Trinh, T. Minh-Ha (Thi Minh-Ha), 1952– Interviews. I. Title.
PN1998.3.T76A5   1999
791.43'0233'092—dc21   99-19959
CIP

CONTENTS

ACKNOWLEDGMENTS

Most interviews come with an introduction by the interviewer, which I have included here. To avoid redundancy, however, I have deleted the parts that give a bio- and bibliographical summary on myself. I would like to take this opportunity to thank all the crew members whose commitment and generosity remain the greatest support for the films. I also wish to thank the interviewers involved, as well as the editors and publishers who have given permission to reprint the interviews. Special thanks are also due to Hilton Tse for conscienciously scanning in all the photographs onto computer disc and doing a marvelous job on the touch-up work. Finally, this book simply would not have found its present intervals had it not been for Jean-Paul Bourdier and his art and design work.

ILLUSTRATIONS, FILMOGRAPHY, AND DISTRIBUTION

ILLUSTRATIONS AND FILMOGRAPHY

Photo design, layout, and story boards: Jean-Paul Bourdier. Photos on cover page: stills from *Shoot for the Contents* (front) and from *A Tale of Love* (back).

TL   *A Tale of Love.* 1995. 108 mins. Color. Distributed by: Women Make Movies; Freunde der Deutschen Kinemathek; Image Forum. (Print with Chinese subtitles at the Golden Horse Tapei Film Festival Archives.)

SC   *Shoot for the Contents.* 1991. 102 mins. Color. Distributed by: Women Make Movies; MOMA; Idera; Cinenova; Lightcone; Image Forum; National Film & Video Lending Service.

Surname Viet Given Name Nam. 1989. 108 mins. Color and B&W. Distributed by: Women Make Movies; Third World Newsreel; MOMA; Idera; Cinenova; Lightcone; Image Forum; National Film & Video Lending Service.

Naked Spaces — Living Is Round. 1985. 135 mins. Color. Distributed by: Women Make Movies; MOMA; Idera; Cinenova; Lightcone; Image Forum National Film & Video Lending Service.

Reassemblage. 1982. 40 mins. Color. Distributed by: Women Make Movies; Third World Newsreel; MOMA; Idera; Cinenova; Lightcone; Image Forum; National Film & Video Lending Service.

International sales for all five films: M&L Banks.

DISTRIBUTION

Cinenova
113 Roman Road
London, E2 OHU, United Kingdom
Tel: (081) 981-6828   Fax: (081) 983-4441
Email: admin@cinenova.demon.co.uk

Freunde der Deutschen Kinemathek
Welserstr. 25
D-10777 Berlin, Germany
Tel: (030) 213 60 39   Fax: (030) 218 42 81

Idera Films
Suite 400-1037 West Broadway
Vancouver, BC, Canada, V6H 1E3
Tel: (604) 732-1496   Fax: (604) 738-8400
Email: idera@web.net

Image Forum
Fudousan Kaikan Bldg., 6F
3-5 Yotsuya Shijuku-ku
Tokyo, 160 Japan
Tel: (81 3) 357-8023   Fax: (81 3) 359-7532
Email: nkj@imageforum.co.jp

Lightcone
27 rue Louis Braille
75012 Paris, France
Tel: (1) 4628-1121

M&L Banks
330 Fifth Avenue, Suite 304
New York, NY 10001
Tel: (212) 563-5944   Fax: (212) 563-5949

National Film & Video Lending Service
Cinemedia Access Collection
222 Park Street
South Melbourne 3205, Australia
Tel: (61 3) 99297044   Fax: (61 3) 99297027
Email: access@cinemedia.net

Museum of Modern Art
Circulating Film Library
11 W. 53rd St
New York, NY 10019
Tel: (212) 708-9530

Third World Newsreel
545 Eighth Avenue, 10th Floor
New York, NY 10018
Tel: (212) 947-9277   Fax: (212) 594-6417
Email: twn@twn.org

Women Make Movies
462 Broadway, 5th Floor
New York, NY 10013
Tel: (212) 925-0606   Fax: (212) 925-2052
Email: info@wmm.com

BEWARE OF WOLF INTERVALS

The relation of word to image is an infinite relation. What is released on the film screen is neither given up to sight, nor put safely under the shroud of invisibility. Between love and death, freedom and madness, the widest range of strange sound harmonies can be heard. Whereas between a passion and a passion, between a desire, a sickness, a pain of consciousness and another, endless modulations of dissonances are to be predicted. An image is powerful not necessarily because of anything specific it offers the viewer, but because of everything it apparently also takes away from the viewer. Nothing and everything, including specifically the ability to put into words what the body feels, to articulate or to name once and for all. Reaffirming the relation of word to image in its infinity is not merely saying that verbal language cannot capture with accuracy what lies on the other side of the discursive border, or that its function proves to be inadequate when the realm of activity involved is, for example, that of looking and hearing rather than of speaking and deciphering. Certainly, in their attempts to verbalize the exacting world of musical phenomenon and performance, musicians have time and again complained about the lack of precision of the linguistic system. But if seeing and sounding isn't saying, it's likely because words work best in relationships when they are taken to the very threshold of language—at once bound to and freed from external reference. The marking (with words) shows its limits, which are always at work in the speech-text. Words as words cannot speak for or be subordinated to the image. They can, however, deploy their own logic to indicate a direction, to bring into relief a landscape through which a film moves, and when treated as a sound world of their own, they render audible and readable the multiplicity of the interpretive process itself.

To keep the relation of language to vision open, one would have to take the difference between them as the very line of departure for speech and writing, rather than as an unfortunate obstacle to be overcome. The interval, creatively maintained, allows words to set in motion dormant energies and to offer, with the impasse, a passage from one space (visual, musical, verbal, mental, physical) to another. To prevent the passage from closing itself off and to preserve the infinity of the task of speaking nearby, a number of conversations developed around specific books and films are here further assembled in an interrelational space of detour. Just as the form a film takes in the creating process can acutely materialize what it says in content, the way a film is talked about can, when circumstances allow in the encounter between interviewer(s) and interviewee, be keenly tuned to the way it is made. It is with this in mind that the reader is invited to enter these conversations, whether he or she has seen the films discussed or not. Knowledge of the specific works is not indispensable, even though it may open up other entries into the texts gathered here. The relation of the discussions to the films is never one of unmediated explanation, but rather one of supplementarity—that is, of outsideness and of substitution, since a reality (filmic) is here replaced by another reality (linguistic) exterior to it. Anyone functioning in a society as steeped in media language as ours today can thus actively follow the interactions, for the questions raised around the works, and the (non-)answers elaborated often also revolve around general issues of ethics, aesthetics, and politics in image making, and require no expertise in film.

"Interval": the word itself does not bring about any tremor like "passion," "death," or "love." Thanks to it, however, a direct relation is possible: a relation of infinity assumed in works that accept the risks of spacing and take in the field of free resonances—or, of indefinite substitutions within the closure of a finite work. In filmmaking, the name historically associated with "the theory of intervals" is Dziga Vertov, whose Kino-Eye and cine-seeing once saved cinematography from "the frightful venom of habit." In his "Kinoks Revolution" manifesto, intervals are what cine-images, cine-documents, or cine-poems are built upon, that is: "upon a movement between the pieces, the frames; upon the proportions of these pieces between themselves, upon the transitions from one visual impulse to the one following it." *Between, between, from, to.* Vertov's sketchy elucidation seems to link the notion of interval primarily to montage experiments. Stressing the gaps between film images, it constitutes the foundation of a filmmaking that is decisively nonnarrative, "unplayed," and engaged in the art of life: a visual study of events, a simultaneous cine-writing of living processes, or as Vertov also called it, "fragments of actual energy (as against theatrical energy)." In his "hall of intervals" where "frames of truth" are minutely edited, all is a matter of relations: temporal, spatial, rhythmic relations; relations, as he specified, of planes, of recording speed, of light and shade, or of movement within the frame. Such a filmmaking is bound to rely, for its meaning and emotional impact, on each distinct image—not by itself in isolation, but in its full interactions with all the other images selected. Rather than limiting the scope of the interval to editing, however, Vertov's call to use the camera for its own properties—making an enthusiastic distinction between the cinema eye and the human eye—serves to further extend it. Like montage and like every single (other) film component, cinematography is in itself a multiplicity of cinema intervals. As the image arises, it vanishes, doomed to disappear for the film to be. But if the lamp is turned around, the nature of this generative container-contained nexus will show itself unequivocally: The cinema interval, which determines the fissures through which light surreptitiously penetrates the fabric of relationships woven in the vision machine, is also all that makes a film uniquely a film.

The gamut of possibilities that can be explored in the interval mode is vast. Intervals allow a rupture with mere reflections and present a perception of space as breaks. They constitute interruptions and irruptions in a uniform series of surface; they designate a temporal hiatus, an intermission, a distance, a pause, a lapse, or gap between different states; and they are what comes up at the threshold of representation and communication—what often appears in the doorway . . . there where the aperture is also the spacing-out of disappearance. For spacing belongs to neither space nor time alone. While the term "interval" is commonly used in music to refer innocuously to the distance between two notes determined by the relation of their frequencies or to the difference in pitch between two simultaneous or successive tones, the important role the interval plays in scale, temperament, and tuning systems can hardly be overlooked. The art and science of making music is largely consumed by the complex task of generating, arranging, altering, arresting, modulating, inflecting, distorting, adjusting, tempering, perfecting, purifying, setting, and standardizing intervals. A sensitive grasp of intervals remains essential to musicians (composers, performers, tuners, and music lovers alike) since melody, harmony, and rhythm are all based on intervals. Hearing intervals is part of the challenge of music education, as one learns to recognize them one by one the way one recognizes faces. Through the identification of intervals one is also conventionally tested for one's ability to locate the historical time to which a Western musical composition belongs. What stands out in each composer's work is his or her ability to control and play with intervals. Musicianship, some would assert, is basically a matter of intervallic mastery.

Each interval can have at least three or four sizes; the naming of these in the West—perfect, major, minor, diminished, augmented—tells of the dualistic and hierarchical system devised to exploit them for established "musical" purposes. Here also, in this part of the world where intervals are classified as consonant and dissonant and made to hate each other, the beats and the howls they release when combined together are called "wolves." Naturally, with the system of equal temperament that has been dominating Western music for more than a hundred and fifty years, the "bad" intervals and the disharmonies tolerated in earlier tuning systems have become aberrant and musically useless to the trained ear. Depending on where one's loyalty lies in today's musical terrain, diminished sixths, augmented seconds, and other disharmonies have come to be either the abhorred or the sought-for wolf intervals that one immediately notices as being out of place or "out there," and that one either avoids playing and drowns with skillful ornamentation, or features provocatively as one's best asset. As with all free play and innovatively unpopular moves, a wolf finding its function effortlessly or a wolf well placed strategically in a piece, has little to do with a wolf reactively or senselessly forced into it. The irony in the whole effort to temper everything equally is the fact that tempered intervals created with tones whose location lies somewhere between consonance and dissonance are intervals meant to fool the ear into hearing a semblance of harmony. Since the invention of equal temperament, to aim for perfection in intervals tuning is thus to yearn for that (unacknowledged) inexactness and impurity.

In the ancient Chinese style of writing—known as the Small Seal Script—the calligraphy for the word *Jian*, which means *interval, space, partition*, shows a doorway with the picture of the moon in the middle. No matter where one is in life, one still has an interval of time to use wisely, advises Deng Ming-Dao for whom, "the time when the moon shines through a doorway indicates both space and interval." In this locus betwixt the worlds of logos and mythos, lunar light has the quiet power to transform sleeptime into awakening time. The taste of the wild arises anew as one follows the call of bewitching forces unleased in nocturnal wanderings. From metamorphoses to metamorphoses, shadows to shadows, one is led, as the night mutates, to one's sudden encounter with one's own abyssal light: the wild self, the infinite self. In this (no)state of intense altered consciousness, one finds oneself being *of both*—of here and there, knowingly knowing not. The image of the moon in the doorway serenely summons up the opening of a passageway. Interval and partition, sleep and wake, wild and tamed, after all, are not a threat to each other when *spacing* is what every movement requires: what enters, exits; what dwells far in, travels far out. It is often said among the wolf people that life is an interval between birth and death—an interval hanging precariously between two seconds: one to die and the other to break through.

PART I

UPWARD

Diving In, Non-Seeing

empty boat passes by

blue light

A SCENOGRAPHY OF LOVE

with Deb Verhoeven

A shortened version of this interview was first published in *World Art*, No. 14 (August 1997) with the following introduction by Deb Verhoeven: "*The man who played an instrumental role in creating the idea of the screen lover, Marcello Mastroianni, described the love story itself as inherently difficult and invariably unnatural. 'The real language of love,' he said, 'is an inarticulate thing.' The difficulty of love stories is, in this sense, a formal rather than emotional matter. For Mastroianni, the language of love is never carried in words per se but can be experienced in the silver of a lover's breath, in the quickening of its rhythms. Trinh T. Minh-ha's most recent film,* A Tale of Love, *is also premised on the idea that love stories rarely capture the true experience of being in a state of love. The film was in part inspired by an epic Vietnamese poem, 'The Tale of Kieu,' written by the early-19th-century poet Nguyen Du. In Trinh's film, the story of a sacrificial woman who supports her family by resorting to prostitution has been extrapolated to the Vietnamese-American migrant experience. Trinh's latter-day Kieu is a freelance writer and photographer's model who sends money to her family in Vietnam. She is also in love with Love. It is Kieu's meditations on love — her conversations with her photographer, Alikan, and her friend Juliet (who firmly believes her Romeo will come) — that eventually unmask the gender issues she shares with her 19th-century namesake. What particularly marks* A Tale of Love's *unique contribution to the cinema is Trinh's experiment with many of those 'formal' difficulties inherent to the love story. Trinh has disconnected and intensified the visual and aural vernacular at her disposal in order to capture the unadulterated and elemental sensations that characterize a state of being in Love. The film presents to its audience partial views, saturated colors, elliptical narratives, sounds separated from context.* A Tale of Love *is a film that must be savored, but in the savoring there is always the unsettling knowledge of absence, of loss, and even perhaps of sacrifice.*"

Verhoeven: *I would like to begin on a self-reflexive note—with a discussion about the importance of the interview itself in your work. Unlike many filmmakers who see the interview as an unhappily necessary aspect of the publicity machine, it seems that you have elevated or emphasized the value of the interview in your films and publications. You use interviews in a quite complex way, especially in* Surname Viet Given Name Nam *in which you stage performances based on previously published interviews. And even in the film that lends itself most easily to the description "fiction,"* A Tale of Love, *you include detailed dialogue exchanges that revisit the structures and shapes of the documentary interview. Could you comment on the reasons for your interest in the interview process?*

T: The interview can certainly be an art, but it is also just one among the many possible forms of relating. I cannot say I'm interested in elevating it or emphasizing it. As with any structure that shapes one's activities—even momentarily—one cannot use it without being used by it, so I would rather explore and push it to its limits than ignore or take it for granted.

Questions and answers can sometimes force both interviewer and interviewee into awkward positions because we often feel compelled to bear the burden of representation. We know we are not simply speaking to each other or for ourselves; we are addressing a certain audience, a certain readership. And since we are framed by this question-and-answer mechanism, we might as well act on the frame. If we put aside the fact that the popular use of the interview is largely bound to an ideology of authenticity and to a need for accessibility or facile consumption, I would say that the interview is, at its best, a device that interrupts the power of speaking, that creates gaps and detours, and that invites one to move in more than one direction at a time. It allows me to return to my work or to the creative process with different ears and eyes, while I try to articulate the energies, ideas, and feelings that inspire it. It is in the *interval* between interviewer and interviewee, in the movement between listening and speaking or between the spoken word and the written word, that I situate the necessity for interviews.

In Chinese painting, Line is action; it is Form's frontier. You have given me here a very interesting line to open with, by linking the question about the interview to the dialogue exchanges in the film *A Tale of Love*. I did not think of the film's dialogues in quite the same terms, but your question reminds me that among the more recent poems I've written, there is one actually titled "Diamonologue." Since I've always worked at the crossroads of several genres and categories, it's true I've often been attracted to what one can call border terms, border texts, border sounds, border images. I've been told time and again in interviews or in public discussions that my "answers" to the questions asked are more like mini-lectures, that they characteristically touch on about five different issues at once. It's difficult for me to stay within the confines of a setup that often does not correspond to the way I think. I have to find a satisfactory way to address the question raised; satisfactory in that it gives something both to the listener and to myself. So it's important in interviews to let one's thoughts come to oneself of their own accord since the aim is not simply to provide answers, but to keep desire, the interval, alive.

When I wrote the script of *A Tale of Love*, I did not want to write mere dialogues. What comes out, hopefully, are not simply questions, answers, opinions, reactions, and so on between two people, but verbal interactions that lie between the soliloquy and the conversation. True, this is the way I've also been working with interviews, slightly enhancing their inevitably fabricated effect rather than hiding it. Both duration and interruption are necessary for certain things to emerge. The verbal events in *A Tale* are at the same time interactive and independent of one another. Each unfolds according to its own story, its own logic. There's no good or bad. I was indifferent to the tradition of psychological realism and was creating dialogues and characters that were not quite dialogues and characters. I used actors, but was interested in the intensity of a veiled theatricality, not in naturalistic acting. And what appeared as conflict never got resolved because there was truly no real conflict in the film. So the story I offer turns out to be in the end just a moment of a no-story.

V: A Tale of Love *was described as your first feature narrative—to which you have responded that you neither agree with the terms "first," "feature," or "narrative." How then would you prefer to describe your most recent film?*
T: The combination of these three terms subjects the film to a hierarchy, a category, and an order imposed from the outside, that is, from a tradition of making narrative and advertising it as a "special attraction" that has little to do with the film's own workings. "First" in relation to what? If it is in relation to my own artistic itinerary, then yes, everything I come up with is a "first." But if it is a question of making a debut in the art of storytelling, then no, because there are ten thousand ways to tell stories. I could never conform to an all-plot, action-driven narrative dictated by the mass-media model, with its unity of theme, time, place, and style, or with its clarity of story line, dialogue and character. I would rather work with film the way, for example, Heinrich Von Kleist describes marionettes and their unequaled dance movements: You find the centers of gravity as they emerge with the work, you give all your attention to where the weight falls, and the rest follows of its own accord.

The film is put together as a multiplicity of movements. Each movement has its centre of gravity; and centers do move, they are not static. This is very close to the notion of *ch'i-yun* (or spirit-breath-rhythm) that determines the vitality of a work and is the artist's sole aim in Chinese traditional arts. It's so easy to fall prey to what Raul Ruiz calls the "predatory concept" of cinema, a normative system of ideas that enslaves all other ideas that might slow down, distract, rupture, or put obstacles in its activity. Because of this exclusive form of centering, no human can come anywhere near a puppet, for Von Kleist, where grace is concerned. This can apply to *A Tale*, both literally or negatively, on the level of acting, and figuratively or positively, on the level of narrative structure. Acting, never free of affectation, should subtly be seen as acting. By subjecting all elements of cinema to serving the plot and to psychological realism, one simply buys into the normalized practice of commercial cinema, which can see multiplicity only as a threat. If I refuse such a classification as "first feature narrative" for *A Tale*, it is to invite viewers to come up with other ways of experiencing film. How they name and describe this experience is ultimately up to them as the naming also tells us about them as viewers.

V: *Why choose "the love story" as a key point of departure for the film?*
T: As a poet puts it, "Experience is an interval in the body" [Mei-mei Berssenbrugge]. It's such a precise statement and, for me, full of love. On the one hand, there's no cinema—only entertainment, document, information, technique, for example—if there's no love. On the other,

the entire history of narrative cinema is a history of voyeurism, and no matter what form it takes, the art of narrative cinema is unequivocally the art of resurrecting and soliciting love. A friend of mine once said that "all the books written and stored in the libraries are in fact one single book." You can never capture love or death on film, they are what I call, in A Tale, the two Impossibles. This applies to both fiction and documentary films the difference between which is more a question of degree. Death is a name by which we draw a limit to the unknown. Death is not bodies falling into a pool of blood, for example; nor is it cadavers, mummies, skulls, or skeletons on display. Death is in every moment of life; it is, crudely speaking, something we live with the moment we step into life. So although there's nothing more old-fashioned than narratives of love, we continue to produce and consume what, in the widest sense of the term, always comes down to the love story. And surely, what is characteristically sought after in societies of consumption is the exceptional-individual love story.

V: *In press material you write that* A Tale of Love *"offers both a sensual and intellectual experience of film." Would you also expect that the film be an emotional experience for the audience? You detail the sensual experience of love as a state of heightened impressions, a heightened separation of elements. Would this also apply to the emotional experience of love? Can these terms "emotional," "sensual," and "intellectual" themselves be meaningfully separated?*

T: Not really. These are all ambiguous terms that designate different spaces. What is emotional changes radically with each viewer. I've been told by many that they were very moved by the film, but I've also heard comments from the audience that suggest how difficult it is for them to identify with my characters, or rather, noncharacters, and how distanced they feel toward them. Of course, this does not necessarily exclude the fact that the film can still be moving. It all depends on what the viewer really sees and hears. Gertrude Stein's "A sentence is not emotional a paragraph is" always makes me smile. I would say that in A Tale, more than in my previous films, what is visible and audible can prevent one from seeing and hearing. What continues to elude us is the fact that the image is in itself a veil; so is the "dialogue," especially when it appears all too obvious at first reception.

When I resort to the distinction made between sensual and intellectual, it is to recall something very basic to the experience of film. If I define cinema as an alchemy of the fragment or an art of the cut—this means one learns when, how, what to cut, not simply by following the script one wrote or media formulas, but intuitively, in the way one conceives image, sound, and silence. If it is the art of the cut rather than that of the suture, then filmmaking is no more the putting together than the pulling apart of fragments. Less a question of consolidating power through unity and coherence, than of transforming at the base with incisive cuts, instinctive distractions and sharp discontinuities. To follow an idea, a story, or a message is primarily an intellectual activity, especially in the context of film where the active reconstruction of fragments and details is constantly at work, if one is to "understand" what is being shown. But the experience of film is also a sensual one, as the reception of images and sound appeals immediately to one's senses before one makes sense of them. Pudovkin did not hesitate to affirm that film is "the greatest teacher because it teaches not only through the brain but through the whole body."

Yet films that resist serving up a story or a message without merely falling into the trap of serving Art, often leave the spectator at a loss. For me, since brain and body are not separable—despite the fact that society, as suggested in *A Tale*, still largely prefers women's bodies without their heads—the nonverbal events in the film and what is not sayable in the actors' dialogues are just as important, if not more, than what is actually said. Often, people who have problems with the content or the performance of *A Tale* and whose rejections can sometimes be fiercely anti-intellectual (not to mention sexist), are precisely those whose viewing of the film remains primarily intellectual. Such a viewing never accounts for the impact of a film on the spectator's body. It reduces everything to the order of meaning and remains oblivious to the way the non-verbal, plastic, musical, sculptural, or architectonic workings of a film interact with its content and verbal performance. For me, a sensual experience is clear and luminous, but not immediately tangible; you don't know where you are exactly, so you take a risk when you try to verbalize it.

I've made a detour to come back here to precisely what the film focuses on: an altered state of the mind and body, the state of being in love, in which our senses are strangely aroused and sillily obscured—hypersensitive; so lucid and so blind at the same time.

V: *At the end of* A Tale of Love *Kieu comes to a realization that her own narrative comprises a series of layers without the "climax" or unifying flourish that ordinarily conclude the conventional "love story." The point is that she "recognize" her own situation, gaze upon it and so "be in love with love—not with a Prince Charming." Then there can truly be a happy ending. How might this observation be applied to the cultural rendering of Kieu—as a metaphor for Vietnam?*
T: There's no truly happy ending; I didn't intend to imply this. But your question is a real challenge, because if Kieu as a literary and mythical figure has been the site of continuous moral and political appropriation in Vietnamese culture, it was more in relation to foreign domination in Vietnam's history and to the Confucian norms that regulate women's "proper" behavior. The conclusion of being in love with Love is one that I introduce in my own tale, one that is informed by the feminist struggle and its questioning of power relationships exerted in the name of love. Kieu's tumultuous and wretched love life, her being forced into prostitution, her passion and sacrifice have all been extensively written about and used as an allegory for Vietnam's destiny. But no one has really linked Kieu's denouement to Vietnam's geopolitical, socioeconomic, or artistic and ethical situation today. Perhaps I can venture into saying that independence entails complex forms of re-alignment, and that Vietnam's opening up, which for many means assimilation of the free West, can be, despite all the mistakes and drawbacks, a way of keeping Her distance from all three power nations: China, Russia, and the U.S. Infidelity to others and to one's own ideals, even when dictated by circumstance, can only lead to difficult places, and hence, there's definitely no simple happy ending here.

V: A Tale of Love *explores the premise that a character/person can have many stories and many selves. Do you consider that you have many selves? What are they? There is a moment in the film where the characters discuss the idea that women in particular are punished for having many talents—is this true of your own experiences?*

T: It's by working with multiplicity that the notion of "character" can be undone. Since the narrative was not conceived as a game of psychological construction, it was important that everyday individualized passions should not be the mainspring of the film, and that each of the protagonists (Kieu, Juliet, Alikan, the Aunt, Minh) should be a multiplicity. They are what one can call disinherited characters, and the actors cannot simply "act themselves." For me my many selves are as real as the fingers of my hand, although the process of naming them can be infinite, if I were to avoid types, roles, and fixed categories. Kieu's miseries have been legendarily attributed to her beauty and her many talents. Although I don't necessarily identify with her, Kieu's life does speak to the lives of innumerable women.

In my case, it has always been extremely difficult. We live in a very compartmentalized world, and people certainly do not forgive you for being more than one thing at a time. Aside from the fact that as a woman, you always have to be twice as excellent for them to accept you simply as "proficient," they also cannot praise you, for example, as an artist without demeaning you as a theorist or a scholar, and vice versa, depending on where the stakes are for each of them. The more accessible I look, the more competitive they tend to be. Age, gender, ethnicity, and appearance have a lot to do in these kind of situations. This holds true even for my closest friends, some of whom simply can't accept my being, independently, every bit as much a writer as a filmmaker, and vice versa, for example. They prefer to give you credit for the area that is clearly not theirs or where they can't claim mastery. Or they judge your work in the light of your other activity, not in its own light. Everything is seen in terms of complementarity—one activity *serving* the other—rather than in terms of radical multiplicity. It's distressing that such an attitude thrives even in highly progressive and informed milieus.

V: *In the past you have commented that, "Light, setting, camera movement, sound, and text all have a presence, a logic, and a language of their own. Although they reflect upon one another, they are not intended to just illustrate the meanings of the narrative." To what extent does a process of cine-symbiosis rather than reflection also have a "formal" role in the cinema?*

T: Symbiosis . . . very appropiate word in love context. I prefer it to the overused term "syncretism," because it implies both intimacy and dissimilarity in living together. I also like the way you evoke it as against reflection. Myself, I have developed a closer relationship with the concept of multiplicity, which is a way of working radically with differences. When I say, for example, each character or each film element has its own story spaces, I mean it literally, not metaphorically. In my films, the relationship between things or events themselves is just as important as the relationship between people, or between people and things. Similarly, the relation between the verbal and the nonverbal, between what is said or read and what is seen, heard, and felt is never homogenized. The center of gravity and the moving force change place with each shot, both within the image and between images. These have their own rules and dynamics, independent of you and me, or of the viewer, the maker, and the actors. It's like coming up with a finite assemblage in which everything holds tightly together, every cut, every segment, every scene is carefully thought out, but nothing works in unison. Not only is the center never the same, but also, as each segment is itself a multiplicity, depending on which segment you start out with, you'll enter and leave the work quite differently. The relation of the segment to the whole is always in displacement.

Let's just take one element of film as example: color—and you know how charged this word can be. What is the color of love in the context of *A Tale*? Yellow, blue, red. These are the primary colors featured in the film, with green as a punctuation. The way Jean-Paul and I [Jean-Paul Bourdier is the codirector as well as the production and lighting designer of the film] work with these colors and the way they unfold their story on the screen is clearly something that has an impact on the reception of the film, whether positive or negative, and whether the viewer recognizes it or not. As mass-media consumers, we are trained to view narrative space predominantly in terms of actors and action. But if you follow these colors in their full mobility, in their multifold relationship—in their contrast, texture, and rhythm—you may get involved in a story-track that can radically shift your reading of the film.

Primary colors stand on their own, and their use can be very exacting. In other words, their relationship on the color scale is not that of complementarity but of multiplicity. The experience of color is rich, and there are many ways to discuss it here. I will not go into the technical aspect of cinematography, but I will briefly mention here lighting design as it is fundamentally relevant to the question of multiplicity. In classical lighting, the triple imperative is dramatization, hierachization, and legibility. What comes first in the image are, obviously, the actors. Actors should always be visible and audible. Since the setting is of secondary importance, if the actors move out of the frame, the decor empties itself and becomes useless. The camera's movement is subjected to the actors' movement and the framing of this, to the immediate legibility of the object shown.

None of these norms entirely applies to *A Tale*. Small differences may escape the inattentive eye, but they are precisely what challenges the perceptual system of moviegoers. Here, the setting stands on its own, its presence speaks volumes, even and especially when the actors are absent from the scene. The camera has its own pacing, and actors are the ones to come in and out of its vision while it stays in place. They also move in and out of the light projections, which appear and disappear accordingly, as their formation and visibility depend on the placement of the bodies in motion. Lighting is therefore neither reduced to lighting the actors nor to filling in the space where the action takes place. If you remember, the lights come in definite colors and shapes. This is something you rarely see, because most people see light as being functional, not as having a form and a force of its own. The lighting here is not used for dramatic effect, to depict some metaphorical or psychological state of the actors, or to create an atmosphere that will serve to advance the plot. Lighting is therefore not discreet or "invisible" because its purpose is not simply to light a subject. On the contrary, the subject becomes lit as it falls or moves into the rays of light. Neither being privileged, both actors and light become visible when the two cross each other's paths.

By maintaining the independence of its elements, the film shows its graphy. It's more a scenography of love than a love story. Lights and colors have their own laws. It's not uncommon to hear painters speak about "veiling a whole picture" to bring out the individual colors, or about "painting a luminous veil over an image" to give a lustrous quality to a color. If we

TL

don't fall prey to the old dichotomy of form and content, voyeurism and the politics of the veil in the film would not only take on many dimensions, their scope would also lead us to a very different place and in a different direction than those that seem most evident. It makes quite a difference, for example, to see the relationships of Kieu and Alikan (the photographer who loves veiling) or of Kieu and Juliet (the woman who creates with smell) in the context of the film's tonality, with its movements of color and lighting, its moments of veiling and unveiling, its changes of contrast and texture, or else musically, with its staging of voices and verses.

V: *Why do so many recent films resound to the strains of Shakespeare? You use Shakespeare in a critical way in* A Tale of Love, *although it could be argued that some recent rereadings might also be repositioning his work to culturally critical ends* (Twelfth Night, Richard III, Romeo and Juliet).

T: I'm not so much interested in Shakespeare as I am in the figure of Juliet and her love relationship with Romeo. The reference to Romeo and Juliet is here a reference to a universalized love story from the West. Its giant stature and popularized verses place it next to "The Tale of Kieu," which has so thoroughly gained the heart of the people among all classes of Vietnamese society that many who know Kieu by heart and who can recite long passages of this national poem may not even know or care to know about its creator, the early-nineteenth-century poet Nguyen Du. This can, in fact, be the best homage to a writer, who can disappear from the scene while his or her work lives on independently of its creator to become common bread.

V: *At the Melbourne Writers' Festival Forum, you pointed out how intentions and pre-conceived ideas have little place in the creative process—what were more interesting were the happy accidents, the impasses that remained unseen to the audience viewing the film. In what ways does* A Tale of Love *deviate from your original premise? What were some of the happy accidents from your point of view?*

T: When you work with accidents and impasses, there are certainly things that escape your control. So the process of not being able to see or not see in advance is a process both audience and makers go through, albeit differently not at the same moment or with the same events. It's not just a question of behind-the-scene, happenings. I have already expanded on one of the ways by which A *Tale* exceeds its intended framework, when I discuss how a carefully thought-out assemblage that has no exclusive center or purpose can remain destabilizing. A novelist like Toni Morrison would affirm truth is random, fiction is not. True, but the two also go together. Freedom and experimentation in the realm of scripted fiction are necessarily different from those in the realm of nonfiction. The falsehood of spontaneity has to be acknowledged at the same time as the work, as thoughtful as it might be in its details, has to come together in an unachieved way—that is, built with ellipses and "story holes" in a process of constant layering and condensation.

The happy accidents occurring during the shoot or the editing are actually anecdotes that have the potential, let's say, to lead you out of an impasse or to shift slightly the meaning of a scene. An example here is the scene of Kieu's interaction with the dog. The encounter was meant to be an opportunity for Kieu to pour out her heart, her loneliness as an exile and a foreigner. But when we shot the scene, Bacio, the dog, was so excited with the sweets Kieu enticed him with to make him come closer to her that he got totally out of control and jumped all over her. The crew burst out laughing in the middle of each take because they immediately saw that the dog was in heat and thought the whole thing was obscene. But I saw none of this, being blindly engaged in Bacio's movements, which I simply read as movements perfect for a context of love. The crew thought the scene was not usable and kept on interrupting it, but I insisted. All this, of course, remains unseen to the audience in the final edit on screen, but what one can certainly see are the excited and graceful movements of the animal, and rather than having only loneliness, what also comes through is a joyful affection that was not foreseen, but was no less relevant to the mood of the film. These little surprises are common to all shoots. What can be different is the basic attitude of the makers toward them in the filming process.

V: *One aspect of your earlier work, especially in the ethnographic documentaries, was your experiment with cinematic rhythm. Did these earlier explorations inform your work on* A Tale of Love? *How did working with actors and a script alter your approach to the question of rhythm? How influential was your background in music composition?*

T: Sure, what one acquires gets internalized and training easily becomes nature. I can never look at a film without being immediately affected by its lack of rhythm or its powerful play with it. It's a very strongly physical experience. I have the same inclination in music. I love classical and folk music from around the world, but the music that has a full impact on me and moves me the most is drum music. Even though my area of strength as a composer is more generally percussive and electronic music—one of the oldest and the newest forms of music—I especially love drums because of their very freedom from melody, their proximity to noise with which they share the ability to create rhythms. Here, all is a question of vibrations. Drummers know how effectively drum sound works on a person's depths as it is intimately related to an altered state of consciousness. A drummer's performance sometimes gives one the feeling of listening to five or six players at the same time. Here, the art of rhythm can reach an ecstatic complexity.

As I have shown in my film *Naked Spaces—Living Is Round*, rhythm is in work, in daily activities, in people's interactions. In Africa, the gesture of work, the movements of labor are always rhythmic, and when a person dances, one easily recognizes this person's occupation, since each job has a rhythm of its own. Rhythm determines the relationship between people, things, and events. Someone who lacks rhythm—not in terms of being slower or faster, but of having no sense or a poor sense of rhythm—while working in groups disturbs the others by his or her insensitivity. But rhythm cannot be equated with the strong or marked beat or even with the weak and irregular one. It cannot be reduced to pattern, cadence, or meter. Deleuze and Guattari nicely summarize this when they wrote "Meter is dogmatic, but rhythm is critical." Rhythm at work is usually very subtle, not easily locatable as it may come with a silent beat, and when you think you have it, it evaporates and returns as a new rhythm.

So rhythm is something that changes from one film to another as the film emerges, whether one works with a script and actors or not. Look at the difference between the two first films I shot in Africa, *Reassemblage* and *Naked Spaces*. And I've heard as many responses on the impact of the rhythms of *Surname Viet Given Name Nam* and *Shoot for the Contents* as I've heard on the two other films mentioned. For me, *A Tale of Love* is essentially rhythm. One can talk about it in terms of the overall course of the film; the shifts of color, texture, lighting, setting, and framing; the movement of actors and events from shot to shot; the editing of music and image; or the choreography of camera movement and stillness.

When we decided to use the Steadicam for the street scenes, for example, Jean-Paul (who is also an architect) immediately saw the potential of its movement in space. A movement free from the exacting constraints of both panning and tracking to which we have subjected ourselves during part of the shoot. And when the camera is further not enslaved to the actors' moves, the freedom is even more overwhelming as the mapping of the camera's movements can be quite intense: It can follow the actors, bypass them, move ahead of them, turn around to look at them and beyond them, wander away from them in a new direction, toward the wall graffiti, and finally end in a motion upward on a shot of the moon, as in the scene where Alikan follows Kieu in the street. The action here is all in the rhythm and the choreography.

V: *Do you "love for a living" as Kieu describes the role of the writer in* A Tale of Love? *What is it the writer loves?*

T: Certainly writing; whether that love relationship takes the form of hatred, of challenge, of escape, or of effacement, for example. All love writing seeks to say and to unsay while veiling itself. Kieu's statement bears a certain theatricality, which I see as a suspension of the flow of meaning and interpretation, an interval in the reflexive power of the word-image, and an intensity of speech caught in the act of subtle acting. "A tale" here should be understood in its modern connotation, as a fabulation. A fabulation of love.

為人民服務

erve the People

(Mao)

PAINTED POWER

with Homi Bhabha

Edited from the public conversation conducted by Homi Bhabha in London, when the films *Shoot for the Contents, Surname Viet Given Name Nam, Naked Spaces,* and *Reassemblage* were shown at the ICA (Institute of Contemporary Arts) in November 1992.

Bhabha: *I take a certain perverse pleasure in welcoming you to a very old country [Britain], where the royal family is falling apart, where there is intrigue, sexual scandal amongst the courtiers, conspiracy in parliament, where the church has voted for the ordination of women and there is a feeling that the church is now collapsing. So, the court has collapsed, parliament is about to collapse, and the church, too, and you have arrived from this new Camelot [The U.S.], what is claimed will be the most culturally diverse, ethnically diverse administration. Do you feel that this will be so, or do you think it will be like Clinton's pot-smoking days: a mouth of smoke that was left uninhaled and never reached the lungs.*

Trinh: One always has to live with hope. Without it, how can one carry on any kind of struggle? On the other hand, one also has to remain very vigilant, especially when "multiculturalism" is officially proclaimed to be an important element of governmental politics, as in the States. In the display of a narrow pluralist stance, there is always the danger of falling back into what multiculturalism was before: a bland melting pot, where all forms of assimilation and of leveling out of differences were practiced, in order to keep those differences at as minimal and harmless a level as possible. And there is the other danger, as in the apartheid policy of South Africa, for example, where divisions and cleavages were kept as intact as feasible, supposedly for the black nations' own good. So rather than challenging the fixed boundaries of cultures within and between nations, rather than questioning [internal] cultural frontiers as related to [external] national frontiers, multiculturalism in this case would merely amount to reinforcing, in the name of cultural diversity, a number of well-defined ethnic partitions. Since it is within these limits that marginalized social groups are required to operate, the change is no more than a cosmetic improvement. These are the dangers we constantly face in the States with multiculturalism, as we are repeatedly reminded through current events that there's no escape from interracial dependency if, in this era of transnational economics, democracy is to be "restored" (to use a term touted as the great achievement in the U.S.).

B: *Philosophically, it's interesting how there's been a new justification of multiculturalism from the neo-pragmatist philosophers like Richard Rorty, who, this year at the School of Criticism and Theory, was actually teaching a course on cultural diversity, or cultural pluralism, I think that word was used. I wanted to ask you to reflect on this notion of cultural pluralism, and I wondered whether you felt as I did that there is a different claim to identity, to communality, to the retrieval or reinscription of history on the part of black or colored people or minorities in a post-slavery culture, like in the United States, where there is an awareness that the soil is soaked with the blood, the formations are there, the buildings are there, where there is an intertwined history.*

This is different from the diasporic postcolonial situation in this country, where clearly there has been great oppression, great violence in Africa or India, but there is the sense that it was in another country and that people have come here for economic reasons or as political refugees. This is one contrast I felt very strongly. I wondered whether the experience of the Vietnamese, which is again an imperial experience in another country and then a return—the experience in America today of the Vietnamese, the migration of Korean communities—whether this is not more like minority communities here, Afro-Caribbean, Asian, and so on, than it is like the post-slavery situation.

T: My first reaction is to agree with that similarity and then to think a little further, mainly in terms of degrees, about the different humiliations and different kinds of experiences marginalized peoples are going through. Talking about that very strong sense of intertwined history in the post-slavery culture of the States, one would also have to make a distinction between the African-American and the Native American experiences. The loss of land may be said to be what both groups share, but the two experiences differ markedly. In one case, one is taken away from one's native land and reduced to slavery; in the other, one remains homeless in one's own land as one is dispossessed of one's very means of survival and made to undergo slow, extensive disempowerment through dependency and culturecide. These are different forms of oppression that also need to be distinguished from the experience of refugees and emigres from the Third World. Most victims of power realignments—who came from a context of colonization and who, for political or economic reasons, either left of their own will or are involuntarily and massively driven away from their country by historical forces—are no less haunted by the feeling of having lost their base for action, their native land. But certainly, the predicament of displacement coupled with the sense of escape or with the hope for a new life is yet another kind of experience.

I think it is also useful to bring these experiences together. The mutilation of a people's dignity takes many forms; however, it seems to me that we're heading nowhere in our struggles if we can't cross the partition lines (geographical, cultural, racial, sexual, gender, generational, and others) to create new alliances. For example, when we talk about border cultures, the first culture that comes to my mind is that of the Chicano community, for which crossing the borderline is such a physical, daily experience of survival. Knowing this should not prevent us from raising questions about the many other borders that make a culture what it is, even if we are aware of the risk of turning a political reality into a diluted catchword. On the contrary, to grasp border politics in its wider scope, we are compelled to deal with more than one realm of reality at the same time. Different levels and degrees can coexist without necessarily canceling each other out. Within the Asian-American community itself, some have attempted to set up a separation between the new Asian immigrants (who are not "American" enough to be "Asian American") and the third or fourth generations of previous Asian immigrants. Further, there is a strong feeling among south and southeast Asians of being a minority marginalized in its relation to the majority, which is composed mainly of members of Japanese, Chinese, and Korean descent. The divisions can go on indefinitely. It's dangerous to dwell on the diversity of these experiences; we should constantly ask whose interest it serves to make these kinds of separations. We can still talk about something that is very specific; we need not forget the circumstances that give rise to each form, content, and context; and yet, from and with that specificity, try to open up to other struggles, whose concerns and issues may intersect with ours and can powerfully transform our own struggle.

B: *The problem is how one maintains a specificity. One begins to see the border as a transgressive boundary, which is also, however, heavily policed, and one sees the border not only as existing between communities and positions of power, hegemonic power, dominant power, but also constituting borderlines within communities. For instance I participated in a panel in Los Angeles during the uprisings, and gang members and their counselors were included on the panel. What emerged there was a very tense situation between African Americans and Koreans, the notion of what my sons call "dis," "don't give me dis," don't give me disrespect, "don't dis me" as my sons say. African Americans were saying "Koreans don't show us respect, they give us disrespect."*

It's interesting that the bulwark against the pluralism you're talking about, the multiculturalist pluralism, does not come only because one can evolve better ways of thinking about how difference can be together, emphasizing its specificity, but also because communities within themselves are setting up certain borderlines of incommensurability. They are saying: We will negotiate together, but these separations we want to keep. It's a very problematic issue: that which prevents you from pluralism, from thinking about it in the pluralist way, can also be a very dangerous borderline within minority communities. The Anita Hill–Clarence Thomas trial was precisely such an event, where minority communities were at loggerheads within themselves and showed up the impossibility of the pluralistic solution, or the multicultural solution.

T: And yet at the same time we believe that a kind of plurality within is absolutely necessary, because there is no such thing as a community that is truly homogeneous. It's nothing new to say that sometimes I feel so comfortable being with the east-Asian communities because we find ourselves walking into each other's heart with a minimum of words exchanged. There is, so to say, a common background or a familiarity in "proper" behavior, gesture, and intent that immediately creates a bonding. But most of the time, I feel I'm utterly a stranger to these communities and their aspirations; to the way, yes, that each group fiercely plays the game of the dominant and denies what links it to other "minority" groups or to other contexts of post/colonization.

This necessity to exile oneself from one's own community and to maintain the differences within is also very much linked to the histories of the diverse communities. It has always been in the interest of the colonizing or "dominant" group to have both the line distinguishing it from the "minority" groups and those lines separating these groups from one another kept in operation. And the Hill-Thomas trial certainly showed with mortifying clarity the state of gender and race relations in our society. Marginalized peoples find themselves caught in a complex dilemma: pushing the divisions to further extremes, fighting by necessity to maintain one's boundary, and to reclaim an identity that continues in certain milieus to make one the object of (refined) contempt, while realizing that the more one is kept busy with the demarcation, the better one ultimately serves the interest of the dominant group.

B: *It's not only when and where and how am I, but, as you put it in your* Framer Framed, *also why am I, what am I in relation to—not even who am I in relation to, but what, why am I here— so that every identity is in a way a response to a certain inquisition.*

Where I disagree with this perspective to some extent is that I would grant more agency, now, to this new borderline that I was trying to talk about within communities. I would not say that that this is because people are put there in that position but rather that people are realizing, even in relation to other minority communities, what their differences are. [Frantz] Fanon once said "I don't want to be accepted as a person only in my presence, I want my negating activity to be accepted too," and that's the kind of thing I'm trying to say. I would credit more agency to the communities who, within themselves, are constituting internal boundaries and limits, too. It could be very dangerous, but it could also be quite productive, and I take absolutely seriously the idea that one has to be able to find a way of talking specificities within communities, specific ideas within communities, and in some way constituting a more communal re-historicization, a more communal representation, which does not end up in a totalized or homogeneous sense of community.

I feel that in a number of ways in your films this notion of history as repetition seems to me the way in which a number of people are working in order to re-inscribe differences without totalizing them, which I know is close to your work. There seem to me to be three, I know there are many more, but roughly three genealogies to this process of history as re-inscription:

1. The feminist psychoanalytic narratives about repetition: the reconstitution of a gendered subject in excess. I think it was a very important historical moment when that emerged. 2. The work on gay sexualities by, for example, Judith Butler in her essay "Inside Out" where she talks about re-inscription and the constitution of lesbian sexuality in the process of re-inscription. 3. The colonial and postcolonial strategies of what has been called mimicry, the inappropriate/ inappropriated other, or something I'm trying to work on now, which I call insurgent iteration: forms of repetition that are constituted in insurgency. Also the work of W.E.B. Du Bois, especially the end of The Souls of Black Folk *when he says that the real problem with progress is not to oppose it to irrationality, but that (he put it very beautifully) there is the swift and the slow in human doing, and who can normalize it, and say whether progress only goes in this direction or only that. It's this historicization through re-inscription that I think is very profoundly and movingly represented in your work, in your films.*

T: Perhaps we can come back to discuss this question of repetition afterward, because I feel it links very well with our elaboration on the notion of differences within the community and between communities, or of difference in such oppositional terms as those of major versus minor cultures, for example.

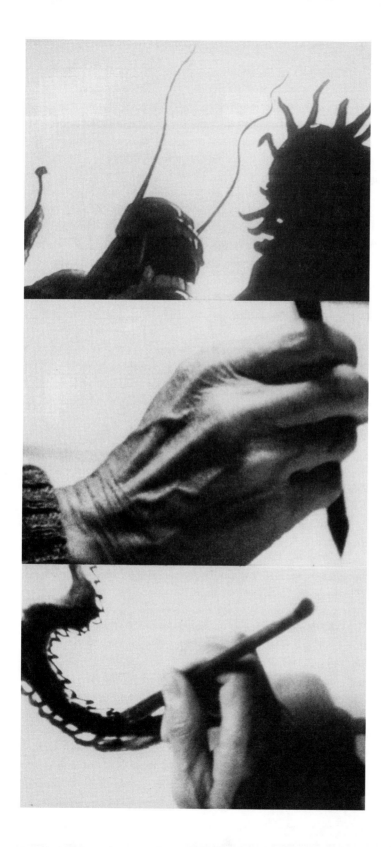

(Screening of excerpt from *Surname Viet Given Name Nam.*)

T: What you have just seen is an excerpt from a film that is quite long, and it takes almost two hours to build up precisely this sense of what you were talking about earlier, Homi, the sense of specificities and of differences within the culture, like the many names that Vietnam has had. The sense also that the more one looks into one's own culture, the more one sees there is no such thing as a place that one can just return to safely. Every time one tries to retrieve or to rescue what is thought to be retrievable and representable—the authentic Vietnamese culture, for example,—it loses itself like ripples widening on the surface of water. It's a reality that cannot be contained, that always escapes, but that one cannot escape. In this very short excerpt, the "you" ("even you") referred to by the women interviewed points immediately to the role of a witness-confidante-listener who, although trusted as an insider, holds a border position in relation to the culture. So there is this constant shuttling across thresholds of insideness and outsideness even for someone who is from within the culture: Just as one exiles oneself from one's culture to inhabit it anew, one also returns to it as a guest, rather than as a host or an owner, to hear its voices afresh.

B: *At the formal level, I find the way in which what I call this re-inscriptive history (which I think is really shown by the film), the formal way in which it occurs across a range of films made about specific cultural locations, minority groups, or diasporic narratives, is in antagonism with the documentary form, that is documentary as a mimetic or realist form which presented, but institutionally, informationally, and conceptually, this notion of emergent cultures or of emergent peoples as belonging to a culture. From there you begin to have the pluralistic multicultural history of documentary filmmaking and even anthropological filmmaking where the distance was established. But the difference was always kept at bay, because those communities were always seen to be somehow self-contained.*

What I find both in Surname Viet *and in* Shoot for the Contents *as well as in a number of films by black British filmmakers, Asian-British filmmakers too, is the use of documentary and then this re-inscription, taking it apart, not obscuring, not saying that that moment does not exist historically, cinematically in representation, it does exist, but continually hybridizing it, righting its margins, reassembling it, disassembling it and so on.*

What's very interesting in your films, and also in the excerpt that you showed us, is the way in which it is women who play this liminal role. The moment in which the repetition goes out and then comes back in, that turn, or fold, in the repetitions, is really a liminal space, which is occupied very much by women.

I'm thinking specifically, for those of you who know the two films, of the woman at the end of Surname Viet *who says "our history is always on the borderline." Sorry, I'm speaking in her voice, in a way much less poetic than hers, but it's something like "our history is always on the borderline of this north and south, but I speak from somewhere in both places, in between, and I will not accept this division, and I will not think truth divides itself in that way." In* Shoot for the Contents *there is a continual calligraphic marking, remarking and unmarking of the dragon, which is being painted, and I think somewhere, both in* Surname Viet *as well as* Shoot for the Con-*

tents, *but even more explicitly in* Surname, *there is a notion of woman and dragon, and Chinese history and dragon. It's almost as if the indirection of Chinese history which you talk about and the liberating indiretion of the woman as witness on this liminal borderline come together. The question that arises is: Does this liminal woman too easily fit in to the formal procedures of the film, in terms of the woman as liminal witness and the way in which we witness the pleasure that the film gives, form that cusp-like moment. Do you think somebody could say that it all fits in too easily, that the reality is much more grainy and gritty than that.*

T: First, concerning the antagonism you mentioned between the documentary form and the activity of reinscriptive history, I think one of the ways of approaching repetition as a political strategy *and* as an aesthetic device—at once as a negating and an affirming activity in its resistance to representation—is to ensure that in the making of documentary (or of any other genre), one does not censor oneself. The fact that the loudest claims to representative truth and information have been voiced and legitimized through the documentary form does not mean that in order to bring about change, one has to banish it and adopt other, more adequate, forms. When handled creatively, repetition is a way of affirming difference. Rather than using it routinely to reproduce the same, one can use it, to continue saying what one has said, to shift a center, to lighten the burden of representation, to displace a form from its settled location, and to create new passages through the coexistence of moments.

For example, as many viewers have expressed in their feedback, there is a disjunction between what one could expect from *Surname Viet*—or from a so-called documentary portrayal of Vietnam by an insider—and what one actually experiences with the film. Rather than constructing one (even when based on several) homogeneous insider's point of view, or a first-person "unmediated" account of the culture, the film engages the politics of the interview while entering Vietnam's history through collective and individual gaps. That is, not in an easily recognizable way, through chronology, linear accumulation, and succession of facts on Vietnam (this is what one can find in any book of Vietnamese history); but rather through popular memory, with its "bold omissions and minute depictions"; through women's personal stories; through songs, proverbs, and sayings particularly telling across generations as to the situations they struggle with; in other words, through nonofficial, undervalued sources of information.

Many times I have been asked why I showed footage of the Vietnamese refugees in the fifties, and not of those in the seventies, when I was dealing with the latter's situation. And I have also been asked why, in focusing on arts and politics in China in *Shoot for the Contents*, I did not make a film more specifically, let's say, on "Madame Mao," as a viewer puts it, on the cultural revolution, or on the post-Mao period. For me, there are many ways to approach history—here we come back to this question of repetition and difference—and one way, as suggested by the film, is to see it not so much as a succession of periods and of governing individual names (through which history is often reduced to neat, straight lines and to a finality), but rather as a manifested field of interrelated creative energies and social individuated forces across specific times and places. Such an approach allows one to unsettle the terms of established hierarchies and to continually reinscribe history while apprehending it in its hybrid dynamics, its density, and multilayered thickness.

When one deals with such a vast culture and country as China, it is necessary—at least for me, for example—to confront such giant, mythical, and political figures as Mao and Confucius, not as individuals, but at once as two passé cultural monuments and as two overlapping fields of historical forces that continue to define China's faces today. Although for anyone caught in the binds of linear history it may appear very contradictory to put these two names together, for me it is clear that Mao ruled through the repetition and adaptation of old popular sayings, or "through the power of rhymes and proverbs turned into snugly capsuled slogans," as one of the narrators in the film said. Because he deliberately resorted to oral traditions to convince the people, he can sometimes sound exactly like Confucius, whose "feudal" vestiges he tried so hard to extinguish. Both of them returned to this treasure of ancient Chinese stories, songs and sayings while blazing new paths. It was through this "verbal struggle," as Mao called it, that Mao succeeded in spreading his words widely among the peasantry and to create his own version of Marxism. I think it's important to show this intensity of experience and density of history which, when split open, yields new possibilities of times spaces in the most familiar realities of the culture.

For this, showing the repetitive but continually changing calligraphic painting and unpainting of the dragon you've mentioned seems most adequate. As a creation of people's imagination, an allegory of both power and change, a symbol of the Word creator, as well as a guardian of immortality in many Asian cultures, the dragon is evoked here in its mutiplicity and perpetual metamorphoses, both through its numerous names, functions, and appearances, and through the stories that indirectly comment on the political transmutations of China. As one proceeds with the film, the moves or the gestures one makes invent the movement and the trajectory one is to take. To paint a dragon is to paint a form of power, which is in itself a multiplicity of powers. But to paint a dragon without clouds, as the calligrapher reminded me during the shoot, is to miss the point and to paint no dragon at all (hence the shot, in the closing section of the film, of the man and his brushwork showing a dragon with water and clouds). Dragons are thunder and rainmakers; they are feared and revered for their power to control the waters or to make themselves accordingly visible or invisible. So without clouds, a dragon lacks dimension, substance and reality. Deprived of the essential elements to survive and to create, it can, literally speaking, neither dive deep nor rise high to take flight. The same holds true for the nature of power. To paint or assume power, one has to paint and assume the elements of change. Otherwise, as a statement in the film says, "the five colors will blind a man's sight." Since the five colors refer to the dragon, one can translate, "power will blind a man's sight"; and since filmmaking involves both a play of colors and the power to direct and create, one can further translate, "the five colors / the dragon / power will blind a filmmaker's / film viewer's sight."

Keeping in mind how power appears from a painting, I'll take up the question you raised concerning the way women occupy a liminal space and how this fits too easily with the formal procedures of the two films. I certainly agree that reality is always more complex than whatever we come up with to frame it. But I would say first, that in my work form and content are inseparable. So to have women fare primarily and precariously in that liminal space is as much a political as an aesthetic choice—a choice that invites rather than excludes other possibilities (even when they seem contradictory) and other occupations by marginalized social groups. The many links suggesting these possibilities are constantly evoked, some of which are manifest and others latent, and some of which tend to situate the subjection of women while others turn out to be liberating despite the difficulties involved. For example, in *Shoot for the Contents* the dragon is not always associated with women, even though the important roles of the translator and the narrators are deliberately given to women. The same may be said of the color red whose meanings are multifold, and while it is stated that "the word 'red' [in Chinese] is a symbol for woman," such a statement adds dimensions rather than excludes them, for it refers specifically to one of the many mutually dependent possibilities of red.

This being said, there is always a danger, in assuming a tone and a position of indirection, that one may simply fall back into the habit of understating and of muting one's voice as expected from women: We are, after all, supposed to abide by the rules of proper feminine speech and manner, never going at something too aggressively and too directly, often taking the back door, the discreet path to arrive at certain locations or to make certain points. But such an attitude can be assumed submissively, strategically or creatively. To see through it is to grasp the situation of marginalized peoples caught in power relationships. One can never go to the ruler in a direct way; in order to voice one's opinion, one has to take an indirect way. Indirection is likely to disturb viewers, including feminists, who expect a film to make a categorical statement, to deliver a positive political message, or to build around a clear story line. But for me, in a context of late capitalism where externalized directness (not to be confused with direct knowledge) is ultimately made to serve reductive and consumerist ends, it is important to work with indirection and understatement, if meaning is to grow with each viewer, and if the interstices of active re-inscription are to be kept alive. One can render the troubling complexities of a situation and still be very specific in one's fight without being totalizing. As women gain agency and move into a position of power, being able to make themselves heard through their own voices, we can't simply occupy that subject position at the center, for this is what we have also been consistently fighting against in our struggle. So we would have to open up that position again, to remark and unmark it anew. What seems very recognizable at first is necessarily displaced with the steps we take as we affirm difference through repetition.

B: *This is not to say that there are not many struggles that just invert the access of oppression and say: I want to be in the place of dominance, I've for so long been in the place of victimage, now I want to be in the other place. I'm not talking about such situations, but rather, situations where, to return somewhere is different from having started off there. What I want to suggest is a way in which we might sometimes misrepresent or misread the moment of agency as being a moment of unicity and inner struggle. For instance, during my discussion here on another occasion with Victor Burgin we were talking about inscribing images, and he had taken images from South Pacific which were entirely in tune with "Bali Hi" "Let's all live together in the fifty-first state of the United States." He had taken all that pluralism and clearly displaced it; through a process of video wizardry all the imagery had been repositioned so that what now emerged was the impossibility of pluralism. At the level of artwork, I think that's possible, so that when you then reoccupy a space that might look centric, it isn't.*

You talked of the repetition of the archaic in the sayings of Mao. I want to just illustrate this with Gandhi for a minute and then move somewhere else. With Mao this repetition was at least repossessing and displacing the Confucian tradition. What I think is wonderful about Gandhi is often not pointed out, because he's caught up in such a nationalist myth, for David Attenborough it is backward. This was a man who continually, in a rather foxy way, used the liminalities and marginalities of various discourses, to claim Indian freedom. He would dress like a yogi with a little loin cloth and marks on his head, and he would sit, in that image of ruralism, spinning the thread every day. He moved politics from the municipal chamber into what he called the ashram, although everybody was running around in this ashram cooking up political schemes. It was not a place of great otherworldly purity. It was absolutely insane. So he did that. And then, of course, he comes to Britain, goes to the bulldoggish Churchill and says "Give me my freedom, not because I'm some great Hindu mystic, but how can you occupy this space, and how can you be part of the tradition of Ruskin and Carlyle and the Lords' Prayer and John Stuart Mill, and still prevent me from having my independence?" So it was that hybrid reoccupying of a center, which I'm suggesting is not a center because of the way in which the repetition occurs.

This kind of liminality touches on another important concept I see in your work, particularly in Shoot for the Contents: *the notion of survival. There are few great discourses on survival and they tend to be the work of novelists, of Knut Hamsun or Raja Rao writing about small south Indian villages. People surviving are often seen to be on the road to somewhere else: If only they "rose up" they would have the new Jerusalem, if only they fought. This in between, interstitial state of survival, which is linked to notions of repetition and liminality, is very important because it deals with the notion of the everyday. It does not share the same logic as progress, it also acts as a block to totalizing contents. There is now a need for a theorization of survival. At present I think psychoanalysis is the one discipline that actually deals with the notion of survival.*

T: Since we are talking about repetition and survival, there is a very familiar story of what happens in the process, for example, of appropriation, expropriation, reappropriation, and so on. In that process one can stop anywhere, one can stop at the stage of appropriation, or of reappropriation, because, let's say, the latter becomes so self-sufficient in itself that one doesn't go any further. . . . This seems to be the case with a notion like "hybridity," which has provided a strategic space for a range of new possibilities in identity struggles, but is being reappropriated in diverse milieus, such as the art milieu. Curators can continue to "collect cultures" from remote parts of the world, but rather than retrieving information and salvaging tradition, they now expertly stage and circulate the "hybrid object." Nothing has really changed. In acquiring, valuing, and ranking this "progressive" object, they simply accumulate more-of-the-same categories of the cultural as they reappropriate hybridity to their own ends. To stop there and to let subtle expropriation take its course is to concede "culture" to those in power again. One cannot merely accept or reject this kind of reappropriation, whose effect is to depoliticize a potential means of empowerment. So one would have to reaffirm difference in working again with hybridity, constantly reopening it and displacing it in order to keep its space alive. This is for me a question of survival; yes, there is always the danger that in any step of this process, liberating notions will be reappropriated and congealed, but then the fight is precisely to go on. . . .

B: *I agree but I think, however, there is a difference. I want to introduce a greater sense of disturbance or disjunction between the moment of expropriation, the moment of reappropriation, I want to concentrate on what actually happens. We can certainly tell the story the way you have told it, and it is the one I like to tell myself, but sometimes in a moment, in this kind of repetition, or in a moment of liminality, something congeals and what it gives rise to is maybe a form of essentialism of one kind or another. Then how you return to the strategy of hybridization might be something different, it might not be part of the cycle of reappropriation, expropriation. The problem that I see, for example, with exhibitions such as the Centre Pompidous' Magiciens de la* Terre, *is that what results as an institutional form is not hybridization but pluralism, I think that is the difference there, a strategy of hybridization does not celebrate cultural diversity, it celebrates, as we've been saying, cultural difference.*

T: Another way to open further the question of repetition is to come back to musical practices of repetition. One can have, for example, a form of repetition like that of the looping of a musical sequence on tape in electronic music, where one hears a mechanical reproduction of the same over and over again. Or one can have the effect of slippage that often occurs in African and African-American music where with each repetition, each return of the familiar, there are imperceptible elements of change; something is slightly off, slightly varied, and these minute differences make the music flow in a state of constant regeneration, so that one never has a static reproduction of the same. Here repetition is accordingly ritualized to allow untamed differences to stand out in a framework of stability.

Question from the audience: *You made a point about the African-American community, that there is repetition without very much re-inscription. I feel that here the notion of duration would come in as something to be looked at, that in a repetition if there is a certain duration, if it is just reproduced, let's say mechanically, without very much thought going into the duration, then I think it just reproduces the same and the same again, but if there is a certain notion of duration, a certain persistence in this kind of repetition, even blindly, I think then the way we hear and the way we perceive it might be slightly different. This is very apparent in contemporary music with someone like Steve Reich or Philip Glass, where the repetition with duration produces a certain transformation in the way that one perceives or hears the music. I think that one can play in the context of history. The idea of duration is very interesting in Steve Reich: Precisely because of the repetition you lose your place and you lose the borders of that which is being repeated, so in conjunction with different parts of what was originally itself the music is transformed.*

T: On African-American music, that's not quite what I said. On the contrary, I was emphasizing the subtle shifts in repetition. But your point on the lack of re-inscription in mechanical repetition and the importance of persistence in duration can be relevantly applied to any community. As with other groups' struggle, we can say of the struggle of African Americans that in spite of the fact that there is a great deal of repetition—even when thought to be "blind"— there is also, whether fully assumed or not, whether historical or personal, transformation that occurs in the way people perceive their fight and the way they establish identity. Such a transformation is due to their very persistence in repetition.

Q: *I wasn't intending to say that it wasn't, neither was I intending to say that I thought that even the blind remembering repeating isn't completely politically necessary because people like to be pressed—so you have to keep reminding them. In order for the progress to take place I feel this other thing has to happen, that's why I was suggesting in terms of the vocabulary perhaps, each time you rehearse for a scene then that's a repetition in the French language and it looks the same except for the accents. Again I feel when it doesn't move anywhere when it's repetition, when it's not re-inscription, then there is the feeling that you are in a rehearsal for something that will take place in the future and, of course, that is only one problem. So there is that other sense of repetition: It doesn't get anywhere because somehow the event is elsewhere, it is in the future.*

T: What I expanded on earlier corresponds also to the way I work with repetition, constantly introducing differences in what seems at first reception to be the same. Perhaps the space of creativity is precisely the distance between two fixed notes, the pitch relationship between two tones. Instead of following the Western way of Equal Temperament and its system of musical training in which notes are tuned by the standard A, one can turn to other systems in which the focus in tuning is not so much on the notes as on the intervals. In many contexts of Asian and African music, for example, an instrument played is tuned, not according to some standard pitch, but as adapted to other instruments or to the human voices that accompany it. There is no standard measurement, and there's no attempt at reproducing the same. What is important is the precision of the interval, not that of the fixed notes. In other words, what are valued in creating and performing music are relations and relationships.

B: *There is also the issue of inundated site, which Foucault brings up in his notion of material repeatability, so that when we have the person in the Giorgio Armani suit speaking about separatism, the same statement made at another site has a different purchase, and that's just the point I want to make. As we know the whole discourse of lynching in the mouth of Nina Simone is so different from lynching in the mouth of Clarence Thomas when he talked about being lynched, which was just a way of saying to the senate, inverting the idea completely, "I might have done all these horrible things but ain't I a man—are you going to let me hang for this?" So there is the issue of repetition and duration, and the other issue is the way in which when the repetition returns it locates somewhere else and that also becomes a site of inundation, a different kind of intervention.*

Q: *What were the reasons for your own return to Vietnam to make* Surname Viet?

T: My return to Vietnam was not a physical return, I didn't go back to Vietnam to shoot this film. I was emphasizing the politics of the interview and I was working with a body of interviews that had been carried out in Vietnam by another woman of the Vietnamese diaspora, translated and published in French, retranslated by myself into English and then re-enacted in the film. So there are many sites of mediation, and more than one step of translation and of inauthenticity involved in the making of this film.

It's not a return in a physical sense, but a return in the sense that I made my two previous films in Africa before making *Surname Viet*—a film in which I have finally been able to come to terms with Vietnam or with a national identity; a film focusing on Vietnamese women or on female identity and difference. That's why it was extremely important for me not to approach it from a legitimized "insider's" point of view, but rather from a number of spaces locating me somewhere between an insider and an outsider. Spaces manifested, for example, in the acknowledgment of the mediator's role; in the multiplicity of translation, of the "you" referred to by the interviewees, and of first-person narratives; and in the exposing of the politics of interviews involved.

It was also important to situate myself as a multiplicity in the multiplicity of Vietnamese culture. For example, I can never work with the Vietnamese language without immediately facing the fact that there are three prominent accents related to the three regions in Vietnam. [Of course, this language issue is only perceptible to viewers who are well acquainted with Vietnamese.] From the outside, one tends to talk in terms of North and South (and this also applies strongly to the Vietnamese community in the States), but actually there is a central region, and even though it tends to be economically the more subdued one, its mediating role, especially since the reunification of the country, is indispensable to the movement between Northern and Southern activities. Here too, one can raise many questions concerning this kind of duality promoted by the media and developed in relation to certain moments of history. I'm saying this with a big question mark, and I have no answer to give, but when I look at my own situation, such a simplistic duality has no reality. Members of my family belong to what can be seen as three political factions—some have always lived in the North, others have been compelled by circumstances to move to the South, and others yet have been shuttling from one place, one region, one country to another, having been part of the leading force of the National Liberation Front from the South. There are so many complex positionings within the Vietnamese reality that to discuss it only in terms of north-south duality is to fall prey to seeing within the most obvious form of power relationship. This is a long detour to come back to the question of survival. One has to remember these things in order to survive.

Q: *Another reason for repetition is simply because you are not heard, you keep repeating because you are not listened to, you are not attended to, so you say it again, and you say it again. At the ICA's [Institute of Contemporary Arts] recent conference on History as Repetition, Repetition as History, Stuart Hall made a distinction between what he calls narratives of displacement and narratives of appropriation, but there were a number of different papers within that context, on the writing of history, the rewriting of history, history as a political project, as a cultural project, as an emancipated project, how one actually writes history.*

There was another set of discourses, which related very much to your own work on the transitional space, the creative imagination, and then there was something that worked in between the two, which often was used as a kind of personal position within the historical, as a way of creating a space, both between the creative imagination and the historical and social space. When we talk about something like transitional space I want to try to see how that actually fits with the notion of a public or a social space. It seems to me it's very easy to slip into the way of talking about something that takes it back into the realm of subjective experience, and I think we can talk about it there, I mean when you talk about transitional space as being a space between the teacher and the student what is happening in that space is that there is a willingness on both parts to actually meet together, but does the creative imagination work in this way in political situations, is there a way in which the transitional space can be used as a metaphor in terms of readdressing or re-creating the notion of a public space?

T: I wonder how that separation comes about. The fact that we continue to ask such questions tells us how compartmentalized our activities can be. Of course, the word "creative" can be used, understood, reopened, and talked about in many different ways, but still, what is that creative space if it is not a social space? What is that space if not precisely this interval, this space of reinscription, of survival we have been discussing all along? I'm reminded here of the question of a Palestinian friend who asked if it is possible to speak about poetry in a context where one works from nine to five everyday, and my answer to that is: It depends on what we mean by poetry and practice as poetry. Although the question and answer are common enough, the art and social context in which they are situated is specific: This friend is rebelling against the fact that whenever he wishes to speak aesthetically about the works of his concern, he is immediately requested, steered, and set up to voice his opinions, and hence to be heard, only politically. In other words, all that he has to say is recuperated in a highly charged context and it is within the confines of an occupied territory that people accept his speaking. Social and political conflicts are, in this instance, easier to consume than aesthetics. So creative space, for me, depends on what we do "creatively." The notion of in-betweenness is something the feminist struggle has for decades worked on in order to challenge the fixed boundary between the private and the public. While pointing to the constant danger of collapsing the personal with the political, we are bound to work with a space in which differences converse and the power of reinscription thrives on the tension between the two.

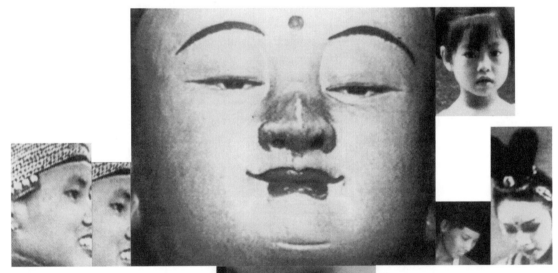

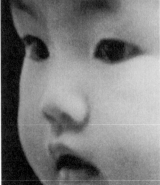

THE UNDONE INTERVAL

with Annamaria Morelli

Interview conducted by Annamaria Morelli at the Istituto Universitario Orientale in Naples, Italy, in May 1993. First published in *The Postcolonial Question. Common Skies, Divided Horizons*, ed. by Iain Chambers and Lidia Curti, London: Routledge, 1996.

Morelli: *When I read your writings, or I watch your films, what often comes to my mind is the image you evoked at the very beginning of* Woman, Native, Other: *the people of a remote village meeting to speak in the marketplace at nightfall. You say, "Never does one open the discussion by coming right to the heart of the matter . . . to allow it to emerge, people approach it indirectly by postponing until it matures, by letting it come when it is ready to come. There is no catching, no pushing, no directing, no breaking through, no need for a linear progression, which gives the comforting illusion that one knows where one goes. . . ." Do you find that this image of the way people discuss in that remote village might describe the way you proceed in the composition of your texts?*

Trinh: Yes. Such a practice not only applies to the approach of the book, but also to its writing. The second chapter ["The Language of Nativism: Anthropology as a Scientific Conversation of Man with Man"], for example, begins with a specific suggestion of how I proceed in theorizing the West's approach to its "others." The work constantly reflects back on itself, and everything written in the book can be said to be equally critical of my own activities as writer and thinker. It is important to remember that if one goes directly to an object, if one tries to seize it, one would always somehow lose it, and this is for me one way to live truth. As I have stated elsewhere, "a creative event does not grasp, it does not take possession, it is an excursion."

With the expansion of a market-intensive economy of movement, there is a tendency in the mainstream media to emphasize speed as a goal of inventive people, or rather, of smart consumers. To save time and energy, one is told to "go at it" and devise shortcuts so as to take hold of the desired object as quickly as possible. So, anyone who makes a detour, opts for indirectness, and takes time to move on his or her own can neither gratify the reader or viewer right away, nor expect any immediate gratification in return. But for me, to be able to maintain a certain independence and to pace one's movement accordingly is always a necessity, if one is to meet cultures other than one's own, and to embark in any artistic or creative venture—theory, for example, is also a form of creativity. One can only approach things indirectly.

Because in doing so, one not only goes toward the subject of one's focus without killing it, but one also allows oneself to get acquainted with the envelope, that is, all the elements that surround, situate or simply relate to it.

To start a story, for example, not linearly "by the beginning," or to come into a story without a preconceived beginning and ending, but rather with anything that emerges at a specific moment in one's thinking process, that relates back to one's intimate experience, and then, to proceed slowly from there—just like the way the village meeting that you have just quoted unfolds—letting things come to you rather than seizing or grasping them. Such an attitude is necessary for any creative venture, otherwise all that one has to offer the reader or the viewer is the empty skin of a fruit. There is, in other words, no reverberation, no resonance. With this, also comes the much debated notion of subjectivity, which has regained all its complexities in contemporary theories. If one merely proceeds by opposing, one is likely to remain reductive and simplistic in one's critical endeavor. Whereas in an approach where things are allowed to come forth, to grow wildly as "controlled accidents" and to proceed in an unpredictable manner, one is compelled to look into the many facets of things and is unable to point safely at them as if they were only outside oneself. It is in indirection and indirectness that I constantly find myself reflecting back on my own positions.

M: *You say that your films are not materializations of ideas or visions that precede them, and that the way they take shape entirely depends on what happens during and in between the processes of producing them. I wonder if the way your written texts take shape is similar to the practice you describe in the making of a film. If so, to what extent and what are the differences, since what happens in the producing of a film has also a lot to do with the fact that one lives and creates with other people, while in the writing process one is unavoidably alone in the reassemblage of voices, tales, thoughts, memories.*

T: I guess I will start with the last statement, which is that one is alone in writing, whereas, in filmmaking one is with other people. I think the difference is very small, actually. It is just a question of physically working with other people, confronting them on a daily, one-to-one basis, whereas in writing, one may be immediately isolated and yet, with every word or every sentence one writes, I think one is always endlessly conversing with a huge amount of people, reading and hearing from as many ears and eyes as possible, whether they are immediately present or absent. Yes, I would say that although images and words are two different worlds, there are many similarities in the way my films are made and my books are written. I am thinking here of *Woman, Native, Other* and *When the Moon Waxes Red*. With *Framer Framed*, it is a slightly different situation since interviews (which form part of this book) are encounters between two individuals and the discussions generated usually deal with the more generalized concerns of a certain audience and readership.

When I write, I never know ahead of time where the writing is going to lead me. I never proceed by having a plan (with an introduction, a development and a conclusion, for example), by mapping out the terrain of the arguments I wish to sustain, or even by compiling ahead of time all the points I want to discuss; I never work that way. Perhaps I can start here with an anecdote and then see where I can go with it in articulating my own practice. It is a story in which the African-American poet and activist June Jordan told us in her recent book, *Technical Difficulties*. June was having a conversation with her aunt whom she loved dearly, but who apparently could only explain June's political stance by accusing her of being "a Communist." Such a label came about when June expressed her desire to go to Nicaragua at a time when she was supposed to celebrate Thanksgiving at her aunt's home. They argued heatedly about the way Nicaragua had been spoken of in the mainstream media via "his Highness, the American King"—Ronald Reagan—and since they strongly disagreed with one another, the aunt simply deduced that June was "a dupe of their [the Communists'] propaganda" and remarked: "It's a matter of East and West, can't you see that?" To which June replied: "East and West! But if I got on a plane tomorrow, heading for Managua, I'd be flying south and west. West!" And this just made her aunt even more angry [*laughs*], as she exclaimed: "That's just geography!"

For me the story is extremely revealing because at the same time as it is hilarious, it also offers a marvelous example of how wars devastating nations are fundamentally linked to the way meanings are produced and fixed. With the playful insertion of one single word—"south"—June succeeded effortlessly to introduce a shift of meanings that remains remarkably plural in its scope. In other words, she not only disrupted the East-West axis by opening it up to a third terrain and by implying the connection between geography and ideology, or between politics and economics, but she also displaced the binarism of such an axis by juxtaposing "south" and "west." For me, the poet in June is always at work. In a rather banal fragment of a family argument, the potentials of politics and poetry are simultaneously woven and unfolded. Such a practice of speech and writing would appeal to anyone who does not use language as a mere instrument of thought and is aware of how the same word can acutely shift its meaning when it is put in a slightly different context, as in this example.

Word as idea and word as word. These two movements of language are interdependent and always at work in the space of writing. When the telling and the told remain inseparable, the dichotomy between form and content radically loses its pertinence. This is how I would try to describe the way I proceed in writing. The way a thought, a feeling, an argument, a theory, or a story takes shape on paper is at the same time "accidental" and very precise, very situated, just like a throw of dice. The fact that, radically speaking, "language only communicates itself in itself" [Walter Benjamin] has not only been much theorized among the so-called antihumanist thinkers today, it is also nothing new to writers for whom writing, which refers to and is drawn from reality, constitutes a material reality of its own. How one renders this reality is another matter. For me, if one of the two movements mentioned is atrophied in writing, if language is subjected to being a vehicle for thought and feeling, or if the focus is only laid on the told, the message, or the object of analysis, then the work will never resonate. And without resonance, writing becomes primarily a form of information retrieval or of administrative inquisition. Its ability to constantly reflect on itself, hence to generate new meanings along the process, to surprise both the writer and the reader, and to lead them to unexpected places remains atrophied.

It is not enough to master a language in order to serve a vision or an idea. There are many dimensions in language and it is by constantly playing with these dimensions that words keep

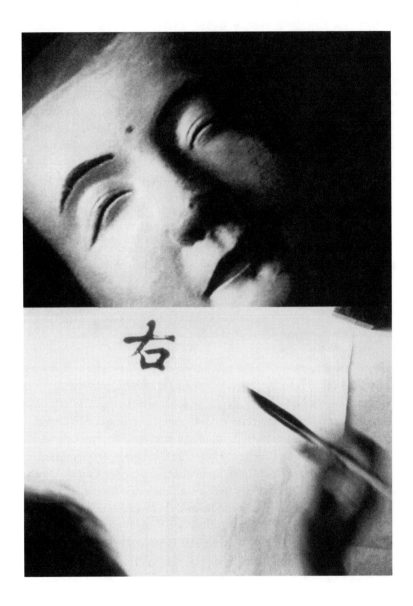

on displacing themselves from their intended or given meanings. And as words communicate among themselves, the writer who is the first reader of her text-in-progress would have to remain *actively* receptive to their interactions, for displacement causes as well as intensifies and multiplies resonances. Because of the sharp balance maintained between these two movements external and internal to language, writing proceeds by scrutinizing itself and by constantly undoing the previous contextual meanings arrived at. What I mean by "resonate" is therefore not simply a question of aestheticizing language or a formalistic concern. Working with resonance is to resist diverse forms of centralization—the indulgence in a unitary self, in a locus of authority, or in words and concepts whose formulation come to govern the textual (and extra-textual) space.

In my case, working with resonance is also, more specifically, to explore and develop the ability to speak to very different groups of people without having to name them all. For example, although *Woman, Native, Other* focuses mainly on the realities of women of color in the U.S. and Third World women, the critical tools it offers have been taken up by many other groups of resistance; these include, not surprisingly, marginalized groups across cultures and nations, which I have not anticipated but which can relate to the situations discussed, whether they are men or women, whites or nonwhites. For me, if the book has inspired readers to use the tools offered to carry on their struggles on their own terms, their responses to the book have also been most inspiring to me as I move on in my work. It's a reciprocal way of resonating. And it is exciting to write, as I said, with many ears and many eyes, even though you do not know exactly where all the possibilities lie.

Because of the multiple dimension of language, I often don't know how a sentence will end; I never know exactly where I will be in the next paragraph [*laughs*], not even to mention the next chapter, or the entirety of the book. This is something that applies on the most minute scale of the book as well as on the largest scale of the book. I have no idea how a book is going to begin and end when I start my writing journey. A story, as I wrote in the opening pages of *Woman, Native, Other*, is headless and bottomless but one has to enter somewhere, one has to go out somewhere, and even though there is a beginning and an end to every story, the readers can actually enter and exit on any page they wish without the feeling that they have missed "the intrigue" or the "main point." By turning yourself constantly into a reader while you write, you can see how your words can always be read differently, how language resonates differently from one context to the other, and according to the way it resonates, I'll decide on the turns I'll be making or the courses I'll engage in. This being said, the book is certainly not chaotic [*laughs*], because you can take the last page of the book and the first page of the book and they do speak to each other in the contextual links created. The process constantly allows things to build on one another, and you as a receptor never lose sight of the many possibilities generated or of the continuous weaving of the many threads initiated. Ultimately one can talk about at least three movements rather than the two movements I mentioned earlier. One movement is to go forward in an argument; another movement is to constantly come back to oneself; and the third, for example, is to create from and with the unintended reflexive communication among words themselves.

M: *It seems exactly what is happening right now, I mean the way you have just answered seems to be articulated in the very movements you have just mentioned. These movements contribute to creating a rhythm that also comes out of different timbres and tones that modulate your voice. Different voices, in both the metaphorical and literal sense of the word, as well as silences also constantly cross your voice, your work. As far as silence is concerned, while in your films, or while listening to you, the crossing and resonance of silences is clearly audible, it is apparently more problematic to listen to them in your written texts. Personally I find them in the way you put images in among the printed pages, sometimes in the way you play with the layout, or in the movement from prose to poetry, and vice versa, or in the overlapping of theorizing and story-telling. For me, all these things create in the otherwise overly compact printed space, different rhythms and cadences, which break the linearity of the composition and invite the reader to take a pause, to stop and listen to the soundless re-creation of her/his own associations, imagination, reflections. Here I'm talking of my experience as a reader, but I would very much like to hear from you about the possibility of creating silences in the written text.*

T: Well, the description is really great [*laughs*], it is an acute way of describing how one can work with silences. Because for me, how should I say this . . . rhythm can only be created if one works on relationships, which means that you do not just focus, as I said earlier, on the object of observation or on advancing an argument, but musically as well as conceptually, on the reverberations and the links created in the process you have initiated. It is in drawing new relationships among old objects that changes can be effected on these very objects and that an unspoken space can be opened up. If I take music as an example, what is important for me in composing a piece of music is not just to select the sounds to be included, but also to select the silences. In other words, not merely to focus on the musical notes, but to have a feel for and to work with the intervals and the transitions between notes, phrases, and movements, and how these take shape in relation to one another. Without an ear for the way tone, timbre, dynamics, and duration (the latter includes both sound and silence) enter into relations with one another, your rhythm is bound to come out weak, flat, or derivative. The piece would be just like a stream of notes and phrases put one after the other, whose relationship—you can hear this immediately—is not working out because they have not found a way of coming together and coming apart.

The same thing occurs, for example, when one reads aloud in delivering a lecture. You can hear how certain sentences are not fully lived, because they don't seem to know how to find their tones, their pauses, their cadences. So, I would say that creating rhythm is a way of working with intervals—silences, pauses, pacing— and working with intervals means working with relationships in the wider sense of the term. Relationships between one word, one sentence, one idea and another; between one's voice and other women's voices; in short, between oneself and the other. What you are creating in relationships is not the mere product of an accumulative process, but rather, a musical accuracy—the precise rhythm and tuning that allow what you say and don't say to find its reverberation in other people. This leads us back to the point that I made earlier about how, when you let things resonate and approach them indirectly, you are opening up a space in which absence and presence never work as mere oppositions. So although you cannot be exhaustive and totalizing, you are not excluding either. Silence here resonates differently; it is not equated with absence, lacuna, or emptiness; it is a different sound, or to use a pertinent word of yours, a "soundless" space of resonance, and a language of its own.

The working with silence is also very much linked to the notion of multiplicity of meaning, which has become a commonplace in contemporary thinking. Of course, a number of people would continue to say "But what's the use of having many meanings; why don't we use words and sentences in a clear-cut manner so that nobody is mistaken about the message put forth?" But here multiplicity of meaning, as I have already elaborated, is not a question of cultivated ambivalence and ambiguity; it does not derive from a lack of determination or of incisiveness. It is radical to language, whose fictional nature is precisely what tends to be denied in every attempt to subject it to the ideological norms of clarity and accessibility. A further example is, let's say, the fundamentally different meanings that may be given to the same word, the same sentence when it is read by a member of the dominant group and by a member of a dominated group of a culture. Since marginalized people are always socialized to understand things from more than their own point of view, to see both sides of the matter, and to say *at least* two things at the same time, they can never really afford to speak in the singular.

This is why the use of the term "West" in the context of my writings is always strategic, because "the West" is both outside and inside me. For example, when I used capital "I" in *Woman, Native, Other* and more specifically in chapter three, I was compelled to use small i, I/i, and, actually, to resort to the whole gamut of personal pronouns—we, they; he, she; you— while addressing the complex issues of identity and difference I was facing in writing from a non-unitary, multi-vocal place of subjectivity. "I" reads as the voice of a white male dominant member in the context of that chapter, but the fact that I chose "I" instead of pointing to "Them" in an "Us" context, was a deliberate gesture to resist such clear-cut division and to acknowledge that the oppressor is not necessarily only outside of "i," "she," and "we," but is also well and alive within each oppressed self. So the use of "I" is very ironical both toward He-the-Master and toward myself, or the He-in-me.

While these tactics inevitably run the risk of being misread and may enrage certain Euro-American readers, they are easily understood by many members of marginalized groups. Not only language radically lends itself to multiple readings, but the plurality of meaning here is also bound to the readers' different socio-political contexts. Recently, actually in Bologna, one of the responses that Paola Bono, who writes for the newspaper *Il Manifesto*, had for the paper I delivered at the Centro di Documentazione delle Donne was that, what disturbed her was precisely the difficulty she faced in trying to figure out when she was being included and when she was being excluded in my use of "they" and "us." Such a reading was very perceptive and I was glad to hear it discussed in public. Needless to say, the feeling *was* disturbing especially when the person who experienced it was a member of a dominant culture and who, as a feminist, also resisted that location. But then, when you think that people of color across nations have always found themselves struggling in similarly charged situations, where they constantly have to decide whether words like "man," "mankind," "human," and even "woman" include or exclude them! When you realize this, you also understand that what I usually offer the reader or listener through my writings and lectures are experiences that are being lived on both sides.

So it was not just Bono who was being put on the spot, it was myself as well, even though our subject positions in the experiencing of that disturbing feeling were markedly different. This anecdote may give you another example of working with multiple meaning and silence. Something was being conveyed that was unsaid in the text—the space, as mentioned earlier, that resonates without being named.

M: *"Hybridity," "interstices," "voids," "intervals," "in-betweeness" . . . these words circulate in all your works and are actually inherent to your practices of writing and filming, so that your texts (politically, strategically) resist closures and classifications. I wonder if you would relate the recurring use and naming of these words, each time in a different context, not only to what someone has called your "theoretical project," but also to another way of playing with differences in repetition; that is, as a further tool to keep on opening up meanings. I mean that these words also probably need to be constantly displaced to prevent them from becoming another set of fixed categories, a sort of theoretical commodity, a fashionable theoretical passe-partout.*

T: Yes, I would agree with that. To give you an example: the word "marginality." In "Cotton and Iron" [a chapter of *When the Moon Waxes Red*], the immediate concern I had while addressing the question of marginality was how to avoid reproducing, in the writing itself, the same model of center-margin power relationship that has prevailed in the existing system of cultural and political representation. So at the same time as the discussion evolved around the notion of marginality, it was not "centered" on it, in the sense that marginality here remained an "empty" site—thanks to which, however, the movements of the text could unfold. "Empty," in that the meaning of marginality, remained constantly in progress or in-the-making throughout the text. With each new paragraph, I began again with a different departure on marginality. The set of specific and contextual meanings arrived at in the previous paragraph was in the next one either refuted or pushed further, to the point of running the risk of losing the term and invalidating its "useful" function in the struggle of "marginalized" people. In other words, there was, with every re-departure, a return and a new take on the same notion, which kept on growing with differently situated meanings as it is repeatedly slightly displaced. What may come out of such a spherical advance-and-return movement are ways of understanding marginality whose complexities can reach us in our heterogeneity, our different everyday situations and thinking habits, and lead us beyond the simplistic negation or assertion of marginality as mere opposition to a locatable center.

But I really share the same concern as the one you have just voiced, which is that after a while, one becomes tired of hearing concepts such as in-betweeness, border, hybridity, and so on. It's like the word "difference": It is so old a word and yet we keep on using it again and again in widely varied contexts of struggle. Diversity, identity, ethnicity. The more these terms are popularized, the more difficult the challenge we encounter when we use them. But we would have to keep on using them so that we can continue what Mao called "the verbal struggle"; and the link to Mao here, for me, is to draw attention to the fact that the theoretical project is not "*just* a theoretical project," but one that, despite its reality as theory, grows out of a social, cultural, and political context. Unless we abide by the prevailing compartmentalized view of the world, our life activities are inseparable. Whether we articulate it or not, many of us are aware

TL

of the fact that the words mentioned and the difficult emerging space we are trying to open up are being quickly co-opted by the mainstream. So the constant appropriation and reappropriation of these terms, as I have stated elsewhere, needs to be further reappropriated, and the struggle is endless because you'll always have to be on the alert to resist easy consumption. You'll have to keep on undoing and redoing what tends to be hastily encased.

Of course, the temptation is always to go and look for new words, which a number of theorists have done. Roland Barthes, for example, came up with a lexicon in which many of the words coined are retrieved from Latin; they are, to quote a number of French thinkers, Barthes' "barbarisms" [*laughs*]. But one can understand such an operation when one tries to invent new words and realizes one can't really invent them from nowhere. A rather common way to take up this challenge is to go back to one's "roots," one's remote traditions, or in the case of people of color, one's denied heritage in order to invent anew. Here one runs the risk, as with Barthes, of coming up with words and concepts that sound so archaic, "backward," or "barbarian" to some people that one is bound to have to negotiate one's ground very tightly.

To come back fearlessly to the "old" in order to bring out the "new" and to re-open a different space of meaning is something that the women's movement has devoted much energy to. Here the same terminology is used with a differed meaning. The notion of "difference" itself is a famous example. Difference on the Master's terms has always been given to His others. But this does not mean that "difference" should be banned from women's language. So, while some of us continue to ask, "What's the use of reclaiming difference when it is already given to us?," some others among us refuse to concede theory and history to the Master all over again and work carefully at expanding the term from within as we continue to displace it. A new hearing may then be produced on our own terms that makes difference not an inherited attribute but a politics of articulation (or disarticulation). For the time being then, we should continue to use words like in-betweeness and hybridity as tools of change, and we should keep on redefining them until their spaces become so saturated that we would have to couple them with other words or invent some kind of hybrid word [*laughs*] in order to go a little further. This is the verbal struggle we constantly have to face.

M: *I think the way you use these terms in different contexts, and for different goals and aims, as I said earlier, might be a good strategy for displacing them and preventing them from undergoing a short-term saturation. In your work you may sometimes use these words in a piece of poetry or among fragments of pictures; at other times you use them while talking about women, or while talking about storytelling. For me, you stubbornly face the verbal struggle not only as you continue to reappropriate and reuse these words, but also when you reuse them time by time in different contexts, so that, repeating them in differences, their meanings continue to be mobile and shifting. I guess this might be one of the possible ways to prevent these words from becoming part of a fixed terminology.*

T: You remind me of the other part of your question, which is the use of repetition. Actually, repetition has been a notion frequently debated in both artistic and theoretical milieus. It is a technique very familiar to avant-garde filmmakers. One of its functions, for example, is to emphasize something that may be lost otherwise, therefore drawing attention to the neglible, the unessential, the marginal. Another function is to fragment, because repetition can interrupt, hamper, or delay the flow of a narrative, an event, or an argument. In musical practices that are passed on through oral transmissions, repetition is linked to collective memory and its social function may be said to be that of uniting a community, ritualizing its cyclical activities, marking its life passages, and providing it with a sense of identity. It is here a process of memorization rather than an individual technique of structuring, as it is often the case in Western works. In the political realm, repetition as a means to gain voice and to reclaim certain rights among marginalized groups can, at times, become so expected to members of dominant groups that it is simply heard as a naive reproduction of the same. Such a repetition consequently tends to block the space of critical thinking, for it doesn't go, doesn't lead us anywhere; it just stays in one place and marks time. For me, this is where the point you made on short-term saturation comes in.

It's very important to understand the diverse functions and effects of repetition. One way of challenging mechanical repetition, as I have said elsewhere, is to proceed by unceasingly introducing difference within repetition. So that, reproduction is never quite the reproduction of the same, and viewers or readers are invited to return to a familiar ground only to find themselves drifting somewhere else. Repetition with displacements means, for example, that one can use again and again the same statement while differing the objectives (if any), the contexts, the tones, the punctuations. In my film work, I did this, let's say, in the soundtrack by working on the whole and the parts of a commentary, a conversational fragment or a musical phrase. A complete statement is written and recorded more than one time on tape. This is a mere point of departure, for in the editing process, that same statement may come out whole, in parts or with certain parts missing. According to the contexts in which it is placed, I may decide to leave this statement as recorded, to make two statements out of it, to cut off a part of it, or to cut just one word in it, and thereby change the entire meaning of the sentence. By letting this statement come back each time in a slightly different form, I may have given the spoken words what a viewer called "a ritual charge." And by repeating a sentence in its multiple and at times, incomplete form, I not only suspend its meaning, alleviating it from the weight of correct syntax and definite affirmation or negation, I also find great pleasure in exceeding my own intentions, "rediscovering" the statement, and by the same token, offering the viewer a wider range of possible interpretations.

Now, in a situation of political activism, whether the repetition of the same slogans over and over again helps to change things or simply saturates the space of critical hearing would have to depend on the ability both of the speaker and the listener to work with difference. In other words, the questions, "Why are they always pounding the same things into our head?" and "Are they really listening? What do they hear?" continue to be raised separately on the two sides instead of being experienced both at the same time on the one side or the other. In certain contexts, one may need to repeat many times in order to be heard; still, one can use exactly the same slogan while diversifying the contexts, the tones, the volumes [*laughs*], and the elements of duration. I'm thinking here, for example, of the many speeches delivered by African-American leaders, which come from places like the churches and other communal settings. It suffices to remember the speeches of prominent figures of resistance like Malcom X and

Martin Luther King Jr., or to attend those of Angela Davis or June Jordan (to name only a few) to understand how repetition works and how complex the social, political, psychological, as well as artistic role it plays proves to be.

What you have is a practice in which not only differences are deliberately introduced into repetition, but repetition is also deliberately used to punctuate and ritualize a speech, thereby optimizing, through the building of rhythmic patterns around pivotal statements, its ability to empower while raising the consciousness of a community. Here, the more times you repeat, the further along you build the ties that bind the listeners. Repetition is thus used to emphasize as well as to create a different kind of relationship both among the listeners and between the listeners and the speaker. Every time you repeat, you also build up, and in the process, people come to understand what you say differently from when they first hear you make the same statement. In my own work, I had to resort to a wide range of tactics and strategies with the use of repetition. One example is the way I work with stereotypes. Sometimes the text of *Woman, Native, Other* is spun around stereotypical English expressions that may irritate certain readers—academics, for example—because these popularized expressions tend to stand out sorely in the context of scholarly and theoretical writing. But to use stereotypes in order to attack stereotypes is also an effective strategy, for irony here needs no lengthy explanations or rationalizations. This is another example of how repetition is used to produce a different hearing. In short, repetition has an important and extremely complex political function, but it can easily be dismissed because it has often been understood and practiced in a very limited way.

M: *Referring to the notion of "writing the body," you also say that "it is a way of making theory in gender, of making of theory a politics of everyday life; thereby re-writing the ethnic female subject as a site of difference." I wonder if you could elaborate a little further on this, in particular as it concerns the making of theory as a politics of everyday life.*
T: It's such a vast question! [*Laughs*]

M: *Well, if you are tired we could have a break or we can talk about that another time.*
T: No, let's try. Just give me a try [*laughs*]. To start somewhere, what usually bothers me most is the tendency to reduce politics to the most evident sites and sources of power, such as institutions or government officials and personalities. Being political, for a great number of people, is merely to focus on things that relates directly to the body politic. I think that the women's movement in the seventies and the gay and lesbian movement in the eighties are, for example, movements that truly opened up a space in which politics is no longer simply to be located in these all-too-visible sites. It infiltrates every aspect of our lives, and this is where your point on theory as a politics of everyday life comes in. For me, if theory has a function, or if the intellectual has a role to play in society, it would mainly have to be that of changing the frame of thought with which we operate in every single activity of our lives; so that, instead of remaining isolated within the family context or within the individual space, these activities reflect our social function—the way we situate ourselves vis-à-vis our society, as well as vis-à-vis the world around us.

So every single tiny action we carry out reflects and affects our politics. In *Woman, Native, Other*, for example, nothing can be taken for granted. Everything, down to the smallest and most banal detail of our lives, can be politicized: the way, for example, we perceive ourselves, the way we define our activities, the way we write, do research, bend down in the field picking tomatoes, interact with others, tell stories, fight with our mothers, and go on transmitting their truths. And here we are led back to the question of relationships we discussed earlier, because to understand the political dimension of our personal lives, we constantly have to look into the ways we position ourselves and the different contexts in which we operate. Thanks to this awareness of our positionality in everything we do, our activities are no longer compartmentalized as if they could be sufficient in themselves, and what is thought to be personal can no longer be limited to the individual and the singular. In other words, what is being constantly challenged are the unquestioned partitions, boundaries, and binary divisions, including those between the individual and the society, or the self and the other. What is political and what is apolitical, for example? This does not mean that we can no longer make the differentiation, but rather, that it has become much more difficult to take the license to decree what is political and what is not, when the criteria that serve to define it have been radically and thoroughly undermined.

Now to relate politics further to the question of body writing that you started out with, you have here another die-hard binary opposition: that of the body and the mind or, let's say, the specific and the general, the personal and the impersonal. The literary and the art world, for example, have been taken to task for having used the term "political" too loosely. As some who are eager to guard the territory for themselves would argue, "political" should be attributed to investigations of specific historical contradictions. Well, the body *is* a site of particularity and specificity, at the same time as it is a site marked by historical "contradictions." As such, it is as intimately personal as it is impersonally social. With all the work that has been done in this area, it is difficult to deny this without reverting to the old dualist frame of reasoning, which opposes the concrete to the abstract, or the body's reality to the mind's unreality. The politics of writing the body precisely breaks down such an opposition because, as many writers have already elaborated on, thinking and writing is a very physical process that constantly speaks of and speaks to the body of the person writing. Again, that body does not simply point to an individual terrain; it is the site where the individual and society meet. And it is by working on this relationship that the tension between the personal and the political is maintained and kept alive in writing.

M: *Euro-Americans' attempts to classify their Other into a unitary and monolithic category have been rightly deconstructed by postcolonial practices and theories. Yet it seems to me that an unquestioned category still continues to survive, that of the West. The West is a sort of unitary category, which perhaps should be further displaced and deconstructed, not so much because of the complex realities of postmodern cultures, as some people say, a notion that might sound and in some cases really is very self-indulgent according to me, but because, once again, it doesn't help to undermine a politics of simple opposition and binarism. Further, and I know you are very aware of this, the act of naming the Other, even if this time it is the Other of the Other, in any case relies on a sense of a delimited and fixed identity. So maybe also this category should be displaced to prevent, let's say, hyphen realities from becoming fixed identities in the moment they name their*

Other. In other words, the naming of this category needs perhaps to be further displaced to let hyphen realities keep on moving and remaining mobile, so continuing to be difficult to be categorized. What I mean is that, since one of the main challenges brought about by hyphenated cultures to the dominant cultures is precisely their capacity to be mobile and baffle categorizations; hyphenated cultures should be vigilant in the act of naming their Other in a unitary way, because the risk is that of freezing their own movement, name, and identity, which leads to the danger of re-creating the conditions in which, once again, they are easily compartimentalized by the dominant cultures.

T: I think it is important that the undermining and displacing of "the West" be carried out on both sides. Although I have already clarified my position on this matter earlier in our discussion, I would add that the situation you raise here is quite complex. Your question could be read, for example, as a critique of the simplistic way marginalized groups, marginalized cultures name the centralized cultures. Such a naming fixes the West in the same manner that the West has been fixing its Others. But the question could also be read more subtly as a form of denial that is necessary to certain members of Western cultures, but that can appear as merely defensive and redundant to members of non-Western cultures. (As elaborated earlier, it may be useful to keep in mind here that terms such as "West," "non-West" and "marginal" are strategically used in my context.) For example, when a member of the dominant culture tries to break down the monolithic concept of the West, isn't it necessary that the person also tries to face — rather than to escape — the historical situation that contributes to undertanding how the notion of the West can, or has become, monolithic to its "Others"?

Members of dominant groups have always defined their subjectivity as mobile, changing, flexible, complex, and problematic — in other words, "safe for democracy." Whereas the subjectivity of their Others remains uncomplicated, unsophisticated, unproblematic, verifiable, and knowable — that is, incapable or undeserving of "democracy." So to say the West is non-monolithic can be a redundancy in this context, and although no culture can in reality be monolithic, one can still talk about an acceptable Western ethos, about Western empires, European imperialism, or about the metropolitan West and its overseas territories. Perhaps nowhere is the residue of imperialism better seen than in the way "natives" are represented in the Western media. It suffices to read the many books by cultural experts and to follow the news or any cultural-economical program, to notice how Western systems of representation continue to assume the primacy and the centrality of the West, how they exclude even as they include, consolidate, and package.

For me, the predicament of naming "the West" is tightly related to the dilemma of naming oneself in the politics of identity and difference. When do we mark our boundaries with markings already given to us, and when do we refuse them? A well-known example is South Africa's naming of its black nations, which serves to control their movements while allowing its members of European descent to move about unrestricted. Naming and confinement go together. But even in the U.S. or in the U.K., for example, self-naming among marginalized groups is no less problematic. When some of us call ourselves Asian Americans, or gays and lesbians, are we simply endorsing the labels that we have been given, or are we re-appropriating these labels, thereby situating politically such namings, not in the phase of assimilation-for-survival, but rather in a phase of struggle where marking is also affirming ourselves critically? Here, what is given rise to is a certain consciousness that empowers second-class citizens and not only allows them to assume without shame their denied cultural heritage, but also to conceive of identity as a political marking rather than a mere inherited marking.

Now the danger, as you said, is that when we name ourselves, we are also bound to work with closures and to use all-encompassing names such as "the West" to designate the site of dominance; or if you prefer, "the non–African Asians" to refer to those who largely occupy this site. Of course, this simply leads us back to the danger of perpetuating binary oppositions and hence, the necessity for members of Western cultures to face the challenge, and to unceasingly undo this monolithic notion of the West through their own disengagement with the most confident master discourses, and with all imperialist undertakings. Just as in the women's movement where, for example, it is important that women not be the only ones to solve women's problems and to deal with gender politics, it is also crucial that Westerners work with differences, and learn to rename and exile themselves so as not to be lumped together under a unitary label. They would have to participate, as an Other among Others, in the process of constant renaming and displacing, which marginalized groups cannot afford to ignore in this moment of history. This is a task that has to be carried out on both sides. The West has been responsible for the reactive, monolithic naming of the West; through its historical imperialist deeds, it has created its own unacknowledged unitary classification. So we are not dealing here with a situation of equal power relationship, and in that sense, we cannot really talk about "the Other of the Other." We have learned this lesson with the feminist struggle, for when men talk about men's liberation, nobody should be led to believe that an equal, reverse form of oppression or of sexism is at work, but rather that men do, indeed, need to liberate themselves from their own privileged status in male-dominated societies.

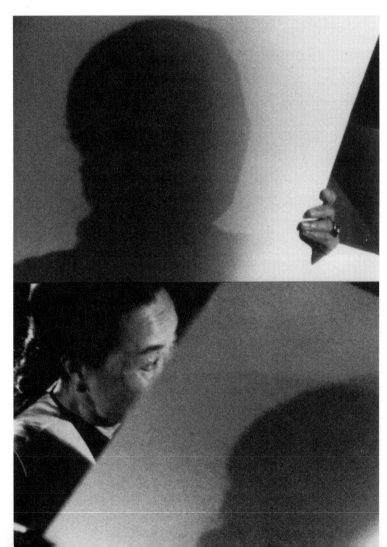

JUMPING INTO THE VOID

with Bérénice Reynaud

Public interview conducted at Hatch-Billops' Artist and Influence Series in New York in May 1992. First published in *Artist and Influence*, ed. James V. Hatch and Leo Hamalian, Vol. XII, 1993, with the following Foreword by Bérénice Reynaud: "*A woman of many talents and many cultures, Trinh embodies with rare ethical elegance the contradictions of a 'postmodern' condition: the fractures of a dominant discourse, questioned by categories of people conveniently labelled 'Others': women, people of color, inhabitants of the Third World. This is sharply described by the director herself: 'What is at stake is not only the hegemony of Western cultures, but also their identities as unified cultures; in other words, the realization that there is a Third World in every First World, and vice versa. The master is made to recognize that His Culture is not as homogeneous, not as monolithic as He once believed it to be. He discovers, often with much reluctance, that he is just an other among others. In this 'horizontal vertigo,' identity is this multiple layer whose process never leads to the True Self, or to Woman, but only to other layers, other selves, other women.' 'Otherness,' though, is not a fixed notion. To paraphrase Simone de Beauvoir, one is not born an 'Other,' one becomes one. Especially in the documentary process, the filmmaker—no matter what is his/her race, class, or gender—takes the position of a unified subject (all the more powerful for being invisible). The object of the cinematic gaze is the Other. Does that mean that we cannot escape the alienation created by the documentary process (alius, in Latin, means other)? What struck me when I first saw* Reassemblage (16 mm, 40 min, 1982) *at the New York Film Festival was its voice-over: unmistakably feminine, unmistakably foreign, hesitant yet resolute, ironical yet poetic, it slightly irritated me. When I related this experience to a group of students at Ann Arbor, I was asked to explain my discomfort. 'It is because, at the time, I was not very comfortable with my own femininity,' I quickly free-associated. The truth is, a first encounter with Trinh's films is often unsettling for the viewer, because it decenters his/her positioning as a subject. Instead of centering the subject/viewer with the comfortable notion that a quantum of 'knowledge' about something was provided by the film, it sends him/her back to his/her own essential displacement—what*

Trinh calls 'the trial of the subject.' So this soft, disquieting female voice was saying: 'A film about what? my friends ask. A film about Senegal, but what in Senegal?' Reassemblage was also unsettling for the viewer, because it could not be pinned down to a genre: Was it documentary, diary film, experimental venture? In a seminal text published in 1984, 'Mechanical Eye, Electronic Ear, and the Lure of Authenticity,' the filmmaker poetically explained: 'Some call it Documentary. i call it No Art, No Experiment, No Fiction, No Documentary. To say some thing, no thing, and allow reality to enter. Capture me. This, i feel, is no surrender. Contraries meet and mate and i work best at the limits of all categories.' This defin-ition of 'intertextuality' is often applied to feminine writing, that takes place '(in) the interstice: that banned place, which remains unheard, opaque, incomprehensible to the dominant's ear.' For Trinh it has many other functions as it defines the 'meeting and mating' of such 'opposites' as: Asia/Africa, First World/Third World, film-ing subject/filmed subject, film/music, voice/text, natural/fictional, Western thinking/Eastern thinking, subject/object—and finally, i/you: it is because 'I' is generically used to express a white male unitary subject that, as a woman of color, a 'non-unitary subject,' Trinh feels its inadequacy and often uses the alternate form i, or even I/i. 'Once, a spectator became really upset after reading my script, because he realized that I had used some Joola music over images of a place that was not populated by Joola people. His reac-tion raises two issues. On the one hand, this seems to me to be a prolongation of the colonial territorial mind: Africans should mind their own business and look at Africa; Asians, at Asia; while Euro-peans can act on behalf of . . . the world. You are not, for example, supposed to cut across borderlines of African cultures. . . . But, if you make a film about aspects of American culture and use a sonata by Mozart, no prescriptive question whatsoever would be raised, because it seems "normal" that the dominant groups share the same cultural heritage. In dealing with Third World cultures, you are thus bound to an extremely reductive ideology of authen-ticity. However, this reaction is understandable, because, in a way, it reflects both the desire of the West to correct its mistakes and the fear to go wrong in trying to "universalize," hence the necessity to stick to the specifics. . . . In Naked Spaces I deal with this question precisely by providing hints and cues that informs the viewer of the use of the same music and commentary across different societies. Repetition in such cross-cultural contexts is used as a strategy, and the notion of difference I work with is one that does not ex-clude similarity. There are differences within Africa, but there is also a link between all the African countries, so one can speak of an African culture, an African heritage.' After spending her first seventeen years in Vietnam, Trinh T. Minh-ha came to the States, where she continued her studies in music composition (she has composed a number of musical pieces), ethnomusicology, and [French and] Francophone literatures. She then went on to teach *musical composition at the Dakar (Senegal) Conservatory of Music, from 1977 to 1980, while doing research at the National Cultural Archives. During these three years, she traveled extensively in Senegal, Mali, and Burkina Faso and became passionately involved in the local culture, especially music and architecture. Naked Spaces—Living is Round (16 mm, 134 min, 1985), Trinh's first feature-length film, starts with a stunning absolute silence, on a close-up of dancers in an African village. But why Africa when one is an Asian woman? 'My refusal to represent Africa while dealing with representation, my desire to show the culture without packaging it, is prone to misunderstandings. I am here acutely caught in the in-between position of an insider and an outsider. I am an insider to this culture insofar as we share the experience of colonialism, and there are many instances in which African and Vietnamese cultures do meet. But on the other hand, I am no less an outsider than if I were a European. It is in dealing with this precarious position . . . that I find myself having constantly to face issues of post-colonialism. From Vietnam to Africa, they have multiplied in dimensions. . . . Speaking about specific affinities, what struck me while living in Senegal was the language of silence. Before going there, I had been living in the United States for some years and had come to accept that silence (which has always played an important role in Asian communicative contexts) could not be communicated and was not communicative. To my great surprise, I realized in Africa that this language of silence could be shared: People understand the complexity and subtlety of silence, and can decipher it. This is what introduced me to African culture.'"*

Reynaud: *Why show Africa when one is an Asian woman? I thought that, with the agreement of Minh-ha, I would start the discussion with her by just jumping in the core of the subject and playing devil's advocate and ask her that.*

Trinh: This is an ideologically loaded question that has been repeatedly asked, not only by members of the Euro-American and African-American communities but even more so by those of the Asian-American community. The first two films I made were certainly very hard for Asian-American programmers to classify, hence to present it as an "Asian-American product" in their exhibition network. For me, there is no such thing as pure culture. Whether I deal with Africa or with Vietnam, my own culture, I would have to deal with the very hybridity of the culture itself. The choice can be viewed both in terms of circumstances and of political motivations.

The thought of making a film in Senegal came to me quite unpredictably after I had lived and taught there for three years. The time spent in Senegal and in several other West African countries was partly marked by the almost routine encounter with the normative discourse of cultural expertism and of anthropology, whose authority made itself felt in the smallest daily events, whenever people talked about the culture—whether they were African city dwellers (that is, insiders to the culture) or local outsiders (mostly foreign researchers, administrators,

businessmen, and technical assistants). Hence, the necessity immediately to question my own position as outsider and as a "hybrid insider" because, despite the differences, I recognize acutely the ethics and the experiences related to colonialism's aftermath, which I myself grew up with in Vietnam. If it was odd, as an insider, to read about oneself being offered up as a cultural entity by experts writing on Vietnamese culture, it was unsettling to look at oneself and others from the standpoint of an outsider-insider in Senegal. The encounter with African cultures thus became a catalyst to think about questions of subjectivity and of power relations.

Why Africa? Why do we have to always limit ourselves to the boundaries that are marked for us? Whose interest do we serve when we abide by them? I think there is something to be said again and again about the complex issues involved in the way dominant identities maintain the flexibility of their boundaries while those marginalized are expected to remain within well-divided, well-defined frontiers set up "for their own good." Since it is only within these "authentic," easily identifiable, hence confining demarcations that members of the marginalized groups can make themselves heard in reclaiming their rights to self-representation, one cannot generalize in black-and-white terms the process of internalizing, rejecting, and reappropriating such apartheid divisions. Furthermore, no member of the marginalized groups can really bypass the burden of representation. Here, whenever you raise your voice you are not simply speaking as an individual artist or thinker, because everything you say is perceived as being gender and ethnic specific, or specific to sexual preference. You are more often than not speaking as a representative of a community, a nation, a people. So those of us who used to be spoken about are now asked to speak, but only to speak as a token—"Don't you trespass the marked boundaries."

R: *I am going to continue in the same vein of attacking you. Even when you talk about yourself in the large sense, meaning your own culture, meaning Vietnamese women, you still generate controversy because in your film* Surname Viet Given Name Nam *you commit the absolute crime. You make a movie of Vietnamese women in English. Second, you make a "documentary" in which you treat the spectator shamelessly. It is only about halfway through the film that the spectator starts scratching the head and says "Wait a minute, this is staged. I have been had!" To create in the spectator this distance from buying in the raw as if it were a documentary. (For those of you who have not seen the film, the women who are used to stage the interviews are Vietnamese women living in the United States, and they are the same women who we later see in unstaged situations, talking about their lives. They are not at all the original women interviewed in Vietnam and the staged interviews are conducted in the United States.) I would like Minh-ha to explain the apparatus of the film and also to comment more on this issue of categorization. How do you position yourself as a filmmaker between the genres of experimentation and documentary?*

T: Even when one speaks about one's culture, one still has to resist the binary opposition conveniently set up between outsider and insider. To follow up on what I said earlier, the first thing one could question here is the authority with which insiders are unquestioningly endowed when they speak about their own culture. A Vietnamese woman making a film on Vietnamese women: What could sound more familiar and correct in today's context of cultural diversity and liberal pluralism? And yet, as I also mentioned earlier, self-representation and representation is a responsibility one cannot afford to merely reject. In order to break away from that kind of authorized subjectivity I went for a number of itineraries that would allow me to show "the culture" without endorsing the insider's authority. This was largely done by avoiding the so-called factual historical information that one easily gets in history books on Vietnam, and by working with the more slippery realms of oral tradition and popular memory: the songs, sayings, proverbs that expose women's condition; the stories that people remember of the historical heroines of Vietnam; and the life stories of contemporary Vietnamese women.

I have spoken at length elsewhere [1] on the varied uses of English and of Vietnamese in the film, and on the necessity to cross boundaries of film categories in dealing with "truthfulness" in representation. It is not always easy to maintain the creative function of repetition, especially when certain questions inevitably call for certain answers as related to the specific context of each film. To avoid repeating myself entirely, I would link here the work on language and on film genre to our earlier discussion on authorized boundaries and subjectivities. It seems that all the controversy generated by *Surname Viet*—as you describe it—is due to demands for authenticity and compliance with conventions that have become naturalized. In such an ideological context, any unfamiliar departure from these conventions, which also asks the maker and the viewer to look at themselves while they look (you speak it, it speaks you), would then be perceived as incorrect or fallacious—a fraud.

For me *Surname Viet* can only accomplish what it sets out to do if its viewing is precisely experienced the way you just describe it. The creative potentials of cinema lie in the showing of this process, in which a form of mediated documentation—the reenactment of interviews carried out in Vietnam—slowly unveils itself as such without taking away from you the compelling mode of direct address of interviews, nor reducing itself to a piece of mere information retrieval (by announcing, as in many TV films for example, right at the start of the interviews and in an unimaginative, formulaic manner with a burnt-in caption, that the material shown is a reenactment). Some filmmakers (Alexander Kluge, Jean-Luc Godard) have affirmed that tales are the best documentary works. Even when they are not "staged," interviews cannot be viewed merely as pieces of oral testimony. In a way, all "oral testimonies" *are* fictions because language itself is fictional by nature. An image of a reality or a word used to point to a reality has to address its "fictive" reality as image or word.

I was not only interested in the stories unfolded in these interviews, I was also working with the politics of interviews. On the one hand, unmediated truth in film is an illusion. On the other, you don't get the intimate stories of people simply by pointing a microphone and a camera at them. So in dealing with "truthfulness" in representation, I used both reenacted and "unstaged" interviews. Thanks to the abundant feedback viewers have given—both negative and positive—it has been possible for me to assess the kind of impact such a process has had on them, and to see its potential to unsettle their perception when the fictional and the documentary tightly act upon one another and are mutually exposed. One may realize more acutely

---

[1] See Trinh T. Minh-ha, *Framer Framed*. New York: Routledge, 1992.

how constructed all "real" interviews are but as with the questioning of permitted boundaries discussed earlier, what one more importantly faces are the fictive nature of every film practice and the normative character of the existing film categories.

All this being said, what remains challenging is how the whole process is brought out in the film. How can one show this imaginatively without hammering the point on the viewer's head, or flattening it out for the sake of clarity? If tale-telling is said to be a documentary practice, then one can easily understand this statement made in *Surname Viet*: "By choosing [interviews which are thought to be] the most direct and spontaneous form of voicing and documenting, I find myself closer to fiction." This was precisely also what happened in the process of shooting the film. In the passage from the staged interviews to the "real" interviews the women involved are supposed to drift from stories of other women in Vietnam told in English to their own stories in the States told in Vietnamese. Since the memorization and the rehearsal of the reenacted interviews in English was such a hardship for the women, I thought that the change to their own voices and to their mother tongue would be a relief. But to speak "spontaneously" and "freely" in front of the microphone proved to be impossible. It was another form of "acting natural," another ordeal altogether. On the one hand, the experience was indicative of women's dilemma of "coming into speech" and of the uneasy relation that women have always had with language. On the other, it is precisely in "real-life" situations that people are most concerned about what they should be saying, hence most eager to be tactical about what they do say. What the women were facing here was not just the interviewer, but a whole community of Vietnamese exiles, especially Vietnamese men or those who claim authoritative knowledge of the culture (not to mention the English-speaking film and television "public out there"). It was extremely difficult for them even to talk about their own lives. Everything that came out was a way of addressing the community. Now we are back to the burden of representation discussed earlier.

R: *What you have said is so rich that it opens up a lot of questions. I want to go back to the idea of the relationship between interview and fiction and the communication of knowledge and interview as politics. About the transmission of the quantum of knowledge, a very powerful male curator, after having seen your last film told me, "Well, you know, nobody really understands what China is about and Minh-Ha doesn't either." I thought that this was a great compliment. This is a film that does not give anybody the truth. Not only about China but about this incredibly difficult and fascinating moment of history that China has been living since June 4. There is also something I would like to say about in* Shoot for the Contents. *A scene that impresses me very deeply on two levels personally and formally and the personal is always injected as part of the viewing process. There is a Chinese filmmaker called Wu Tian Ming. He was put as the head of Xian Film Studios a few years ago and made it possible for what became the fifth generation of Chinese filmmakers to make their first films. This man has lived outside of his own country since 1989 and teaches the history of Chinese cinema. He is an older man and has problems with English, and he basically speaks to people in Chinese and when he teaches he has a translator. This man appears in a few scenes interviewed by Minh-ha and the apparatus is quite wonderful. First of all, we see this man from the back, and he is lit in a certain way, and we hear his voice in*

Chinese. Because of the way the film is made it is obviously directed mostly to non–Chinese-speaking audiences. It is clear that the speech that this man is uttering is opaque for most of the intended viewership. Then the camera shifts very slowly and as it shifts we hear a female voice in English we gradually understand is the translator and that she is translating the words of that man. The face of the speaking woman is gradually revealed and she is a young pretty woman. So we have in space, in the image a very powerful sweeping movement that reveals a situation in which, in order to make himself understood, a man who lives in very particular conditions outside of his own country has to borrow the voice of another. I think it is highly significant that this other is a woman. Can you talk about that scene and maybe tie it up with what you said about coming into speech? I think it is not only women that are coming into speech, I think that speech is difficult for all of us and especially before people who are put in situations of censorship and historical displacement. They don't have in front of them the intended audience that their speech was originated for.

T: Speaking about intended audience, it depends on what we mean here by Chinese people. Does this naming refer only to the people living in a specific geographical location on the world map, or does it address the Chinese people all around the globe? It would be very expected of me to make a film on China and have someone residing in mainland China talking about Chinese culture. But in *Shoot* what is offered to the viewer is a wide range of what one can call border people who are right at the edge of being an outsider and an insider to the culture. Wu Tian Ming has exiled himself because of his being too outspoken during the Tiananmen Square event. So as far as the film is concerned, even the person who is the most directly involved in China's political situation is now someone who speaks from the hybrid place of an insider-outsider (being outside the country even though his outsideness is an intimate part of the event). I consider his role as being at one end of the outsider-insider spectrum. At the other end of the spectrum is Clairmonte Moore, an African-American interviewee who is only indirectly involved with the politics of China (via his anti-imperialist Marxist stance in world politics), but whose role is to give a direct analysis of the changes in China and to situate Her politically in relation to Russia and Africa. In between the two ends of the spectrum are the voices of the Chinese-American women and my own voice, which comes through the written text (composed of personal reflections and a wide selection of quotes from ancient popular stories and from Chinese artists, thinkers, and politicians) and which the women also bring out as narrators.

One of the questions I consistently get is: "Why the African-American man in a film on China? Who is he?" Again for me, Clairmonte's role is politically and personally significant, not only because, Asian as I am, I have been making films on Africa but also because this is a film that deals with varying degrees of outsider-insider hybridity within each of the voices involved. To have a "layman," a non-academic, who is very well versed in politics speaking directly about China's political moves in the film is to offer you (the viewer) an analysis whose value is not dependent on nor validated by an institutionalized position of authority. Viewers coming to see a film on China always expect information to be given by either a "real insider" (an insider-insider) to the culture or an academic "scholar" whose opinion is immediately validated by his expertise and authority in Chinese matters. "Is he a professor?" is also a question often asked.

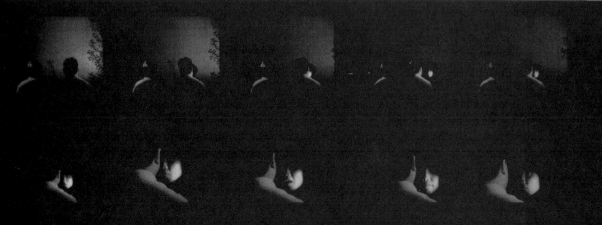

There is nothing in the film that tells you that Clairmonte is a professor. No burnt-in caption, no academic title in the final credits. Such reactions to his role tell us how well-trained we are with the media to look at culture only through experts and supposedly through insiders. Insiders are apparently empowered, but in a limited way—within their own "homelands"—only to serve the purpose of validating someone else's process of retrieving information.

Although the film may be oriented toward an English-speaking audience (including the Chinese), it is not made without the Chinese-speaking viewers in mind. There are many little instances in the film that are only accessible to Chinese speakers (for example, Wu Tian Ming's answers in the scene you just describe are heard in Chinese before they are translated; some of the Chinese poems and signs are not translated, nor is the calligrapher's reply at the end). However, what Wu Tian Ming says is only accessible to the English-speaking viewer through the voice of a translator. So it was important for me to emphasize the role of the translator. Viewed in a wider scope, films are translations and filmmakers are translators, whether the culture they show is their own or others'. The situation is not that Wu Tian Ming's words can only be accessible when we borrow the voice of another person, but that we are constantly in a state of translator-translated whenever we do anything. The question of translation is not limited to the transfer of meaning from one language to another. It is involved in the very production of meaning within one or across several contexts, mentalities, and cultures. One works here with both internal and external differences. The work of translation is performed when a Chicana writes on Native Americans, for example. But it is also performed when she writes about her own culture. Translation is here understood in the multiple, wider sense of the term.

R: *There is an Italian proverb that says that every translation is a betrayal. I wouldn't go as far as that but I think that what is somehow poignant that is articulated in your films, especially these two instances that we are talking about is that in every translation something is lost. There is a lost object that cannot and shouldn't be retrieved. The original Vietnamese women, you haven't tried to reconstruct the way it really happened. In the situation with translation what is lost is the immediacy of being in contact with the speech. I would like you to elaborate on that in relationship to your refusal to represent something but to deal with the process of representation. Meaning again this idea of not conveying a quantum of knowledge but to reflect on the politics of knowledge.*

T: I will counter your Italian quote with a quote from India (and I quote by memory), which says that sadness does not result from an unwanted loss, but also from an unwanted gain. In the process of translation I think that it's not just a question of losing something but also of gaining something. This is where the role of the mediator comes in. Whether the mediator here is the filmmaker or the Chinese translator. The best translation of a text is precisely a translation that can take off and depart from literal meaning. In taking off it creates for itself another space. This occurs so that it can remain loyal not simply to the letter, but also to the spirit, the music, or the poetry of the text. I feel the same with filmmaking. If one loses the kind of immediacy inherent to first-hand experience (the "original" text), one gains in the creation of a third ground because, in the encounter of the "over there" and the "over here," one has to come up with something that belongs neither there nor here, but is able to translate the spirit, the rhythm, or the lived quality of that experience. The process involved in the work of translation is in itself a creation (or a re-creation) rather than a mere illustration, imitation, or transfer of meaning. That process is what interests me in making a film. Here, what is told is in the telling and the conventional divide between form and content can no longer apply. Translation leads us, as with the earlier discussion of interviews, to the fictive nature of language and image — that is, to the politics of filmmaking and the politics of knowledge, as you have pointed out. What the viewer confronts then is not ready-made knowledge, but a different way of knowing — one that does not depend on diagnosis and reification, hence does not limit itself to mere representation.

R: *In your work in general I am very aware that you constantly question the place one is speaking from, whether as an audience or as a filmmaker or writer. Can you talk about the place you are speaking from, which involves many mediations as a woman, as an Asian woman, as an Asian-American woman, etc.?*

T: The place of mediation is precisely the place where you can question this "speaking as." Members of the dominant groups always expect members of marginalized groups to "speak as" because that seems to be the only way they can tolerate difference. When internalized, such a marking of the dominant becomes a form of self-marking. Sometimes this self-marking is used matter-of-factly to quickly point to a temporary representative place from which one speaks. But most of the time, the self-marking or the speaking as so-and-so turns out rather to be a form of validating one's own voice within permitted boundaries. Hence the necessity, as discussed earlier, to always question these boundaries because, at the same time as we have to "reclaim our identity" — an identity that had been denied and undermined in the past — we also cannot be confined to it.

What seems more challenging to me in my work, both artistic and theoretical, is, again, *how* one situates the place from which one speaks or produces meaning. So the questioning of that place is always double-edged. It opens a critical space in which both the maker and the viewer are exposed in the way they read or look at the material offered. It is most important on the one hand to look at the tools that define ourselves and our own activities (the politics involved in filmmaking or in writing), and on the other, to question the representative space that one occupies. The unquestioning acceptance of the Master's tools and technologies is likely to perpetuate the established power relations that see to it that the knower continues to go unnoticed (moving invisibly in unmarked zones) in speaking for others, while the person known remains unproblematically knowable and locatable within pre-marked boundaries. If we do not focus on the tools that define our activities, then the danger is that we will reproduce fixed meanings that are apt to become pawns in the game of power. We have been witnessing throughout history that battles for human rights have always been battles carried out because of the way meanings are imposed and perpetuated. Hence, the need to question the fixity of these meanings as well as the way they are construed, appropriated, and naturalized, defined on terms other than our own or the ones we would like to explore.

R: *My favorite story on that matter takes place during the parade after the Gulf War. There were various groups of veterans who wanted to march as separate entities, and there was a group of gay veterans who thought they really had the right as gay veterans to march. Then there was a group of orthodox Jews who contested the rights of gay veterans to march. The whole issue became ludicrous and also was simply a way of empowering the powers to be. It was "us" being marked as different minorities, that people had the right to participate in the action of a government that had oppressed the people in the Gulf, etc. It is a funny story but it is a horrible story at the same time, and I think you are alluding to things like that. Especially in the U.S. the marking and the sub-marking also at the level "I am an experimental/documentary filmmaker" is also a mode of sub-marking that is a way of playing the strategy of power and forcing it as well as trying to deal with it and making the best of a bad situation. Would you agree with that?*

T: Yes, I think that there is an active level of reappropriation involved. For example, the terms "third world" or "women of color." "Third world" started out as a downgrading term that designated countries lagging behind in the economic competition between the two power blocs. Such a term also tends to focus on economic wealth as the most important or as the only criterion for the advancement of a society. Knowing that, one need not simply reject or censor the term. One can also politicize it by reappropriating it or turning its negative connotation to advantage, which is what actually did happen. This process of reversal and displacement of values applies to many other racially derogatory names. Another example is the term "women of color," which never fails to surprise outsiders to American culture. One has to understand the contexts in which these terms have been reappropriated. Even when we reappropriate them we can never forget who uses them, for what purpose, and in what interest they are being used.

Question from the audience: *How can we be in this contradiction between the necessity of naming ourselves and the fact that these namings are basically corrupted?*

T: It seems to me that no strategy should remain exclusive of the others. Any tool available to you, any strategy that proves useful in a specific circumstance should be taken up. The only danger is that the means often becomes an end in itself, and transitional boundaries run the risk of being solidified. One loses sight of the strategic necessity of a naming or a stance, and starts advocating it as an essential point of arrival. If you say "Today I am speaking to you as so-and-so" and this is used as a strategy, what you are telling your listener is not that "here is my territory, and my specific attributes entitle me to speak authoritatively on this matter." What you tell your listener is simply that "Here, I am speaking from this point of view or this representative position." Understanding a strategy as strategy changes the way you speak. Each one of us has more than one subject positioning, and the demarcation of "speaking as" is always shifting according to circumstances, contexts, or historical moments. It implies that "if I represent another point of view I will have to speak differently." So what you offer is not a solidified boundary but a positioning whose ability to shift and to remain multiple defies all reductive attempts at fixing and classifying.

This kind of subtle displacement in positioning one's voice often provokes anxieties, because people usually think that if you are not committed to a clear-cut position, then everything is opened up to anarchy. And that, in order to be effective politically, you have to be definite in your answers. I would reply here that there are differences to be made. As historical moments, the sixties are very different from the nineties. In the nineties we have learned from previous struggles, from international historical events and from the many critical works on issues of power and knowledge, that we cannot just oppose institutions. Liberation is not obtained simply by eradicating these institutions. Our target is not as clear-cut as it was thought to be. We used to think that we could just make a tabula rasa of everything and start from zero again. Unfortunately, that attitude has also led to many oppressive projects, of which the colonial enterprise remains a most devastating example. In the name of civilization, conquerers set out to raze the cultures of their conquest to the ground in order to implant their own, spread their values around the globe, and expand their territories. Keeping that in mind one would have to remain skeptical of all dogmatic stances and, by necessity, to adopt positions that are precise and to the point, but remain transitional and flexible because they take into consideration the specificity of each circumstance, each political context, and each particular historical moment.

Q: *[Inaudible on tape]*
T: I certainly see that in many spheres of American culture, with all the power of such an exclusive appellation. If you go into the sphere of music, for example, and you talk about American music while focusing mainly on African-American music (which was largely how American music was initially known outside of the U.S. anyway), I would say this can be a form of resistance. The way we articulate the culture would differ with our education and our background, but also with the way we locate ourselves—as Americans. And if you locate my writing between something Asian and something French, then I would insist again that the point precisely is *how* I *translate* French theory and Asian thought. One of the areas that has been bothering a number of academics reading my books is the weaving of the latest critical continental theories with traditional Asian philosophies. It's difficult for someone who has very definite boundaries to accept that a work that can be so critical in terms of theory and yet come back to traditions as old and as mystifying as Zen and Taoism. What interests me is not a return to the roots nor an assimilation of French theory but rather how I can use all the tools that I have in their radical resistance to one another; how I can read French theory in light of Zen Buddhism or Taoism; and how to a certain extent, I can reread Zen Buddhism and Taoism in light of contemporary critical continental philosophy. The process of cultural and theoretical hybridity gives rise to an "elsewhere within here"—a space that is not easy to recognize, hence to classify.

Hybridity is not an entirely new phenomenom here because as an African writer, Paulin J. Houtoundji said, "The alleged acculturation, the alleged 'encounter' of African civilization with European civilization, is really just another mutation produced from within African civilizations." And that "Far from having come to Africa from colonization, it is highly probable that cultural pluralism was checked and impoverished by its advent, which artificially reduced it to a confrontation between two poles: one dominant and the other dominated." So with colonialism, multiculturalism has actually been flattened down to a form of oppositional demarcation between dominant and dominated cultures. It seems that before its advent, instead of being homogenized or merely polarized, the interactions in Third World contexts between different cultures and within the same culture have had their own lives, about which we know very little. We have to question all these hegemonic concepts that tend to be taken for granted and to negotiate almost every territory that we happen to cross. These are little examples to point to the recalcitrance of certain American pragmatists when faced with anything that may have to do with European theory. But if you look at American culture a bit closer, you will be able to locate all the existing potential sites of resistance, and it's how we articulate and relate them to one another that makes all the difference.

Q: *Can you tie up the question of class to your questioning of race and gender? Also, how it is possible to go through the preestablished notions that academia has put together?*
T: The question of class. In almost every page of *Woman, Native, Other* the question of class is addressed without necessarily being named so. Instead of invoking the name mainly for the sake of classification, as it is often done, it seems more important to discuss the issue carefully as it arises in each specific context. We are talking here, for example, about the difficulty a woman writing a book experiences as she goes through diverse passages of guilt, because she is always writing at the cost of someone else's labor, or because she comes from a family context in which time to write is always a luxury and taking up the pen means having a bowl of rice less to eat. And we are talking about the complex positionings of the subaltern and the postcolonial subjects in relations to notions of commitment, of nonalignment, or of "separate development" in apartheid language. These questions are brought up all along the pages of *Woman, Native, Other*. Class is dealt with not as an issue in itself but as part of the issues of gender and race (actually, race is another site, which I discuss without naming it so).

How useful is the banner of class when it is used unquestioningly to reinforce ready-made classifications? I think if you are comfortable with an analysis of class by naming it explicitly, then you should do it. But if one goes back to the writings of Marx, one can already say that his analyses of the class struggle, which have been pertinent to the societies of his time and to the cultural context in which he operated, constantly need to be reread in our time and carefully differentiated according to different contexts since Marx himself refused to be a "Marxist." Today, what can one say about class without immediately posing the problem of postrevolutionary societies, or inquiring about the histories of migration for example? And what about the question of gender? Some see it as a class of its own. A woman can be from an upper-middle class one day because she is married to a upper-middle-class man and be a proletarian tomorrow because the man dies or she gets a divorce. What happen then, let's say to the daughters of this woman? When viewed in feminist terms the notion of class struggle has silenced and suppressed a lot. The same thing applies to the situation of migration. People shuttle between classes or undergo class mutations when they move from one country or one context to another. If there is a phenomenom that is particular to postmodern times, it seems that it would have to be the discontinuities of mass immigration, refugeeism, and displacement. It is precisely these histories of migration all over the globe that we have to address. Here the question of border class—the place between two classes that one often inhabits—is at once impossible and enabling. What can one say about class in this kind of context?

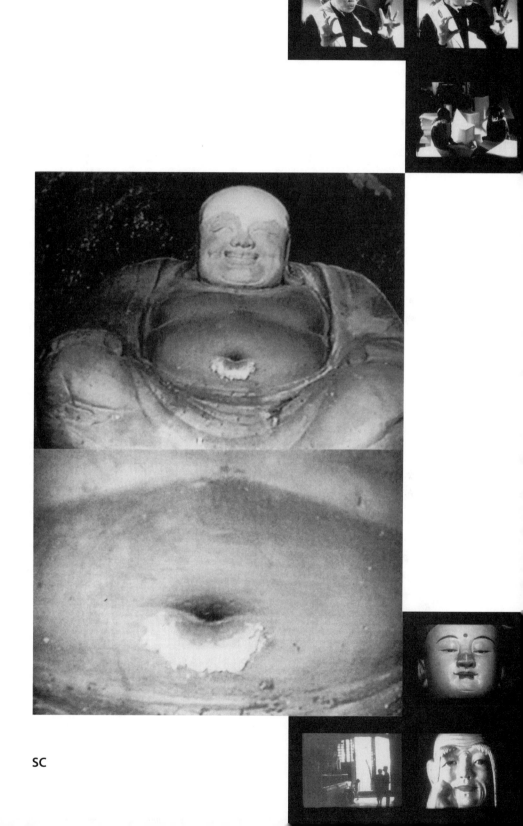

SC

Q: *[Inaudible on tape]*

T: Well, it is necessary to point to our own location precisely if you think, as you said, that for many people class is not negotiable. For example, what does it tell you about a person when that person, who is in a position to negotiate his or her space, ignores or bypasses this position and goes on speaking righteously for those who cannot negotiate it? This kind of work overflows in the market. You just point to another and say "look at these poor people" and you give yourself the license to speak on their behalf. This is for me a very dangerous place to occupy. For years such a practice has actively contributed to the denigration and silencing of certain peoples or certain groups, who kept on being spoken for (even when they are "given voice"). So it is very difficult for me to talk about class or poverty the way it is pervasively talked about—class mainly as classification, and poverty only as economic poverty. Yes, what kind of poverty after all? When you really live through poverty you don't necessarily want to talk about poverty in the terms that have been defined for you. When I was in India, a cab driver told me, "If you are going to make a film on India look at this country very carefully and tell us if you see any poverty." How you do take that statement? Poverty is here given a very different meaning. He went on saying that his friends have gone to the States and that "they see poverty everywhere." Each one of us has a different location. Any reflection upon class would have to take into consideration the shifting complexity of subject positioning, rather than simply reiterate the economic categories, maintaining thereby intact the existing boundaries.

R: *I want to point out my own deficiency in not giving out a list of Minh-Ha's books.* Woman, Native, Other *is a book published in 1989 about the literary production of Third World women. This book took quite a few years to be published because it couldn't fall into any established academic category.*

Q: *Can you elaborate on the way you approach each project?*

T: Perhaps I can do this by going a bit further into the question of location and positioning. It all has to do with how one understands the notion of critical work. In the process of showing and informing, more often than not our critical finger tends to point exclusively to those over there but it does not point back at us. Or else, when the pointing back is done, it is limited to a form of self-criticism that aims for better improvement rather than radically questions established power relations. If we criticize ourselves and humanize our "errors," then we can continue to do the work—as before, albeit with some ameliorations in "methodology" and approach. You would have films, for example, that show the native shooting with a little super 8 camera, while the filmmaker shoots the native for us—the viewers—with a 16 mm camera. This could have been very interesting if you see a parallel analysis or a treatment of the film that would substantially work with these super 8 and 16 mm footages together. You would go back and forth between the 16 and the 8, and you would see how the eyes involved look at things and frame life differently, for example. But no, there's none of that in these films. What you see is a little sequence with the native shooting in super 8, a little insertion of the super 8 images, and then the rest of the film goes about its own business of retrieving information. The native's brief presence serves to salvage the conscience of the filmmaker, who can then continue his or her task of anthropologizing. This tells us immediately how the notion of self-reflexivity could be depoliticized and reduced in its function to a harmless, decorative device. Reflexivity in this case, is used as a trick to bypass the problems of representation as related to the politics of location. These problems are precisely what interest me and what I have incorporated in my work while remaining committed to the unique subject matter of each project. To be critical is not merely to say what is wrong in the state of things, nor is it to expose errors in order to correct things.

Q: *Where can one find your texts, and where can one see your films? What are you working on now since* Shoot for the Contents *is obviously complete? Do you work from other people's scripts and books when putting together a project as a starting point? What is the process of making your films? Do you start with a script? Does the script come later? How do they generally start?*
T: The first book I wrote *(Un art sans oeuvre)* is out of print. The book of poems *(En minuscule)* has only been published in France. The more recent books are available here in bookstores. *Woman, Native, Other* is published by Indiana University Press; *When the Moon Waxes Red* and *Framer Framed* are published by Routledge. These books can be ordered directly from the publisher or via a bookstore. As for the films, since they are not made for any commercial purpose, it really depends on where they are being programmed. One has to have an eye and an ear for things that are exhibited in alternative venues. If one searches for them one would find them. One really has to keep oneself informed of the one- to three-night-stand programs to catch them when they are scheduled. Except for *Shoot for the Contents*, which is presently having a theatrical one-week run at Le Cinematographe (in New York), my films are usually only shown for one or a few nights at repertory movie theaters, community centers, museums, film and media arts houses, educational networks, and more seldom, on public television.

I am at present cowriting a book on Senegalese architecture[2], focusing on people's houses rather than on any kind of monumental architecture. It is a vast project because you never know where the ending line can be drawn. Where does the house stop? Where does living stop? Each group of people whose architecture is studied has their own history, their own spiritual and aesthetic context, their own tradition of building, so each group offers the possibility to compose a unique story of dwelling.

As to the question of how I begin a film, there are many ways to approach filmmaking. We are always made to think that the normal or the only course to take is to follow the linear process of writing a script and blueprinting it before you can shoot the film and go through all the steps of production and postproduction. Or, if you make a documentary, you would, roughly speaking, do some research and decide on a specific topic such as a local trade, a wedding ceremony, a dance, or a ritual event performed by a specific ethnic group. With this, you set out to retrieve "visual documents" according to a preconceived ordering of events. You proceed in such a way as to present the viewer, not with the disorderly way in which you experience the

---

[2] Jean-Paul Bourdier and Trinh T. Minh-ha, *Drawn From African Dwellings*. Bloomington: Indiana University Press, 1996.

event, but with a coherent process that reconstitutes this event from A to Z, and reduces the thickness of lived experience to an uncomplicated line. To take the case of a dance in a village, you would, for example, construct a narrative that "begins from the beginning" and show the preparatives with all the related rituals during the months that precede the dance, preferably by following one "representative" person and his family through the different stages of communal activities. Then, the narrative reaches its climax as it leads to the long-awaited dance and ends on the return to normal life after the event.

This has never been my approach to filmmaking. There are films that do not need any script or any preconceived topic and preplanning before the shooting. Here, you are at the same time very free and very constrained in what you can do. Free because what you have opened in front of you is a wide range of possible starting points, and the subject matter you decide on is not really known to you ahead of time. When you are on the working site, the "zone" and the points of your focus come to you intuitively while you shoot, just as they are also carefully developed while you create with your camera. It is a mutual process of designation—you are inspired by something that designates you as you designate it in the way you look at it or listen to it via the tools you use to record it. I think the only thing that gives me some confidence in what I do is not what I know ahead of time, but the trust I have in working with "nothing." This "jump in the void" is a most exciting moment of enablement, when you know that everything fragmented and seemingly unrelated around you can become the film, whose coherence—in discontinuity—is due to the fact that "I" constitutes a site where incongruous things can meet. You only have yourself and the idea that relationships can be created (or that old relationships can be altered and new ones formed) to work with, so you can go and shoot anything you want. One needs to be curious and alert, rather than be a body of information or a pattern of projections.

During the process of making the film you see, you hear, you feel, you witness, you participate, and this is what dictates to you the form and the structure of the film. In other words, the subject matter is in the way you record and create it. Such an approach works best for me, but I know it doesn't necessarily work for everybody. This is where one can talk about the constraints mentioned earlier. When I started teaching film, I used to tell my students with much conviction that they didn't need any preconceived schema, they should just go ahead and shoot, and they should be confident in their abilities to work with relationships. But since then I've changed, because for many, this approach leaves them at a loss. So now I have come to a point where I say they should start wherever it is best for them. If they want a script, they should start with a script. The script is not in itself a confining frame. It can just be a starting point from which people can depart. As this anecdote shows, freedom is not easy to assume, and it does not lead to mere anarchy—it is a form of commitment. Like every commitment, this commitment, let's say to yourself, to the film, and to the subject matter generates its own principles, limits and constraints. And these are unique to each project since they have little to do with the standardized professional criteria that apply to mainstream filmmaking.

This is the general process I go through with each film, in the shooting as well as in the editing. You give the same importance to the verbal text, the image, and the sound in the film. You don't have such a thing as a preexisting text or music to which you then cut the images.

Similarly, you don't give priority to the image and use the sound only to illustrate or explicate the visuals. One can say that when you come to the editing table, what you have are: the raw visual footage of what you shot, an amalgam of "raw" unedited music and environmental sound, and an unorganized body of verbal fragments (quotations, reflections, and snatches of conversations). All three materials are equally loose at the cutting stage; neither one of them comes first as a unified whole, and neither is given priority over the other. They are all worked on together as the film takes shape. This is one way of making a film.

Q: *What can one come up with to replace the word "linear"?*
T: I would not try to exclude it. I think linearity is in everything we do. To use the word "circular," for example, can also be very limiting. It implies closed repetitive movements, something that goes round and round and does not lead anywhere. So the best thing that one can do is probably to use simultaneously several terms at the same time. So you have the linear process but you also have the spatial process in film, for example. You have something that is very linear because of the successive unfolding of images in time, but these images also result from a spatial assemblage—the way they are spatially conceived (in terms of composition as well as of relationships) and the way intervals between sequences are worked out in the making of meaning and of rhythm. Instead of excluding, you can use all elements in their unique potentials.

Q: *I thought of asking you if you ever thought of making an autobiographical film, and then I thought your answer was going to be, based on the way that you place the ideas of the self in subjectivity in your writing and your films, that you probably would say that in fact you do make autobiographical films. Taking that into consideration, can I still ask you? Have you ever thought of making an autobiographical film in the way that we think of a traditional autobiographical film?*
T: Of course, I would say that everything I did was autobiographical; even though I certainly have problems with the conventional form of autobiography in which the personal either remains personal, or even when the personal reaches the social, the story offered is one that the viewer can consume as a mere story. In other words, if the telling is conventional, the self presented is unavoidably a centralized, unitary self. The question is not so much to reject traditional forms as it is to work with them differently. Even if you make a film explicitly about your own life, I think that what you choose to include will have to be very specific to your own location and yet be shown in such a way as to constantly exceed that specificity. This is a challenge for everyone who makes autobiographical films. Where do you draw the line between what is personal and what is social or political? How do you politicize the personal? These are questions we constantly have to work with. If I make an explicitly autobiographical film, I will not be able to say in advance what form the film will take since as I discussed earlier, you don't fit a content into a pre-existing form. In other words, you don't impose a form on a film; the form emerges simultaneously with the making of the film. A Moroccan filmmaker [Smihi Mouhen] did not hesitate to say, for example, that "just as every film is political . . . every film is autobiographical." Placed in the context of Third World filmmaking, such a statement immediately reminds me of the burden of representation, which I have just discussed earlier in relation to

marginalized peoples. At the same time as you are telling your own story you also face the task of representing your community and your people, whether you intend it or not. This certainly informs the kind of choices you make even in the most specific and intimate biographical details.

R: *I was extremely interested in what you said about the filmmaker being the site on which all these different threads of a fragmented reality can come together. But now I am going to be gross and say that filmmaking is a collaborative venture. Even your own films. Even in most of the cases you shoot your own footage, however, you work with people. Not only do you work with people as crew and as artistic and technical collaborators, there is also a collaboration on the field as an ethnographer would say. I am absolutely intrigued by how these different threads of a filmmaking process itself are conjugated to create a site and at the most practical level, but also maybe at a more theoretical level. It is a question about your process of filmmaking and how and when you shoot, which immediately means isolating a part of reality and not seeing the whole picture, how do you conjugate this to the existence of people who are necessarily collaborating with you at that level? Also, when making up an image like in* Surname Viet *you worked with somebody to create the artistic composition of the image, and what does that mean in terms of creating that site?*

T: I don't see any contradiction with what I said before. The self here is an empty center, that's why the filmmaker is a "site" of meetings. Of course, there is a process of filmmaking typical of the mainstream, which is entirely dependent on the division of labor. And, this notion of division of labor, through which "crews and technical collaborators" are made indispensable, has almost nothing to do with any form of collective work. Such an "industrial" working process is so impersonal that in a large number of cases, you wonder whether the director truly remains in touch with the material and how much of his experience with it really shapes the film. But in my own way of working, having someone else shoot for me instead of shooting myself (as in *Surname Viet*) has simply been part of the process of making a film with no preconceived unifying structure. Since the material is obtained with people whose activities are bound to circumstances that I do not wish to control, to have a cinematographer who may be very different from yourself in the way she shoots, but who understands your sensitivity, is certainly an enrichment. In working with materials you do not "script," you as a site remain quite empty, because you have to be very attentive not only to what happens within and in front of you but also to possibilities. The site has to remain empty for anyone to feel comfortable with fragments from all over the place. The question of having other people work with me on the film does not really raise any problems for me. Of course, it still depends on how one can work with a person, but the collaboration is just another way of working with things that are inside you, with you, and outside of you.

R: *You answered only one half of the question about the collaboration with people behind the camera, but what about the collaboration with the people in front of the camera? Especially in a film like* Naked Spaces *where there are images that obviously have been taken not only with the knowledge and consent of the people in front of the camera, but with a certain work produced for* *the film by the people in front of the camera. I am using "work" in the large sense, I'm not saying that they were "working" in terms of performing for the camera, but there had been a certain space created between you and the people in front of the camera, which I call "work" in a materialistic sense. I would like you to comment on that.*

T: It is a bit difficult for me to answer that question just because the space in which they are presented is a space in which I am not entirely absent. I would say that the way I work with people is not something that is outside of them—I do not dictate to them what to do. It is a process that grows with the coexistence of two or several presences. For example, if I wish to film a woman performing her daily activities, and the woman is ill at ease, and she doesn't really want the camera to be next to her, then I will not shoot. Sometimes documentary filmmakers come into a situation or an event and they feel that if they don't shoot it right away, they are missing something, or they are letting interesting things go by without catching them. For me (at least in the context of West African rural life, like in *Naked Spaces*) there is nothing that one misses, and there is nothing worth shooting if the person doesn't want me to shoot, so I simply do not shoot. Also for me, very often the shooting does not begin when the camera is operating. It begins, for example, with the way I look at things around me as I enter a house or a village. By the time I pick up the camera and shoot it's just one moment or one fragment of the shooting that has been going on already. So when I shoot, the person has most likely become used to the presence of the camera. There is a moment when you feel something going back and forth between you and the subject, and that's also when you start shooting.

Q: *[Inaudible on tape]*
T: Whether my work is of direct use to the people concerned or not is not really a question to which one can answer. Both the claim to and the denial of its usefulness would appear to me as irresponsible. I think that if one makes the kind of films I have been making, one would have to assume the responsibility that one's work offers no immediate gratification—whether to the viewer or to the maker. However, I do see them as a form of contribution to the people because what they offer are not solutions, but contributions to changes in the long term. Changes in the way we define ourselves and look at others, and changes in power relationships that pervade all spheres of our daily life are not changes that occur overnight with a single work.

As to whether people remain subjects or not, one way for me to approach another culture without reducing people to objects is, as discussed, to raise questions on the representative space that the onlooker occupies. This questioning informs the way you frame people and the way you speak while reflecting on their culture. It makes it difficult for you to simply "speak about" or to speak on an "other," hence to objectify them. As I have repeatedly stated elsewhere, the paternalistic notion of giving voice to the people is not a solution. So what you can do best is to constantly locate the place where you stand in every step you make, in everything you record. This way, you can't objectify the person in front of the camera without being objectified yourself by your own tools. It's a mutual responsibility.

I was speaking earlier about reflexivity. This practice does not limit itself to the exposing of the filmmaker, it has to operate in the filmmaking process. You are never in a position where you say "I'm not objectifying." You are always doing it to a certain extent, and you are always a voyeur, so what do you do? I think the predicament of that position has to be brought out in the open, and it can only be so when the workings of the film are constantly disclosed in the film for the viewer—in other words when power is constantly seen in its limits. Hence, the difficulty encountered when such a film is shown to someone who has gotten used through the routine productions of the media to only look at the content and never at the way this content is put together for them. On the other hand, one cannot be too illustrative or too didactic in the way one exposes the filmmaking process either. The challenge one always faces is how to keep the process "alive" so that it becomes integral to the film itself.

R: *Talking about objectification, I think you have also become a cultural commodity. I remember going to an opening at the Bronx Museum and people were talking very doctorally about Trinh Minh-Ha! I want to go back to the situation of the interview that we have here. There are a small number of filmmakers whose work doesn't stop once they've said, "Cut." What kind of site does that create for you, and what is the work that it involves for you? Of being put on the stage as a cultural commodity to talk about the work. On the one hand, you are a cultural commodity, on the other hand, it involves a real work that is part of the filmic work and also of the writing work. This apparent contradiction is something that I am very interested in discussing with you.*
T: If I am a commodity, who commodifies me? When I am sitting here speaking and exposing my process of working, who listens to me? Who allows me to be here? Questions raised constantly points back to the place each one of us occupies. We are all complicit in this process. The work continues, in other words. That work is the most challenging, because we don't know where exactly it leads us but we have to do it.

R: *In other words, you are saying that your films are opening up the space, the non-closed text that opens up spaces in which you are going to be dragged out of your hiding place to be put here on the stage where I am asking you all these questions.*

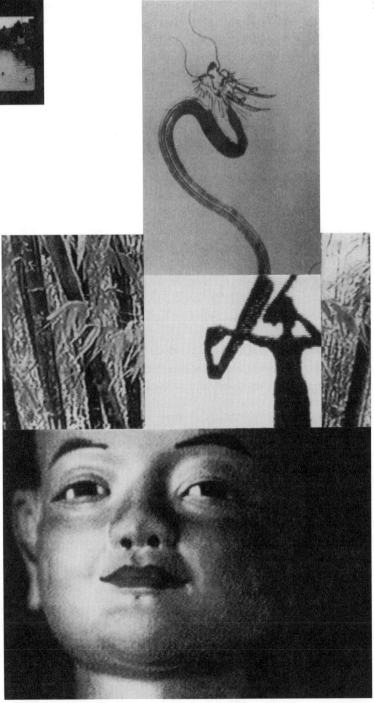

THE VEIL-IMAGE

with Margaret Kelly

Edited excerpts of this initial version of the interview were first published in *The Independent*, July 1998.

Kelly: *Your most recent film,* A Tale of Love, *has been showing throughout the States and at many film festivals in Europe and Asia, including the Berlin International Film Festival. How has the film been received?*

Trinh: It's always difficult to generalize. The overall reception of *A Tale of Love* among programmers and film reviewers in the U.S. reminds me in many ways of the film milieu's response to *Reassemblage* some fifteen years ago. Exhibition venues are first and foremost categories of perception; they are all occupied territories. You can always be the intermittent exception and temporarily fit in here and there with each work achieved but commitment and loyalty remain rare—something more and more out of step in a context where all is geared toward sales and markets. I am talking here about the marketing mind as an instrument of social control, hence, as all-pervasive, which is not only evident in the film industry but also widely established in independent milieus. Permeating the mainstream discourse, which the film industry has been feeding via money power, this mindset does not merely rule the selection, production, promotion, and programming processes of media people and grant makers. It widely determines moviegoers' criteria of "good" and "bad" and the way we think of "success" and "failure." It reflects the triumph of a dominant lifestyle and accounts for all the current financial cutbacks shortsightedly imposed on education and on the arts in this country.

How does *A Tale of Love* fare in such a context? It's surviving in between thrills and rattles. As with my other films, it's actually doing better with time, as it finds its viewers and reaches different audiences. The difficulty is to learn how to be one single self while being with the crowd and to be a crowd when it comes to being oneself. I remember the trepidation of a few crew members at the initial stage of production, not so much in relation to the film itself as to their own hidden desire for a blockbuster-type of film, which they thought this one might well be. But by the time the film reached its final editing phase, such expectations subsided leaving room for frustrated remarks such as: "Oh, com'on, com'on . . . give the audience what they want!" [*Laughs*] Yes, it would have made my life much easier to abide by common habits. The fact that the film used fictional material and was shot in 35 mm was never due to any commercial consideration or to a desire to "make it" into the film industry. Shooting in 35 mm (which was mainly prompted by Panavision's donation of the camera equipment for the entire shoot) means above all working with a different set of constraints, aesthetics, and politics of filmmaking.

Certainly, the film met with rejection from a number of venues that had at one point or another been favorable to my previous films, but it also met with serious support from other venues that had been closed to my work up to then. Probably the place where A *Tale of Love* was shown the longest was in Tokyo, where it was included in a two-month-long exhibition of my films at the Metropolitan Museum of Photography. In Japan, where cultural activities seem far less compartmentalized than in the States, discussions of the films were not merely voiced by "film reviewers" or "film critics." They were also written by novelists, poets, historians, musicians, or music lovers, for example. What a breath of fresh air this was for me. The screenings were very well attended, as my Japanese distributor informed me, and the immediate responses to A *Tale of Love* by curators, art historians, intellectuals there were generally praiseful. They saw it as my best film, enjoying its complexities and especially what they called its "very stylized" unfoldings.

There have been other exhibition contexts in which the film met with discomfort and, occasionally, with either sharp hostility or raptured enthusiasm from a few viewers. This was what happened, for example, at the Berlin Film Festival, where it was shown in The Forum section. Except for one screening, which had technical problems, all the screenings of the film were fully attended, the most memorable one being the screening at the Delphi-Filmpalast, which has a large sitting capacity. You could feel people's responses coming in waves and you could sense the vibrations of the room quite intensely. It was impressive to note, for example, the difference between the press screenings at most festivals and those at the Berlin Forum. Here, you didn't have restless journalists leaving every ten minutes during the screening of the film; almost all stayed until the end. Ironically, it was at the Arsenal, the very place that showed experimental work, that the film met with strong hostility from a couple of male viewers.

At the time, A *Tale of Love* was just released, so I wasn't sure where precisely the hostility was coming from, but with more exposure now, patterns of responses have emerged. It takes time to locate it even though this kind of hostility has happened consistently with every work I've made. But with A *Tale of Love* there is, in addition, this inviolable line that people draw between narrative and documentary. The politics of gender and the play of certain clichés in the film also seem to have caused unavoidable sparks of hostility.

K: *Can you comment on that? What were some of the questions that were posed by male objectors in the audience and how did you respond to them?*

T: I specified *male* earlier because that was where the more blatant hostility first erupted, but it's obvious that the problem as I locate it now is not simply with male viewers, even though, as I said, the politics of gender is very much at stake, both in the film and in its reception. I think it has much to do with viewers' thought habits and the kind of expectations they carry into the film. These are the first screens we encounter: our own areas of expertises, our own veilings.

Whatever we think we already "know" often prevents us from fully experiencing it. Not only do we remain blind to the instance of consumption but also to what images and sounds can offer other than what is evident to the eye and ear. This has also at times prevented viewers from doing what seems most obvious to me in love's romance: laughing at its commonplaces and its utter silliness. So what we have in the film-viewing process is the layering of one kind of veil over another, or the encounter of an indefinite number of screens: mind screen reacting to film screen, and to other mind and body screens.

A viewer once told me, "It helps to have been in love to see this film. There's a lot of quiet laughter in all of your work." People who "see through" the veils are precisely those who neither ignore nor try to bypass these veils. They can seriously engage in any question raised without losing the ability to laugh at themselves while laughing at others and with others. This was what A *Tale of Love* invites the spectator to do, both on the smaller scale with the relationship, for example, between Alikan and Kieu in the film, and on the larger scale with the interrelations of film elements, including makers, actors, viewers, and the tools of creation.

Most people who give themselves the license to judge a film praise or condemn it for reasons that are foreign to what makes a film *a film* (and not a book, a pamphlet, a flyer, a sculpture, a file drawer, or a hammer, for example). Everybody can have an opinion—no more no less, and this has to be acknowledged as such. But to "criticize" a work, you have to engage in it on its terms while creating new terms. This is a very difficult task, which is why it's difficult to find a "critic" who contributes, challenges, and opens doors rather than indulging in the conformity of judging, simply by reifying conventions, formulas, and the state of servility of film.

There are, for example, many ways to deal with what appears too typical or clichéd to one's eye. Exclusion and censorship are not the solution, because one always gets rid of too little or too much. The purge can never be thorough enough, especially when one deals with what, in terms of representation, is the biggest cliché, the most stereotypical subject: the love story. Sometimes you just can't jump over the water to get to the other side, you have to get your feet wet. The love story being all-present in narrative films, you can't move forward without wading across familiar ground even while shifting it. So you are bound to develop endless nuances and to work with "small differences." But if subtleties are necessary to avoid reductive moves, they are also easily missed. Much of the hostility to the film has been coming from viewers for whom these small operational differences are invisible, and some even took the film literally as a love story, albeit one, of course, that would have to fail by their *standards*. [*Both laugh.*]

K: *Right.* A Tale of Love *is actually a tale of many things, a tale of a modern Vietnamese woman researching the continuing impact, in the diaspora, of the national poem of Vietnam,* The Tale of Kieu, *which can in many ways be seen as foreshadowing the destiny of Vietnamese people. In the poem, she is a martyr for love, she is characterized by her endurance and oppression, but in the film, today's Kieu said only through resistance can there be change. How is this true for Vietnam's future, Vietnamese people, and women in general?*
T: The main character(s) is always the spokesperson for the filmmaker in films that center on plot and message. But in my films, what an interviewee or a character-performer says eloquently

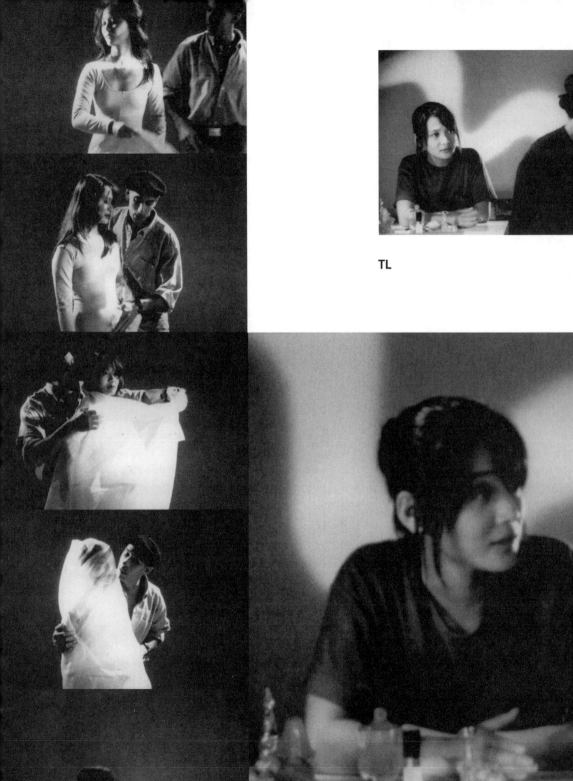

TL

is not necessarily representative of my views. It's simply one among the voices and the possibilities the film offers. Each voice has its own space, not to be subjected to any central conflict, nor to be edited out because it does not fit into the usual pro and con types of answer, for example, or because it is politically inappropriate. Rather than being merely located in Kieu's statements, the "message" moves in the intervals between what is being said or done by each of the voices featured, and the "truth" of the film situates itself in the multiplicity of relationships it sets in motion.

For me, it's exceptional that the national poem of Vietnam is a love poem rather than an epic poem, and that the figure her people persistently choose to represent their collective self is that of a woman. To understand *The Tale of Kieu* is to understand Vietnamese culture in all its subtleties. The ethical, political, and aesthetic values upheld by the poem are part of the Vietnamese psyche and identity. What people see in the character of Kieu is a model of loyalty, sacrifice and victimization; one they fully apply to their personal situation and to that of their country, which has been geographically and historically a much coveted prey to foreign dominators. As stated in my previous film *Surname Viet Given Name Nam*, each government, each political community, each social group remembers and reappropriates Kieu accordingly. But the tendency, in both popular memory and official narratives, is to lay emphasis primarily on her endurance and sacrifice—hence, to preserve the image of Kieu as a woman constantly in tears, torn between circumstantial betrayal and eternal loyalty.

Vietnam would not, however, be where it is today with its international reputation if it were not for its persistent spirit of resistance. *Surname Viet* contributed to reviving this by focusing on the historical deeds of women of resistance and their stories today. This is taken up again, albeit very differently, by *A Tale of Love*, for what the film refuses through the performance of Kieu, among others, is either to dwell on her victimization or to advocate her liberation. What it works with, as mentioned earlier, is the difficult interval between using commonplaces and letting them use you to go elsewhere. The point is not simply to correct the disempowering image of the sacrificial woman in tears. It is to fare precariously in this rarefied zone of love and resistance.

In the film you can still see that Kieu is a victim of many forces, and that the role she plays is problematic as it carries with it many of the attitudes feminists have questioned, such as behaving "femininely," resorting to seduction, exposing herself to the male gaze, and serving male pleasure. Similar points may be made concerning the way the film deals problematically with gender and the Orient in its obvious use of the veil and of perfume. But all of these constitute the so-called *explicit* or *obvious* text of the film. There is always a latent state—the *obtuse* meaning—of things that develops alongside. What is so essential to the success of the conventional screenplay and its predatory concept of cinema—character, action, conflict, plot—is here of marginal importance. The margins, the nuances, the multiplicity of threads and centers are precisely what makes all the difference. There is nothing that is entirely "natural" or that conforms to the tradition of realist psychologism in *A Tale of Love*.

Kieu's interaction with Alikan is not the usual one-way interaction between a photographer and his model. In other words, she is not just a victim; she questions aloud, she talks back, she "looks without being looked at," and she speaks up about her conditions. As for Alikan, he never touches his models while he photographs them. He only *looks*. (Some viewers have seen him as gay in the film.) Everything is displaced. Every bubble can threaten to disrupt the surface of calm water, and nothing, in this intimate struggle for change, is functioning as smoothly as it may appear to the undiscerning ear and eye. The Orient may be feminine and veiled, but it does not only resist and play with its veiling while being circumstantially bound to it; it also looks back and "loves improperly."

Alignment in the Third World has its own laws of fidelity and infidelity. For foreigners and for the younger generations of Vietnamese today, it can be very boring to read this nineteenth-century poem *The Tale of Kieu*. Its language and style belong to another historical time. To be able to appreciate its full significance, one would have to activate it creatively (rather than illustratively or imitatively), that is, to work on its aesthetics ethically and politically so as to make it come to life in a different context. The same applies to Vietnam's opening up of today, which has been unavoidably viewed by outsiders and foreign investors as a subscription to the free West. By the speed with which economic changes have taken place in Vietnam these last years, one can say that such a view is not false. But if things do not always work to the satisfaction of all parties involved, it's also due to Vietnam's resistance to this dominant model of "free" marketing. And hence, while subtle dissidence continues internally with the hope for "a new political dawn," veiled tension persists externally between those who think the world should abide by *their standards* of "freedom" and "opening," and those who obsessively check and brake for fear that what they fought for all these years would just go to dust.

K: *Right. I like the multiple meanings imbued in this "place of resistance." Kieu "never gives in." To quote Alikan's response to Kieu's remarks on his dissecting/dismembering shooting technique, "You really resist not having a head don't you?" Resistance and the ways in which it unfolds and plays out differently with each situation is very captivating. Also to link with a passage you hinted at, "Vietnamese people all around the globe recognize their country in the image of a woman. Kieu is here a folk symbol of love and she is both passionately admired and blamed for having loved improperly. . . .I can't mention her name without feeling somewhat implied. Isn't a writer someone who loves for a living?" And this is spoken by the main character, Kieu. In what ways are you as a writer implied? When you think of the reflexive circle of Kieu investigating* The Tale of Kieu, *in what ways do you feel that you, in making the movie, are also implied in that circle?*
T: It's true that there's nothing in my work, whether books, poems, music, or films, that is not strongly and intimately part of my life. But at the same time as I see myself in everything I come up with, I also never identify myself personally with any of them. These works also have a life of their own, independent of me. In a film conceived not with a single center (be this center a story, a message, or a self) but with a multiplicity of centers, I am implied in every moment, every element, every fragment of the work. And I'm saying this with the understanding that the whole is contained in each fragment; it is not the totalizing sum of the fragments as conventional narratives have it. With each character and with each element of film (Kieu, the cricket, the dog, the mosquito net, the rain, the framing, or the colors of the film, for example) I am both myself and *more* than myself.

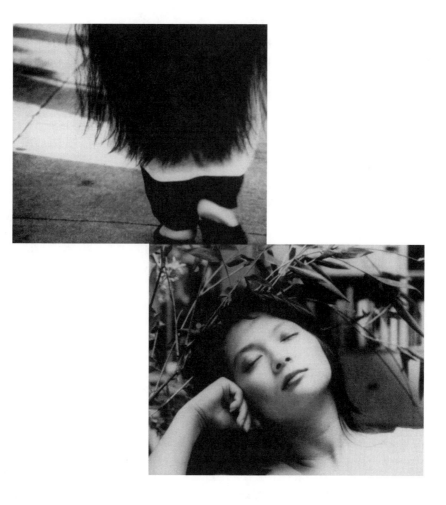

This is why writing requires a lot of love, just as making films as an "independent" requires a lot of passion and active endurance. I don't know how many people I've met among independents who asked me about the "secrets" that keep me going, while many others are falling out of their love for film in these trying times. Depending on where you are, you may think of Kieu's question about a writer being someone who loves for a living as partaking in the marketing mind mentioned (a form of prostitution, which links her to the monumental Kieu of the poem) or precisely as resisting it by making of writing a question of living and dying. As in all of my works, statements, and events in *A Tale of Love* are always both what they are to your senses and more. Again, in the relation between Kieu the model and Alikan the photographer, the politics of veiling applies altogether to women, to photography, and to the many mediated spaces indirectly offered by the film. To work with moments of veiling and unveiling, the film is bound to have a part that is all exposed and *all too visible*. This is the part that makes a number of viewers hate Alikan: He veils her and forbids her to look back (that is to reflect); he secretly follows her to the dressing room and even outside in the streets, and he doesn't hesitate when it comes to photographing nudity at its most exposed. In brief, he has no qualms about being a voyeur.

But since everything is so linked in the film and in my activities, if you speak about character and acting, you are also speaking about the makers and the viewers. We are all in the film, not safely outside it, when we watch Alikan and Kieu. Their relation is the relation between filmmaker and actor, actor and spectator, actor and acting, in brief, between voyeur and voyeur. Voyeurism and visual regulation are inscribed in the directing, performing, and consuming activities of narrative cinema. If we find Alikan offensive, then we should find ourselves all the more offensive. For what he does is no more, no less to be criticized than what we do all the time in making or consuming images of love stories. We follow actors on screen to their most private places, to their closet, their bed, their bath, their toilet. And we demand that the gestures of love be exposed down to their most intimate details and to the widest number, for the more "natural" they are, the more we revel in watching them and the better consumers we prove to be. Voyeurism unveiled and barefaced repels us, but we are in total complicity with it. As you probably noticed, there is no lovemaking scene in my film [*both laugh*]. Despite all, I could not get myself to reproduce this kind of requisite commonplace in love stories. It's hardly surprising that the most intimate event of sexual love is also the most poorly represented in commercial cinema. As a love-image maker, I can only fare with difficulty and discomfort, exposing critically our complicity in this all-inclusive context of voyeurism, so that neither makers, nor spectators, nor actors find it "natural."

K: *I noticed in some scenes, in the more intimate ones between Alikan and Kieu, you matte those scenes, one of them being when they are blindfolded. Is that to make it more noticeable?*
T: It's actually not Kieu but Alikan's other model. In fact, the blindfolded woman can be any woman. But for Asian viewers, the hint that she is not Kieu may be more obvious because of the color of the tips of her breasts, about which Alikan made a remark, albeit a remark more toward the professional retouching of photographs. The matting of the image, which suggests getting a peep at a love scene through . . .

K: *a doorway . . .*

T: Yes, a doorway or a partly closed aperture, the rest being all black. The matting is then another form of veiling the image. And since spectators are the only ones to *see* the scene, such a matting also shifts the attention to their own voyeurism. Here one can also say that there is a situation of equality, where both Alikan and the woman are blindfolded, and that's the only time when he touches rather than looks. You have many kinds and levels of voyeurism in the film. One that is quite explicit is in the dialogue when Alikan says, "Don't look at me when I'm . . . "

K: *"shooting." [Both laugh.]*

T: You see, in Berlin a film critic[1], who immediately saw into this, said, "But isn't every *cinephile* (cinemagoer) a voyeur?" Yes. That's exactly where Alikan's request can be located right from the start, even though not all forms of voyeurism are equally objectifying and repressive. I loved it when the critic also told me he got this feeling from one of the very opening scenes: In the slow tracking of the camera, the critic felt as if he was some kind of Frankenstein monster looking through a window at the two women talking. Alikan merely verbalizes what the camera was already doing graphically and spatially. "Don't look at me as I shoot you" is the golden rule of cinema. Don't look back at the camera (or at the killer), don't look around (or you may see yourself being watched), don't get off role, don't damage the power of cinematic illusion. Well . . . don't lift the veil. The dark room or the collective darkness of the theater proves to be the ideal place where we can [purchase our ticket to] look without being looked at. The idea that cinema is founded on voyeurism is nothing new; many screenplays have featured the voyeur as the hero of the film. But the fact that Alikan is not the usual story character whose visual pleasure one can unconsciously identify with, and the fact that the instance of consumption is embedded in the exposure of voyeurism put viewers to great discomfort. The unified space between spectators and the screen is here being intermittently split apart. For this, there are also female voyeurs in *A Tale of Love*. You remember that scene where voyeurism is also highlighted, there is a woman who climbs down a ladder . . .

K: *to go to the car . . .*

T: Yes, to sneak out with her lover, who is waiting at the car. The scene is seen through another woman's eye. This woman first looked out the window, but as she realized what was happening, she closed the window's lace curtain before lifting it again so as to look out without being seen. To use Maya Deren's concept, this is a "controlled accident"—a gesture that the woman performs instinctively without my directing her, but that works perfectly for this voyeuristic scene.

K: A Tale of Love *is quite vibrant. You use a lot of primary and secondary colors, they're prevalent in much of the lighting, clothing, and props of each scene. I also sense an affinity for trines in*

---

[1] Rudiger Tomczak, who is also the editor of the film journal *Shomingeki*.

TL

your piece—three primary colors; Kieu's "three lovers, three different loves"; the three characters named Kieu, the main protagonist, the fictional character from the epic poem, and the old woman who claims to be the Kieu from which the epic was written. Your film has opened many doors to our senses and our mind. It is quite multidimensional and operates on several levels simultaneously. One of the first qualities that one can appreciate about your film is that it is stimulating as an "intellectual" as well as a "sensual" piece. The list of characters could almost be a list of sensory representatives: Java as the voice of love; Juliet and her perfumes—through which scents and the sense of smell are explored; Minh, who is also associated with the sense of smell of the rain, but more with the sense of nostalgia that rain can evoke; and Alikan, of course, being so visually dependent, interesting . . . like film and voyeurism are so visually dependent. In a way, you diffuse this sort of conventionality, you create this diffuse realm, and . . . how your film rides in-between the boundaries of the experimental and the narrative is that you also diffuse the senses, you allow time for the exploration of sound and smell and touch. One sensually absorbs these moments while one passes through the film. Perfumes, like music, like veils are all things that exist in-between truth and perception . . . clouding . . . a misty veil that lies in-between like a hypnotic perfume, in different ways. . . .

T: [*Laughs*] It's like hearing someone in love. You actually touch on that silly side of the film we discussed earlier. I'm not really giving the viewer a love story with a beginning, a climax, and an ending, but I do offer a fabric of the senses as they manifest themselves in the state of being in love [*both laugh*]. When you are in this state, you walk around talking aloud to yourself, you cry, laugh, and sing for no reason, you smell things that you don't usually smell, you hear them with oversensitive ears. In brief, you see everything in such a different light that people around you who are in their right mind cannot believe they are dealing with the same person. The film certainly plays on these moments of veiled and clear perception, of daylight and night-light or of the heart's and the mind's intelligence. Sometimes you persist in keeping the veil, and you're quite content to remain in the dark because you are experiencing another kind of light.

This is for me where the main tension of the film lies . . . what I see as my frontiers. I'm constantly working at the edges of several "logics": those, roughly speaking, of conscious knowledge, of intuition, and of wisdom. As I mentioned, there's a realm that I can easily talk about and others that are very difficult to put my finger on and to materialize. In an itinerary scripted down to the smallest details, you also work intensely with your intuition and with non-knowledge. You invent while encountering errors; you work with people's strengths and weaknesses during the production process; and you remain alert to accidents that can accurately find their way into your film. This is what constitutes its fabric. Every love story is unique, not because of the course of events or because of any single individual involved, but because of the way reality speaks to you differently. No matter how many times you repeat the same gesture, when you are in love, it is unique to you. Unfortunately, when you work with this diffuse realm, as you put it, a number of spectators tend not to recognize it as it is—magical, silly, and irrational, while having its own exacting laws. Instead, they react all too squarely and leave themselves no room to breathe with the film.

K: *It must be exciting. Your film is so controversial, and it is evoking so many emotions in people. I find it interesting, because I believe an artist would rather receive a strong emotion of one type than degrees of apathy for their work. I'm thinking here of a statement in the film, which you've mentioned: "People always find fault in women with many talents and loves. No matter what they do, they can never escape criticism." You are a woman with an abundance of talents and loves: writing, composing music, and teaching, in addition to making films. And although you touched on this, maybe you could expand upon what particular or reoccurring criticisms you have encountered, which personally affect you, which you consciously fear or anticipate when you're making a film?*

T: The famous Chinese story that Kieu tells us in the film about how women were trained to the art of war is most relevant here [*laughs*]. Remember how the general (Sun Tse) had to behead two of the King's hundred wives because instead of following orders to become soldiers, these women kept on falling about laughing? This is how war and death are introduced into the realm of laughter and disorder. You either lose your head on your own by conforming, or you will be decapitated. Society widely rejects films that think aloud, especially when they are made by women who hold on to their head. So the practice of veiling one's head when one wants to operate in a male economy does not belong only to certain parts of the world such as the Middle East. It's very common for intellectually gifted women to downplay their ability and to appear less sharp than they really are so as not to be a threat to their peers. The headsman covers the victim's head for fear that the latter will stare back at him, challenging his self-confidence and preventing him from following an order.

With the work of feminists all around the world, the new forms of sexism that circulate are much more difficult to pin down. It takes constant alertness and a lot of careful work to articulate them, as nothing can be taken for granted. You can't go too fast without appearing reductive. You have to resist through slowness and work subtly with "small differences," since those who put you down use the same language as the one you use to free yourself. And this profoundly internalized prejudicial attitude may come from the very people who strongly affirm that they have nothing against feminism. There where it hurts the most is when it comes from people of your own political attachment, your own ethnic community, your own gender, and worst, from your closest friends—men and women. Every effort is made to find arguments that would deter you from thinking their assessment of you and of your work has anything to do with the politics of gender.

This is why it's very difficult to name exactly the kind of criticisms I've got. They are not solely to be found in the manifest but also in the latent meanings of what people say. Since I refuse to let the role of victim dominate my thoughts and activities, discrimination is not something I readily acknowledge even when I am confronting it. But no matter how much you try to get away from it, there will be instances where you'll be facing it squarely. You'll then be bound to recognize the extent to which your being a member of the second sex, the minorities, the marginalized, or the Third World is ingrained in the way people situate, criticize, or praise your work. The terms by which the work is circulated and talked about are often the very terms by which restrictions are devised to contain it.

Just look at the way national and geographical categories function in most international film festivals. There is Arab cinema, Iranian cinema, Chinese cinema, Hungarian cinema, and what have you. And then, there is contemporary cinema or world cinema. Films from marginalized cultures are presented for their ability to show spectators a different slice of life or a story with an unfamiliar cultural backdrop. Or else, they offer them a particular angle—a "feminist perspective," for example— that has to do with ethnic, gender, and sexual identities. As such they fit well into the notion of "alternative cinema" that prevails. Films from the diverse diasporas or the "alternative geographies" are even worse off when it comes to fitting into one of these categories. For example, what a representative of Cannes looks for when he selects films from American independents often has to do with what he—the European eye—sees as most representative of "America." So the chances are slim that he will choose here some "ethnic" films or films that deal radically with difference. Why did Tran Anh Hung's prize-winning *The Scent of Green Papaya* enter international film competitions in the Vietnamese rather than the French category (when it was entirely shot in French studios)? You don't need an explicit answer to this question to see what these divisions truly imply and how thoroughly political they are. A "minor" can hardly measure against a "major"; he or she can only compete with other minors. Films from national, gender, and sexual categories are almost never discussed in terms of cinema, that is, presented for their contribution to the art and language of cinema. Form and content remain separate, and the dominant continues to own culture while the marginal remains marginal even when visibility is granted. For me, it is aberrant to think of feminism as a perspective. Similarly, it is vain to divide my films into those that deal with film politically and those that are concerned with its so-called formalistic aspects. These are, in fact, the kind of comparisons and comments that I've invariably been getting with each new film I've made.

K: *As stated by the Museum of Modern Art's New Directors/New Films festival in New York, your film* Surname Viet Given Name Nam *is "a challenging and rewarding work that places Trinh T. Minh-ha as one of the leading American independent filmmakers of the eighties." What do you see for yourself? . . . As artists at times do, when they come from one work to another, did you feel that there were things that you wanted to address in this film that maybe you hadn't, and that couldn't be included in your previous film? What do you see as your next project, how do you see yourself finishing out the nineties . . . and beyond?*

T: It's funny how markings are always so dramatic. When you work on a daily and minute level at changing relations and offering new possibilities of existing, grander narratives that come with these evaluations by decades have a rather limited role. If each work is a work of love, then it is a unique event in itself. It doesn't compare itself. People have always asked me which film of mine I like best because they each have their definite choice, but I myself have always been innately unable to make a choice. I've *never*, not even when I'm talking to myself, seen one film as being better than the other. The body of work I've completed is radically a multiplicity. They all resonate with one another but are neither consonant nor dissonant in their relationships. They are all different moments of my social, historical, artistic, and ethical self, and each has generated its own criteria. There is no real necessity for any measurement in terms of quantity, hierarchy, time scale, or linear progress. I don't come into a project with a desire to address something specific. It is always in exploration and encounter—with a place, a group of people, a thought process, a force, an energy, for example—that ideas and images take shape. What I can certainly say is that I am constantly developing new dimensions in my work.

The next step after the fall: the freedom of a self-decapitated body

Breathtaking are the intervals during which time stands still as I
look on headless, bodyless, selfless, cleared of all residue of "me,"
finding room for nothing and everything

"I am that wretch comparable with mirrors
That can reflect but cannot see
Like them my eye is empty and like them inhabitated
By your absence which makes them blind." —Aragon

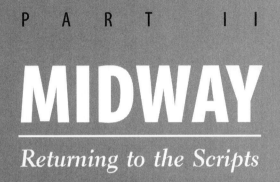

P A R T   I I

MIDWAY

Returning to the Scripts

A TALE OF LOVE

filmscript

USA, 1995. Released 1996. 108 minute color film

With: Mai Huynh as Kieu; Juliette Chen as Juliet; Dominic Overstreet as Alikan; Mai Le Ho as the Aunt; Alice Gray-Lewis as the Model; Thai A. Nguyen Khoa as Minh; Verse Singer: Kieu Loan
Directed & Produced by: Trinh T. Minh-ha and Jean-Paul Bourdier
Written & Edited by: Trinh T. Minh-ha
Production & Lighting Design by: Jean-Paul Bourdier
Line Producer & Production Manager: Erica Marcus
Director of Photography: Kathleen Beeler
Art Director: Angela D. Chou; **assistant editor & location manager:** Corey Ohama; **postproduction consultant & re-recording mixer:** Jim Kallett; **music** by: the Construction of Ruins; **constructors:** Greg Goodman & J.A. Deane; **sound recordist:** Lauretta Molitor; **assistant director:** Lori Kay Wilson; **script supervisor:** Sofia Babiolakis; **Steadicam operator:** Craig Peterschmidt.
Distributed by: Women Make Movies Inc., New York; Freunde der Deutschen Kinemathek, Berlin (Germany); Image Forum, Tokyo (Japan); print with Chinese subtitles at the Taipei Golden Horse Film Festival Archives (Taiwan). International sales: M&L Banks, New York

Appearances: Kieu (writer, model); Juliet (editor of a women's magazine, Kieu's mentor and confidante; Alikan (photographer); the Aunt (Kieu's Aunt); Minh (Kieu's former lover); Woman Model (Alikan's other model); Java (man's voice on the phone); Little Girl in Water (Kieu in her childhood); the Aunt's three children; the Aunt's neighbor (friend of Martha, the battered woman); Mistaken Lover; Woman on Ladder and her Boyfriend; Street Woman with Umbrella; Woman Voyeur; three Library Extras; the Cricket; the Parrot; the Dog.

. . .

Epigraph on screen:

> *"May these crude words, culled one by one and strung,*
> *Beguile an hour or two of your long night"*
> —THE TALE OF KIEU, BY NGUYEN DU (1765–1820)[1]

1. EXT   FIELD OF GRASS   KIEU   DAY

LONG SHOT of golden field of grass against blue sky. Kieu is running in the field toward the camera.

2. INT   (ALIKAN'S APARTMENT   WORKING WITH KIEU   DAY)

EXTREME CLOSE-UP of Kieu with conical hat.

3. INT   AUNT'S HOUSE   KIEU   DAY

Bed with mosquito net. A shape covered with a white sheet is seen through the net. Whiteness of sheet and net are predominant in the frame.

> AUNT (OS)
> Kieu, con da day chua? Con da day chua, Kieu? Ngu gi ma ngu suot ngay vay!
> *(Kieu, are you up? Sleeping all day long!)*

Shape moves slightly. Awaking to her aunt's voice, Kieu pulls down the sheet from her face, her eyes blinking with the brightness of the light.

> KIEU
> *(calling out)*
> Da, con vua day!
> *(Yes, I'm up!)*

She glances at the clock, looks surprised, and hurries out of bed.

4. EXT   COURT   KIEU AND AUNT   DAY

Kieu comes out of the bedroom, waking up.

> KIEU
> Sao gio nay co chua di lam?
> *(How come you're not at work at this hour?)*

> AUNT
> *(scolding)*
> Hom nay la Chu Nhat, co ai di lam dau! Nhieu luc co thay lo cho con lam! Khong biet con song nhu the nao ma luc nao cung nhu la vua o trong con me buoc ra. Toi hom qua chac lai thuc suot dem viet bao, chang ngu gi phai khong?

---

[1] All translations from *The Tale of Kieu* are by Huynh Sanh Thong (New Haven: Yale University Press, 1983).

(pause)

Gan 12 gio trua roi. Thoi uong ly ca phe roi an trua, chu con an sang gi nua!
(Today's Sunday, nobody goes to work. Sometimes I really worry about you. I don't know how you live, but you always look as if you have just stepped out of some dream. Yesterday you wrote all night and didn't sleep, did you?

(pause)

It's almost noon, too late for breakfast. Get your coffee and we'll have lunch.)

KIEU

(smiling)

Viec gi ma co phai lo, con da gia dau roi, ma co cu lo cho con nhu dua con nit vay!
(Why do you have to worry, I'm old enough, I'm not a kid any more.)

AUNT

(listening to outdoors sounds)

Tui nho no di sang nha ban choi, den chieu moi ve. It khi nao ma minh lai duoc yen tinh nhu the nay?
(The kids are playing with their friends next door. They won't be back until late this afternoon. The house isn't often so quiet.)

KIEU

Da.
(Yes.)

The aunt gets up and brings back a pile of mail. She picks out an envelope and hands it to Kieu.

AUNT

Day, tho cua me con tu ben nha.
(Here's your mother's letter from home.)

Kieu reaches for the letter and puts it beside her. Kieu puts two spoonfuls of ice cream in her coffee.

AUNT

Sang nao cung an kem. Bo cai tat xau ay di. Sua thi khong uong.
(Ice cream every morning! Get rid of that bad habit. Why not use milk?)

The aunt gets up and leaves for the kitchen. Kieu then tears open the envelope, smells the paper before unfolding it, and silently reads it. When she finishes reading, she absent mindedly folds the letter down to a small square. Then she applies herself to caressing with both hands the warm cup of coffee.

5.   INT   (ALIKAN'S APARTMENT   WORKING WITH KIEU   DAY)

EXTREME CLOSE-UP of Kieu with large hat and white veil.

6. EXT COURT KIEU AND AUNT DAY

Kieu looks up when her aunt, as she comes back with milk, speaks to her.

> AUNT
>
> Thoi minh an! Co it com nguoi tu hom qua, lay ra an not. An o ngoai nay cho mat.
> (*Let's have lunch. There's some leftover rice from yesterday. Let's eat outside, it's cooler.*)

Kieu stands up and leaves for the kitchen. She comes back from the kitchen with bowls of rice, vegetables, and pickles on a tray. The conversation continues while they eat.

> AUNT
>
> Thang nay con da gui tien ve nha chua?
> (*Did you send money home this month?*)

> KIEU
>
> Da, con da gui ve roi.
> (*Yes, I did.*)

> AUNT
>
> (*facetiously moralizing*)
>
> U, con gai nhu vay co hieu lam. Ca chuc nam nay qua day lam viec toi ngay de gui tien ve cho gia dinh, khong thang nao quen ca. Co the chu! doi song o nha qua kho khan, gia dinh con da trai qua bao nhieu chuyen dau thuong, bay gio ba me gia roi, cuc den dau thi cuc, con cung phai hy-sinh de lo cho ba me duoc day du.
> (*Good girl. For the last dozen years, you've been working to send money back home every month. You never forget. Good, because life is far too hard there. Your family has gone through a lot. Now that your parents are old, no matter how hard it is, you have to sacrifice so that they can have a good life.*)

> KIEU
>
> Trong cong dong viet o day hau het gia dinh nao cung gui tien ve giup do nhung nguoi o lai.
> (*Almost every family in our community here is sending money back to help their relatives.*)

> AUNT
>
> Nguoi minh xoay xo cung gioi. Qua day tim viec dau co phai la de. Nho troi thuong, mac dau doi song kho khan voi biet bao lo lang hang ngay, minh cung du song. Nhung co chi la mot nguoi *social worker*, luong khong duoc bao nhieu. Tui nho cang lon thi gia dinh cang ton kem. Nhieu luc nghi den dien dau. Co dang tinh co gi don dep lai cai phong cua tui nho de cho thue cho do tien nha.
> (*We people have to fend for ourselves. It's not easy to find work here. Thank God, despite all the worries of everyday life, we have got enough to eat. But I am only a social worker with not much of a salary. And, things get more expensive as the children grow up. Sometimes I go mad thinking about it all. I'm thinking of renting the kids' room to help with the house payment.*)

KIEU

The thi may em o dau?
(Where will you put them then?)

AUNT

Thi mot la con chia phong voi tui no, hai la con chia phong voi co.
(Well, either you share your room with them, or you move into mine.)

KIEU looks surprised and horrified, but says nothing. Silence. She looks at her aunt, then stares down in front of her.

AUNT

(looking quickly at her)
Co moi du dinh vay thoi. Khi nao chac chan, co se cho con biet. O nha, muoi may nguoi ngu chung trong mot phong thi da sao? Co ai ma co phong rieng dau?
(I'm only thinking about this. When I make a decision, I'll let you know. What's the big deal? At home, we sleep together ten to a room. Nobody has a room of her own.)
(brief silence, then changing the subject)
The me bien tho noi gi?
(What did your mother say in her letter?)

KIEU

(slowly looks up, then at her aunt)
Co . . . Muon viet van de song, thi phai co phong rieng.
(Auntie—to write for a living, you have to have a room of your own.)

AUNT

Con be nay lam cam that. Co co phai la nguoi la dau, ma cu phai rieng biet nhu the. Cung lam, neu tui nho no qua on ao, thi con vo thu vien viet. Mieng la cong viec nha lam xong chu dao cho co, la duoc roi.
(You're such a pest. We are not strangers to each other. Why do you have to be separate? If the worst comes to the worst and the kids are too noisy, you can go to the library to write. As long as you keep up with the housework.)
(changing subject again)
Nao, the me bien tho noi gi o nha?
(What did your mother write?)

KIEU

Me con gui loi tham co. Ba me con van binh thuong.
(Mother sends you her best. She and father are fine.)
(smiles)
Me con luon luon nhac con ve vu lap gia dinh. Me rat lo con se tro thanh gai gia.
(She always reminds me about getting married. She's afraid I'll become an old maid.)

7. INT (ALIKAN'S APARTMENT WORKING WITH KIEU DAY)

EXTREME CLOSE-UP of Kieu in black kimono. We HEAR Vietnamese singing of verses from *The Tale of Kieu.*

8. EXT COURT KIEU AND AUNT DAY

Return to scene as before.

> AUNT
> Thi nhu ho thuong noi o nha, "gai co chong nhu gong deo co, gai khong chong nhu phan go long danh." Co khong phai noi nhieu, con cu nhin hoan canh cua co thi con cung hieu. Voi phu nu, song doc than la mot cuoc tranh dau sinh song con moi ngay, va nhung loi dem pha cua thien ha luon luon vang vang ben tai.
> *(As they say at home, "She who is married wears a yoke on her neck, she who has no hus-band is like a bed with loose nails." I don't have to tell you, just look at me and you'll understand. For women, living independently is an everyday struggle for survival, and people's gossiping never really stops making your ears burn.)*

> KIEU
> Ho noi gi cu de ho noi, con khong ban tam. Lam nghe van si hay ve, con thay song mot minh rat thoai mai! Con la ke "si tinh" trong nghiep viet!
> *(They can say what they want, I'll not be bothered. Working as a writer or as a painter, I get on better living alone! It is writing that I'm "in love" with!)*

> AUNT
> *(points at her with chopsticks)*
> Nay, con gai ba muoi may tuoi dau roi ma con lang bang nhu the, nguy lam day. Khong la gi ba me con lo lang.
> *(Listen. You're already over thirty, and you're still drifting. No wonder your parents are worried.)*

The two of them eat silently.

9. INT ALIKAN'S APARTMENT WORKING WITH KIEU DAY

From EXTREME CLOSE-UP of Kieu with large hat and white veil to MEDIUM SHOT during the conversation.

Kieu attempts to take her hat off. Her eyes are closed.

> ALIKAN
> Relax. *(pause)* Okay. *(pause)* Don't take it off, will you? Just leave it on until I tell you can take it off.

Kieu follows Alikan's instructions and strikes a number of poses for him as he goes on circling her, taking photographs.

KIEU
(*softly*)
Can I look?

ALIKAN
(*abruptly*)
No, don't spoil it. All right? Don't let me see you watching me while I shoot, otherwise we may as well forget the whole thing.

They go on working for a while, with some directions from Alikan. Kieu seems increasingly irritated. Alikan stops photographing and tiptoes toward Kieu. She waits silently behind the veil. Instead of rearranging her for another pose, he stoops, lifts the veil on her face.

ALIKAN
(*smiling, softly*)
Every story of love is a story of voyeurism. Don't you agree?

Kieu looks at him while he moves away from her, and takes off her hat as they talk. Alikan goes behind her and takes off her kimono. As he speaks, he begins to wrap her in white gauze.

KIEU
Why make such a statement? Because you can only make love with your eyes?

ALIKAN
(*highly amused*)
Is that what you think of me? So if you were to capture love on photographs, how would you do it?

KIEU
There are many ways to show love. Do you always have to be the one looking? Why all this hiding, these veils and semi darkness?

ALIKAN
You know why! You hate harsh light.
(*smiles*)
Love making and image making do not mate. Tell me, who loves *naturally* in front of a camera? All is performed for. . . nothing is unforeseen. Here, love and death are the two Impossibles. Show them and look at them, and we all become *voyeurs*.
(*He finishes unwrapping her and lays her down.*)

10. INT AUNT'S HOUSE KIEU DAY

Kieu hums as she does housework, scrubbing the floor in the bathroom. She coughs as she spreads the cleaning product. She tidies up here and there, picking up dirty clothes as she sees them, then throws them into a basket. She picks up the basket and walks away with it. As she walks, we HEAR verses from *The Tale of Kieu*.

VERSE SINGER (VO)
Hai ben y hop tam dau,
khi than chang lo la cau moi than.
(Two minds at one, two hearts in unison—
unbidden, love will seek those meant for love.)

On her way, Kieu passes a telephone and suddenly remembers something. She goes to the telephone and puts the load down on the floor. She dials a number.

KIEU
Hello? Lynn?

MAN
(barely awake)
Hello, yes?

KIEU
Oooh . . . can I speak to Lynn please?

MAN
(still sleepy)
She's not here.

KIEU
Sorry, did I wake you up?

MAN
(pleasantly)
It's alright. You have a beautiful voice!

Kieu smiles.

MAN
(continues)
Lynn's traveling.

KIEU
Do you know when she'll be back? *(pause)* Here's my phone number in case she calls in the next few days. Tell her it's Kieu calling. Yes, K, I, E, U at 555-6618. Thank you. All right.

KIEU hangs up the phone, smiling to herself. She sings a high note and hums to herself.

11. EXT   CITY STREETS   NIGHT

Traveling shots of night activities in the city—street scenes, shops, restaurants, people behind panes of glass. The camera TRACKS Kieu as she walks.

> KIEU (VO)
> Will love find an outlet, will it weave its own stories in the shadows of the city?
> (OS *from a conversation*)
> Juliet, I need more work. My aunt is having financial problems, and I'll have to move out soon if I want a room of my own.

> JULIET (OS)
> I wish I could help. But you know, the research you are doing now on "The Tale of Kieu" for us is the best I can do. I know it's not a lot, but with the financial situation we're facing now, as a women's magazine, it's very hard for me to do better than that.

> KIEU (OS)
> I'll do anything, really. How about . . . house cleaning? Because after all, that's what I do at my aunt's place in exchange for my room.

> JULIET (OS)
> (*surprised*)
> Why house cleaning rather than any other job?

> KIEU (OS)
> Flexible hours.

12. INT   JULIET'S HOUSE   KIEU AND JULIET   DAY

> JULIET
> But house cleaning doesn't get you very far, and besides, how can I hire you as a house cleaner, when I know what a fine writer you are? What about your other job, modeling for some photographer? How's that going?

> KIEU
> (*looks up and smiles, touches Juliet on the arm*)
> I'm a freelance writer and a sex worker. How does that sound?

> JULIET
> (*smiles*)
> Nothing wrong with that, as long as you know what you're doing.

Kieu begins to walk away from Juliet.

> KIEU
> It pays well. That's why I hold on to it. But, as you know, I got into it by chance, and I haven't tried to look for other modeling jobs. I'm only doing it twice a week. It's not enough.

Kieu goes out into the courtyard.

JULIET

And you're still in charge of your parents and family back home?

KIEU

(from the courtyard)

Yes. I do want my younger sisters to have an education, rather than to work at the age of 13, like my mother.

JULIET

Why don't you give me some time, and I'll see what I can come up with. Okay?

(picks up the manuscript Kieu brought in)

So, what have you brought me today?

Kieu comes back into the room.

KIEU

Well, I start out by introducing the importance of this national poem of Vietnam, *The Tale of Kieu*. I highlight the fact that Vietnamese people all around the globe recognize their country in the image of a woman. Kieu is here a folk symbol of Love, and she is both passionately admired and blamed for having loved "improperly."

(pause)

You know, I never made the connection before, but ever since the day I started doing research on the impact of *The Tale* for the magazine, I can't mention her name without feeling somewhat implied. Isn't a writer someone who loves for a living?

13. INT   ALIKAN'S APARTMENT   MEMORY   NIGHT

View through a narrow opening. A male hand is caressing a woman's chest and unbuttoning her blouse. When she turns her head toward the camera, she is seen blindfolded in red, and when the man lowers his head to kiss her breast, he is seen also blindfolded in red.

ALIKAN (OS)

Her breasts . . .

I could have stayed longer. Were the tips as red as those I've seen? If not, we'll have to use some makeup.

14. INT   APARTMENT   ALIKAN   NIGHT

We SEE Alikan standing with his back to the camera. We hear the end of his previous statement. He is speaking almost to himself and he is holding a slide sheet. He lowers the slides and speaks to a person offscreen.

ALIKAN

(on screen)

People put makeup on their face all the time, why shouldn't they do the same for the tips of their breasts when these are shown in public?

(*pause*)

I'll work on these and deliver them to you later.

The camera PANS slowly then rests on a veiled mannequin.

15. INT   KIEU'S BED ON THE DECK   KIEU WRITING   NIGHT

Kieu is writing, bent over a table near her bed. A cricket keeps her company. She is seen through the mosquito net of her bed. Kieu writes, then stops, puts her pen down, stares in front of her, or continues to think, then picks up the pen again and keeps on writing. We HEAR verses from *The Tale of Kieu*, then Kieu in VO reading aloud the content of her writing.

> VERSE SINGER (VO)
> Nang thi coi khach xa-xam.
> Dam khuya ngat-tanh mu khoi
> thay trang ma then nhung loi non-song,
> Rung thu tung biec chen hong,
> nghe chim nhu nhac tam long than-hon.
> (*She traveled far, far into the unknown.*
> *A road that stretched into the hushed, still night.*
> *She saw the moon*
> *Felt shame at her vows.*
> *Fall woods—green tiers all interlaid with red*
> *Bird cries reminded her of her old folks.*)

> KIEU (VO)
> A narrative poem, *The Tale of Kieu* was written in the nineteenth century by Nguyen Du. Kieu's love life has repeatedly served as a metaphor for Vietnam's destiny. People remember Kieu and the names of the many characters that live on through *The Tale*. They praise her piety and loyalty and say she has had a wretched life, but they never seem to remember she spent fifteen years surviving as a sex worker.

16. INT/EXT   HOUSE NEXT DOOR   NIGHT

View from inside a room with windows open. A moonlit night. CREAKING NOISES from outside. A woman's silhouette moves toward the window. She veils herself partly behind the curtain and bends slightly over the windowsill while looking out.

An Asian teenager in shorts and sleeveless top, with her long hair swinging while she moves, is swiftly climbing down the ladder propped against the window of her room in the house next door. Further down, a young man is waiting for her. As soon as she reaches the ground, they briefly and passionately embrace, then they run away together toward a car parked on the side of the street.

VERSE SINGER (VO)
Cho hay la giong huu-tinh,
do ai go moi manh cho xong.
(How strange the race of lovers! Try as you will,
you can't unsnarl their hearts' entangled threads.)

17. INT   JULIET'S HOUSE   KIEU AND JULIET   DAY

From underneath the floor, we see Kieu bending over, looking at a pile of books. Juliet joins her. They pick the books up and carry them down a flight of stairs to another room as they talk.

KIEU
Oh, Juliet, guess what, I just interviewed a woman in my community this morning, who told me I should write about her life, rather than doing all this research about The *Tale of Kieu*. She felt that she was the real Kieu, not a national symbol, not a figure from a poem, but Kieu herself. It was both funny and scary at the same time. You should have seen her.

JULIET
Why scary?

Kieu and Juliet stack the books on the floor, then go back up the stairs as they talk. They return with more books.

KIEU
Well, she was deadly serious. *Kieu* isn't a story to her. But she herself looks like someone from a story. Somewhere in her sixties, with heavy makeup, and long, long (longer even than yours) floating hair right down to her ankles. She knew I'd come to discuss *The Tale*, so she dressed up for it. Beautiful white *ao dai* with colorful embroidery. Almost like in a fairy tale, you know?

JULIET
So is that how she remembers *The Tale*? Just imagine, women of all ages still feel that passionate about a fictive character — enough to get their identity from her . . .

KIEU
Yes, and not just women, but also a lot of the older generation of men. Today illiterate people might not remember the poem, but they've certainly not forgotten the poetry. They feel a kind of affection, respect, and even fall in love with Kieu as if she really existed.

JULIET
No wonder you said that she's dwelt in millions of Vietnamese hearts.

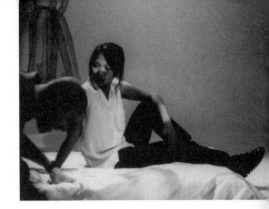

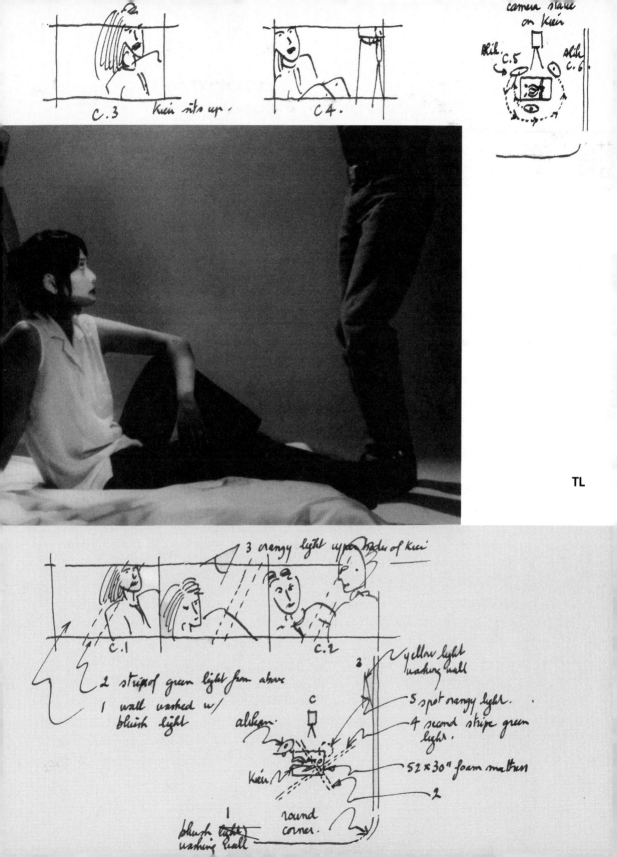

TL

> KIEU

People even tell the future using *The Tale*. They open the poem at any page and pick a verse at random, then predict what's going to happen to you.

> JULIET

That's wild. You know, I've just finished reading *The Tale* myself. It's a real tearjerker. It runs the widest and most complex range of emotions.
> *(carries an armful of books into another room)*
I mean, here's a love poem that talks to its readers as victims and survivors. *(pause)* And what I, like your people, see in Kieu is an all-compassionate heart—one that beats for everyone who's ever been oppressed. *(pause)* But what I think is interesting, though, are the passionate controversies her life has always raised. How do people really remember her story? Have you looked more into that?

18. EXT   WOMAN WALKING   DAY

EXTREME CLOSE-UP OF a woman walking with her long, long hair down in white *ao dai*. We see her only from the back and the undulating movement of her hair as she walks.

19. INT   JULIET'S HOUSE   KIEU AND JULIET   DAY

Kieu removes a scarf from a free-standing shelf. Underneath she finds a multitude of perfume bottles. Taken aback, she exclaims softly while taking her time looking at them.

> KIEU

Juliet, why all these perfumes and colognes?

Juliet comes over to Kieu.

> JULIET
> *(looks very carefully at them as if she is discovering them for the first time)*
Do you think I should simply throw them away?

Kieu shrugs.

> JULIET
> *(continues)*
I wonder sometimes. . . .But you play music. You should know better. What does a musical note bring to your life? . . . It's captivating, sensual, free. Some women wear a perfume the same way others wear the veil. Worse, they can't do without it, not even in bed.

> KIEU

But . . . you don't use them all, so why keep them?

JULIET

Yes . . . why keep all these memories? Fragrances are so precise in what they evoke and provoke. They are merciless.

KIEU

So hopelessly romantic?

JULIET

I don't know what that means. But I know that I've always wished that science and progress will one day invent a pill that will allow us to forget, *selectively*.

CLOSE-UP OF KIEU as she opens a bottle of perfume and moves it in circular motions under her nose while inhaling it with her eyes closed. Smiling, she makes a gesture toward Juliet.

KIEU
(*lightly*)
Like being in an iris mist at the height of summer.

JULIET

The irrational world is always tempting, but it's so easy to unleash melancholia.
(*then, slowly and almost tenderly*)
Behind every perfume lies a love story. . . .

Juliet walks away leaving Kieu where she is.

JULIET
(*as she moves away*)
I forgot, I have to leave for an appointment today. Why don't you stay here and work? Enjoy the place. Just lock the door when you leave.

20. EXT KIEU IN JULIET'S PATIO

CLOSE-UP on Kieu as she comes into frame leaning back, closes her eyes and daydreams.

21. INT KIEU IN LIBRARY

Camera TRACKS along library stacks, finding people reading books, mainly turned away from the camera, before showing Kieu. Kieu is reading book titles, her finger following the letters imprinted on the spines of the books as she goes from one row to another. We SEE a man passing and briefly pause at the end of the aisle Kieu is in, then continues to walk on.

EXTREME CLOSE-UP of Kieu as the steps move further and further away from her, she turns her head abruptly, as if she has just been hit by something. Looking emotionally disturbed, she smells around her, hesitates, and seems at a loss as she tries to understand what is happening to her, her eyes darting around.

TL

Back to FULL SHOT of Kieu as she sets out to follow the steps she just heard. Meandering walk from one aisle to another, through the bookshelves, all the time letting herself be led by her sense of smell. She hesitates in her meandering, clasping the books on her chest, and stops searchingly at a man crouching in an aisle, his back toward her.

> KIEU
> *(in a soft tone)*
> Anh Minh?

The man looks up from the book he has just opened, slightly surprised. (The man is Asian.) He turns around.

> KIEU
> *(stops, quite embarrassed)*
> Oh, excuse me. I thought you were someone else.

Kieu turns around and leaves, while we see the man following her with his eyes, amused. She hurries away.

22. INT   ALIKAN'S APARTMENT   DAY

> KIEU
> *(calling out)*
> Alikan? Alikan? Ali . . .

Kieu walks up the stairs to the apartment and enters the apartment, touching a jacket and stopping to inhale a fragrance hovering in the room as she slowly makes her way in, as if she's following the trace of an odor.

From behind a blue curtain, we HEAR Alikan's voice OS and a camera clicking. Kieu approaches the curtain and turns her profile to us. Half-hidden, she follows the scene, peering around the curtain. A woman is lying back on a motorcycle, naked. She is holding a magazine over her head, far enough from her face to enable her to peep behind the magazine and see in front of her while speaking. We see her slightly on the side. Alikan is not visible to Kieu from this angle, we only hear him and catch glimpses of his hand and arm as he gets excited while he speaks.

> ALIKAN
> *(at once authoritarian and gentle)*
> No, not like that. Why are you watching me?

> WOMAN
> *(amused)*
> But you're the one watching me!

> ALIKAN
> Are we both spying on each other?

WOMAN
(laughs, then spreading her legs gracefully)
It's more fun that way! But now, isn't this exactly the position that you want me in?

ALIKAN
(nervy)
Yes, it is. Get busy and read that magazine. Don't pay any attention to what I am doing, and everything will be alright.

WOMAN
(pulling the magazine toward her face, thereby hiding it from Alikan's view)
I don't know why I volunteer to do this for you, my dear voyeur. You don't want a nude. What you want is a female body without a head.
(silence, while we hear noises of camera clicking)
I'm curious. What's so exciting about sex with no head?

ALIKAN
Don't ask. Just spread a bit further and let me see it, will you?

We see Kieu walking slowly downstairs toward the camera and the entrance door. Pensive look, her head slightly hanging and her shoulders drooping; she caresses the walls dreamingly as she moves downstairs; when her arms are extended she stops, presses her hands against the wall, leans back and holds her head thrown backward.

23. EXT   STREET   KIEU   DAY

It's raining. Kieu comes out of the building, closes the door behind her, and then stands on the sidewalk, oblivious to the rain wetting her. We SEE a woman pass by, looking curiously at Kieu and hurrying with an umbrella. Kieu stands pensive, unaffected. We HEAR verses from *The Tale of Kieu*.

VERSE SINGER (VO)
Dau-don thay phan dan ba!
Loi rang bac-menh cung la loi chung.
(How sorrowful is women's lot!
We all partake of woe, our common fate.)

CAMERA at EYE LEVEL shows Kieu slowly feeling the rain, throwing her head back, smoothing her soaking hair and clothes. She smiles, holds her hand out to catch raindrops.

24. EXT   AUNT'S HOUSE   CHILD PLAYING WITH WATER   DAY

A girl, about 4 years old, sits naked in the sunshine playing with buckets and water, moving the water from one bucket to another.

KIEU (VO)

Where does it lead me? I never know. When a forgotten scent hits you, it coils up in you, and by the time you realize it, it's too late. You're hurled into the dark corridor of buried memories. And you walk around crazed, feeling like a murderer again.

VERSE SINGER (VO)

Nho tu nam hay tho-ngay,
co nguoi tuong-si doan ngay mot loi:
"Anh-hoa phat-tiet ra ngoai,
nghin thu bac-menh mot doi tai-hoa."
(Back in my childhood years, I still recall,
a seer observed my features—he foretold:
"All charms and splendors from within burst forth:
she'll live an artist's life, a life of woe.")

The little girl looks at the camera. We HEAR Minh calling the name "Kieu" and laughters.

25. EXT STREET KIEU AND MINH DAY

Kieu is walking in bright, harsh daylight, accompanied by Minh, who has a bicycle with him as he walks. Kieu puts her hand out to feel if there are any drops of rain falling. She inhales and smells the air.

KIEU

Anh Minh, hinh nhu troi sap mua.
(Minh, it's probably going to rain soon.)

KIEU (cont'd.)

Khi troi mua, mui dat va co luc nao cung lam em that nho nha.
(When it rains, the smell of earth and grass always makes me homesick.)

MINH

Co voi dat gi! Leo len xe di, mau len khong thoi sap mua uot het bay gio! Mau len, mau len.
(Don't talk rubbish! Hurry up and get on the back of the bicycle, it's going to rain and you'll get all wet. Hurry, hurry.)

Minh sits on his bicycle while Kieu gets on behind, hesitating as she lightly puts her arms around him. As the bicycle rolls, Kieu tries to keep balance. She looks slightly disturbed, then closes her eyes, inhaling the smell in the air. The ride happens silently on both sides. It suddenly starts to rain. Kieu throws her head back to enjoy the rain. They enjoy the ride, laughing at the rain. We hear SOUND OF RAIN.

26. INT   KIEU'S ROOM   KIEU   NIGHT

SOUND OF RAIN continuing from previous scene. Kieu wakes up from her sleep. She remains still with her eyes opened and listens to the rain outside. We see her with the mosquito net lighted above. She turns around in bed a couple of times, then decides to get up. Goes to the sliding door and steps outside and stretches her arms to feel the rain. She enjoys getting wet. With both hands, she spreads the water on her face and neck, making her nightshirt cling to her body. We SEE her absorbed in feeling the rain falling and wetting her chest. She sensually spreads the water on her arms and chest.

> KIEU (VO)
> *(warm, but matter-of-factly)*
> A woman said it all: "It is romance I loathe, the swooning moon / of June which croons to the tune of every goon." (Marge Piercy)

27. INT   ALIKAN'S APARTMENT   KIEU AND ALIKAN   DAY

Kieu enters as Alikan drops down from a ladder.

> ALIKAN
> You didn't show up last Thursday. What happened?

> KIEU
> *(taking coat off)*
> I got confused. I came on Friday.

> ALIKAN
> *(as Kieu walks past him)*
> What do you mean, you came on Friday?

> KIEU
> *(arms folded)*
> I did. I came in at three, as usual. You were busy.

Alikan looks at Kieu with surprise, then walks toward her and scrutinizes her in silence, as if remembering something.

> ALIKAN
> *(very slowly)*
> You came in and . . . you saw me? . . . and you left.

Kieu walks away.

CLOSE-UP on Kieu, seen in shadowed profile, sitting. She nods her head yes. Alikan moves in and out of the frame.

ALIKAN
(*unpleasantly*)
Why didn't you say something when you saw me?

KIEU
I did what you would have done. I looked without being looked at.

Pause while Alikan comes into shot and squats beside Kieu.

ALIKAN
(*highly amused*)
Kieu . . . you always surprise me. You always do.

ALIKAN (OS)
(*decisively*)
Let's do something different. Let's break our agreement just for today. Okay?

With inquisitive eyes, Kieu looks at him steadily. Alikan gets up and indicates a place for her to lie down.

ALIKAN
(*same resoluteness*)
Don't change clothes. Don't take off anything. Just lie down over here.
(*indicates the place*)

CUT to Kieu sitting on a mattress at the place indicated, looking at Alikan inquisitively.

ALIKAN
Now simply unzip your pants, casually spread your legs, look up at the ceiling and dream. Okay? Just let yourself go.

Alikan comes over to the mattress and squats beside Kieu.

KIEU
(*shakes head*)
You can't be serious.

ALIKAN
I am! Nobody's going to touch you. And you'll see how exciting this can be for both of us. Beauty awakes when she's looked at.
(*pause while he stands up.*)
The difference with last Friday is that you know you're being looked at. I didn't. And I know that you know this while I'm looking at you.

KIEU
(*firmly*)
We agreed that I'd never pose naked from the waist down, and this is too close.

How strange, the race of lovers!

ALIKAN
(moves closer to Kieu)
You're not naked. Nobody is really naked in front of a camera.

Kieu turns away from Alikan.

ALIKAN
(continues softly)
Don't be afraid. Just unzip them and go on dreaming. It's so simple!

Kieu shakes her head (negatively) while getting up, ignoring Alikan. She slips on the sheet around the mattress and Alikan reaches out to keep her from falling. Kieu pushes his hands off. She breathes quickly, but does not look angry. Alikan is sitting with spread legs and Kieu is on her knees.

As Alikan speaks, Kieu lowers her gaze.

ALIKAN
I didn't mean to frighten you. I only need to look. I want to really see you.
(pause)
You know, it's strange but I have come to love my Tuesdays and Thursdays. They're my dreamtime.
(pause)
I've had a lousy weekend. Sounds silly, but I realized I missed our session. I don't want to stop dreaming. I don't want to lose you.

KIEU
(looking down, gently)
You were busy.

ALIKAN
I didn't plan what happened. Don't get offended about what I've been asking you to do. An image is best seen when it doesn't give everything away. You know this Chinese proverb that says, "The darkest place is always right underneath the lamp"?

KIEU
(looks directly at Alikan)
Is there really such a thing as an innocent veil?

28. INT ALIKAN'S APARTMENT MEMORY NIGHT

View through a narrow opening, as before. The same scene as before of a man and a woman in a silky red blindfold. We HEAR a man's voice humming and singing, lightly aping words. At the end, we HEAR the same voice calling Kieu's name.

29. INT   KIEU'S BED ON THE DECK   KIEU WRITING   NIGHT

Kieu is writing, bent over a table in her bed. SOUND OF CRICKETS in background. Kieu writes, then stops, puts her pen down, stares in front of her, or continues to think, then picks up the pen again and keeps on writing.

> KIEU (VO)
> One night I saw you in a mouth I tenderly devoured.
> (reading)
> In *A Tale of Kieu*, Kieu becomes a prostitute to save her family from disgrace. Pimps, traders, villains, she moved them all to tears at the sound of her talent and her music. Talent and destiny often ran into conflict. What I find most interesting are some of the details that elderly men of letters in our community find questionable. For example, Kieu dares to visit her Romeo, Kim Trong, at night at his place—a very unusual move for a well-bred woman. Then the poet also treats us to an erotic scene where one of Kieu's lovers catches a glimpse of her bathing naked under the moonlight. Last but not least, Kieu remains, despite her pathetic life, a passion-driven creature who has loved not one, but three men—a different love for each man.

30. INT   JULIET'S HOUSE   KIEU AND JULIET   DAY

Juliet is making a Japanese bouquet while conversing with Kieu.

> JULIET
> They think the older a woman gets, the more she resorts to perfumes and other acces-sories to seduce. No, a perfume is something one creates, like a story. A story with a touch that can be light, fluid, and limpid—or, captivating, sumptuous, and sensual like velvet.

Juliet gets up and walks out of shot. The camera PANS slowly to find Kieu busy looking at some of the ads Juliet has displayed on a table nearby.

> JULIET (OS)
> (continues)
> It's an olfactory voyage, a subtle blend of many emotions. Some break into your life whether you like it or not. And others gently tease you and you grow to like them despite yourself. Others pass with time, you forget the fragrance, until one day, it returns as the trace of a relationship, blurs past and present, makes time stand still.

> KIEU
> (looking at the ads)
> Speak volumes, don't they? It's about work and pleasure.

Juliet joins Kieu.

CLOSE-UP on ads.

> JULIET (OS)
> *(leaning on table)*
> Some of them truly make you dream. Look at this. . . .

The camera PULLS OUT to show other green, nature, and sexy ads as Juliet speaks. The women's fingers showing up from time to time, pointing or gesticulating.

> JULIET (OS)
> Today, women want to wear a scent for themselves, not for some man whom they want to attract or seduce. Look at all these new fragrances put out on the market—the focus is on green. On the great outdoors, on fresh florals and fruity scents. Green is selling.

> KIEU (OS)
> A forbidden garden is always an extraordinary garden. Green sex. Girls are always half-naked in advertising, and sex has always sold in photographs.

We SEE Kieu and Juliet face on, from the other side of the table. There is a bright green parrot in the foreground.

> JULIET
> A perfume tells you who you are—the woman you want people to see in you, your personality, your taste, your style.

> KIEU
> What about women who don't care either for perfume or makeup? You don't use much on you either. The natural look is "in" with this back-to-nature trend.

> JULIET
> Sure. As they say, "the beauty biz has seen the future—and it's green, the very shade of a million-dollar bill!"
> *(to parrot)*
> Right Green Boy? Right?
> *(strokes parrot, then speaks to Kieu)*
> But don't confuse natural and nature. The natural look is creative and nature wears its own veil.

> KIEU
> What do you mean?

> JULIET
> I don't have to tell you about the power of a fragrance. Wear it and make it yours. Natural or not, there it comes, ahead of you. Your fragrance signals your arrival, enhances your presence, and leaves a vibrant trace of yourself. It's a strange alchemy of a body in love.

31. EXT   AUNT'S HOUSE   KIEU IMAGINING   DAY

Kieu is sitting on a jetty outdoors staring at the water and at the surrounding landscape. She closes her eyes to dream.

32. EXT   AUNT'S HOUSE   KIEU   DAY

Kieu leans on a fence, daydreaming. Singing a song to herself, she listens attentively to the BIRDS CHIRPING, and suddenly smiles without reserve, amused and happy as if unable to contain her mirth.

> JAVA (VO)
> *(same as from earlier telephone call)*
> It's alright. You have a beautiful voice.

33. EXT   AUNT'S HOUSE   KIEU   DAY

Kieu sits on the deck, peeling mangoes. She hears a sound and turns around, stares insistently in the direction of the sound.

> VERSE SINGER (VO)
> Tuong nguoi duoi nguyet chen dong,
> tin suong luong nhung ray trong mai cho.
> Ben troi goc be bo-vo,
> tam son got-rua bao gio cho phai?
> *(He'd shared the cup with her beneath the moon—*
> *now, day by day, he longed for news of her.*
> *Cast off and stranded upon a distant shore*
> *when could she ever purge her heart of love?)*

34. INT   KIEU'S ROOM   KIEU AND MINH   NIGHT

Nighttime. We barely see Minh sitting in the dark with the back of his head toward the camera and toward Kieu. We see only part of the mosquito net in the frame. He turns to the side from time to time as he talks and we see his profile lit against the dark. Kieu is pacing behind him and we see fragments of her face and body appearing and disappearing in the frame. Camera is set at Minh's sitting level.

> KIEU
> *(coldly)*
> Mai may gio anh phai di don . . . ?
> *(What time do you have to pick them up tomorrow?)*

> MINH
> Vao luc 2 gio chieu.
> *(Around 2 pm.)*

ORANGY LIGHTS
ON LANDING   2

J&K ARE ½ A STAIRCASE APART

PERFUME
SHELVE

1

ORANGY LIGHT
FROM OPPOSITE
ROOM ON BOTH
K & J

JULIET

kieu

LANDING

5 ORANGE LIGHT ON
WINDOWS AROUND
PATIO

6 ORANGY
BACKLIGHTING
ON SOME PLANT

CAMERA

PATIO

3 2 1

4

WASH ORANGE
LIGHT ON WALL

3

CAMERA REMAINS FIX
IN A3 POSITION ONLY
& STARTS PANNING SLOWLY
WHEN K & J REACH
TABLE AT ③ ; CAMERA
TURNS TOWARD PATIO
& ACTORS EVENTUALLY
APPEAR ON/OFF FRAME

1

3

2

DOOR

TL

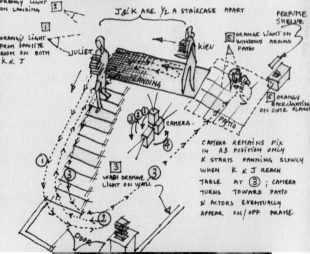

KIEU
(voice getting coarse)
Sao anh khong cho em biet truoc? Gia ma em duoc biet . . .
(Why didn't you tell me before? I wish I had known. . . .)

MINH
Anh chi duoc tin gan day.
(I only learned about it recently.)

KIEU
Anh biet tu lau ma anh chang noi gi cho em biet. Ca mot nam troi quen than nhau ma
anh lai dau em . . .
(You knew it about it long ago, and you didn't tell me. We've been together for a whole
year, but you've been hiding it from me. . . .)

MINH
Khong. Chang bao gio anh nghi se gap lai gia dinh. Vo anh no van noi la no khong
muon qua o tren dat la nay. Va lai, anh cung khong hieu no xoay xo nhu the nao ma lai
co du tien cho hai me con cung qua day. Tin den qua dot ngot, that khong ngo. May
hom nay anh chang ngu duoc dem nao.
(No. I never thought I'd see my family again. My wife always told me she didn't want to live
in a foreign land. And I still can't understand how she's managed to pay the fare for both
mother and daughter. The news was so sudden, I couldn't believe it. I haven't slept for days.)

Kieu stops pacing.

KIEU
Em dai that . . .
(I'm so naive. . . .)

35. INT   AUNT'S HOUSE   SHRINE   EVENING

Kieu lights candles and burns incense at the ancestor's shrine in the house. Kieu inhales the
smell of incense and enjoys it. Spirals of smoke unfold while she agitates the incense sticks in
circular motion. We see her lingering with the smoke, closing her eyes as if she is forming a
wish. She opens her eyes with a start when her aunt calls her.

AUNT (OS)
Kieu, thap huong xong thi con, mang thuc an ra ban nhe!
(Kieu, once you light the incense, bring the food to the table!)
    (impatient)
Kieu!

KIEU
Da!
(Yes!)

AUNT (OS)
(impatient)
Kieu!

36. EXT   AUNT'S HOUSE   DINNER TABLE   EVENING

At the dinner table outside, Kieu, the Aunt, a girl, and two boys (the Aunt's children) are sitting and just beginning to eat.

DAUGHTER
Can I go watch TV?

AUNT
Khong. Ngoi day an, khong di dau het.
(No. Sit here, don't go anywhere else.)

SON NO. 1
May I go watch TV, please?

AUNT
(giving up)
U thi thoi. Neu muon vo xem TV thi di di, de me voi chi an com cho yen.
(Alright. You can go and watch TV so we can have dinner in peace.)

The Daughter and Son No. 1 get up and leave the table.

AUNT
(to Kieu)
Buon qua. Khong biet chung muoi hay hai chuc nam nua roi tui con nit minh no ra sao? Ca mot the he tre qua day, tieng Viet noi khong ranh, cang ngay cang kem di. Khong biet sau nay tui no con nho tieng me de khong?
(It's so sad. I wonder what's going to become of our children in 10 or 20 years? A whole generation of youngsters is losing their Vietnamese. Will they still remember their mother tongue in the future?)

Kieu and the Aunt eat as they talk.

KIEU
Co dung lo. Muon sinh ton tren dat My thi minh phai noi tieng Anh luu loat. Du sao di nua co cu tiep tuc noi tieng Viet voi tui no. Chuyen noi tieng me de hay khong la mot chuyen khong nen ep buoc. Con nghi phai hoa minh voi ngon ngu thi moi duy tri duoc tieng me de.
(Don't worry. To survive in America, we have to speak English fluently. No matter what, you should continue to speak to them in Vietnamese. You can't make them speak it just by forcing them. I think you have to love language if you want to keep your mother tongue.)

AUNT

Noi tieng Viet da kho, giu duoc van hoa phong tuc minh lai cang kho nua. Do con
xem, tui nho no xem TV roi ra ngoai hoc toan thai do cua tre con My, ve nha chang
con biet tren duoi la gi, xung ho voi bo me ho hang nhu la xung ho voi nguoi la. Y niem
lien he gia dinh tieu tan het.

*(Keeping the language is difficult, but keeping our culture is even harder. Look, the chil-
dren watch TV and pick up American children's manners. They no longer know how to
address their elders, they speak to their parents and relatives as to strangers. The whole
idea of the family falls to pieces.)*

KIEU

Gioi tre ben nha cung chang kha gi hon. Theo nhu ho noi thi sau khi My bo cam van
tu thang hai vua qua, nuoc minh khong con phai lo lang con cai an khong du no. The
nhung dieu ho thay dang lo hon het la can ban dao duc cua xa hoi va gioi tre minh sau
nay.

*(The young generation at home isn't doing any better. After the U.S. lifted the embargo
last February, people said Vietnam wouldn't have to worry about feeding its children. But
what people really worry about is the new generation and its social values.)*

AUNT

Dung the. Ho noi la nuoc Viet Nam moi se hoan toan thuoc ve gioi tre. Noi chuyen voi
may ong o trong gioi doanh thuong, ong nao cung deu tuyen bo la tuong lai kinh te
thuong mai khong nam trong khu vuc nuoc My va cac nuoc Au Chau, ma trong cac
nuoc A Chau. Ho con noi thang la nguoi cua the ky 21 la nguoi Trung Hoa.

*(That's right. They say that the new Vietnam is going to belong to the young generation.
All the businessmen here claim that the future of economics doesn't lie in America or in
Europe, but in Asia. People aren't slow to say that the twenty-first-century man will be a
Chinese.)*

KIEU

(laughing)

Da, doi voi phan dong dan My thi nguoi A Dong dien hinh luon luon la nguoi Trung
Hoa hay nguoi Nhat ban. Neu may ong thuong mai o day nghi rang the ky 21 thuoc ve
nguoi A Dong, thi doc cac bao phu nu o nha, ho noi la the ky 21 la the ky cua phu nu.

*(Anyway, for most Americans, "Asian" means Chinese or Japanese. If businessmen here
think the twenty-first century belongs to Asians, the women's magazines back home claim
the twenty-first century belongs to women.)*

AUNT

Oi thoi. The ky phu nu phu niec gi! Con cu mo mat ra ma nhin. Dung qua ly tuong mo
ho. Coi chung mat ngot chet ruoi do! Ai noi gi thi noi, trong hoan canh hien nay cua
minh, con thay co bao nhieu phu nu duoc dat trong nhung cuong vi then chot cua xa
hoi?

(Oh, no! What do they mean, a women's century? Just open your eyes and see for yourself. Don't be such an idealist. How many women are appointed to key positions in today's society?)

KIEU

Mot xa hoi ma tren 200 nam van con yeu men say xua *Truyen Kieu* nhu xa hoi minh thi bat buoc la phai thay doi trong cach doi xu voi phu nu. Khong le hinh anh Kieu chi la hinh anh mot phu nu bac menh khoc suot muot trong nhung hoan canh toi tam?
(Well, a society like ours, which still loves The Tale of Kieu *after 200 years, is bound to change the way it treats women. Kieu's image can't simply be that of an ill-fated woman crying her eyes out in tragic situations, can it?)*

AUNT

Day, thi nuoc minh dep nhat co Thuy Kieu, nhung ma kho nhat cung la Thuy Kieu. "Dau don thay phan dan ba!" Co khoi noi thi con cung hieu ro cau tho nay. Con cung la mot co Kieu do. Con nen can than, khi gap nhung kho khan trong doi, dung roi vao manh luoi cua nhung ke So Khanh.
(The most beautiful thing in our country is Kieu, but the most woeful thing is also Kieu. "How tragic the fate of women!" I don't have to tell you what this verse is saying clearly. You are also a Kieu. Be careful, when facing life's difficulties, don't fall prey to those So Khanh treacheries.)

KIEU

Khong, con nghi neu Kieu la tam hon cua nguoi Viet Nam nhu moi nguoi van noi, thi dieu quan trong khong phai chi nam trong su ap buc va suc chiu dung cua nang, ma con nam trong suc phan khang cua nang. Dieu nay moi co the mang lai nhieu thay doi.
(No. If Kieu is the Vietnamese people's soul, as people say, what seems important is not so much her oppression and her endurance, but her resistance. Only through this can there be change.)

AUNT

Thay doi gi con! Da co nguoi noi, doi Kieu co the tom tat lai trong may chu da: da tai, da tinh, da nan, da sau da cam, va ke ca da dam, da benh luon! Phu nu ma da tai da tinh thi lam gi thien ha cung tim cach buoc toi. Loi ra noi vao, chang bao gio thoat duoc ca.
(What change, girl? As our elders said, Kieu's life can be summed up in a few "many" words: many talents, many loves, many misfortunes, many sadnesses, many emotions, many prostitutions, even many illnesses! People always find fault in women with many talents and loves. No matter what they do, they can never escape criticism.)

37. INT   KIEU'S ROOM   KIEU DAYDREAMS   DAY

Kieu is sitting reading in her bed with the mosquito net lifted above. She looks out the window.

> VERSE SINGER (VO)
> Gio chieu nhu giuc con sau,
> vi-lo hiu-hat nhu mau khay-treu.
> *(The breeze at twilight stirred a mood of grief—*
> *the reeds waved back and forth as if to taunt.)*

38. EXT   AUNT'S HOUSE OUTDOOR   KIEU BATHING   NIGHT

View of a woman washing herself outdoors under the moonlight, pouring, cup by cup, water from a basin over her body. She enjoys feeling the water on her skin. We SEE part of the silhouette of someone (the Aunt) fully absorbed in watching Kieu bathing. Kieu is not aware that she's being watched.

> VERSE SINGER (VO)
> Nghe rieng nho it tuong nhieu.
> *(A lover's mind is full of the loved one.)*
> Duoi trang quyen da goi he,
> dau tuong lua luu lap-loe dam bong.
> Buong the phai buoi thong-dong,
> thang lan ru buc truong hong tam hoa.
> Day-day san duc mot toa thien-nhien.
> *(Beneath the moon, summer cuckoos cried.*
> *Above the wall, pomegranates kindled fire.*
> *Now, in her chamber, at a leisured hour,*
> *she let the curtain fall for an orchard bath.*
> *Her body stood as Heaven's masterwork.)*

39. INT   KIEU'S ROOM   KIEU DAYDREAMS   DAY

Return to Kieu as she looks out the window and lies reading in her bed with the mosquito net lifted above.

> KIEU (VO)
> I thought I would fall sick the last day we saw each other. But I simply went blank and spent two days walking endlessly in the streets. For months, the shock left me drifting and feeling the indifferent passage of time. Then one day I woke up and tears started in my eyes. I knew then that I was starting to heal. But the thought of healing doesn't make the wound any less painful.

She plays with the cricket in the cage, then starts to read again. She closes her eyes as if daydreaming, eventually opens her eyes and smiles to herself a little. She lowers her eyes, and then looks straight at the camera, smiling.

40. EXT   INDUSTRIAL SCENE   NIGHT

FULL SHOT of a factory site with the silhouette of a man (Alikan) standing. We HEAR the blasting sound of a train passing at full speed.

41. EXT   CITY   NIGHT

Traveling shots of night activities in the city—streets scenes, restaurants, people behind panes of glass, sex shops.

> KIEU (VO)
> I'm peopled with echoes and voices. Speaking to myself endlessly, just like old people do when they walk down the street.
> *(pause)*
> It was a loving relationship. But was it love?
> Kieu's life is replete with details that lie in the gray area of what is inappropriate morally. She is at the same time praised to the sky for being a model of Confucian piety and loyalty, and fiercely blamed for having strayed from the norms of proper feminine behavior.

42. EXT   INDUSTRIAL SCENE   NIGHT

Same shot as before of a factory with silhouette of a man standing.

43. INT   ALIKAN'S APARTMENT   KIEU AND ALIKAN   DAY

CAMERA ABOVE Full Shot. Kieu sees a book in Alikan's studio. She leafs through the book (CLOSE-UP) and stops briefly at some of the pages. She sees a painting of a headless nude with her sex exposed to view, Courbet's *L'Origine du monde*. TIGHTER CLOSE-UP with painting becoming blurred—an out-of-focus patch of color. Then she closes the book and throws it back to where she found it.

Kieu looks around. CAMERA PANS from the left to the area with transparent curtains and STOPS ON some clothes left in the area. She hesitates, then instinctively walks toward them and kneels down to inhale the shirt lying on top. She holds her breath, stands up, and quickly moves away from them, as if she had been caught in the act. As she leans against a wall catching her breath, Alikan comes in.

> ALIKAN (OS)
> Sorry I'm late.

He looks at her in silence. She looks embarrassed and frightened. He slowly moves toward her. As he comes close to her, she closes her eyes. He raises his arm to corner her against the wall, but in a sudden and unexpected manner, she ducks underneath his arm and escapes, laughing. He turns around, follows her with his eyes.

KIEU
Let's get to work.

Alikan furtively follows her to the changing room.

Kieu prepares herself for the shooting session. Camera PANS from Kieu getting dressed for the session to Alikan, who, unseen by Kieu, is looking insistently at her shadow and movements through the curtain.

44. INT ALIKAN'S APARTMENT KIEU AND ALIKAN DAY

Continuation of previous scene. Kieu strikes horizontal poses while Alikan takes photos and squats, looking at Kieu intensely. Kieu wears a coarse sack dress; she puts a conical hat on.

KIEU
(tilting the hat over her face)
A headless body. Women aren't supposed to have a head, are they? How convenient for the both of us.

ALIKAN
Yes, the rules of the game say that you either look or you're looked at. But you can't do both at the same time.

KIEU
She's all flesh and body. He is the head, the mind, the thinking eye. That's not new, is it?
(pause)
Just look at the Egyptian myth of Isis, right up to the story of Adam and Eve—women have always been made to lose their heads. Decapitated, just like Sleeping Beauty, so the Prince can play his role.

Alikan moves closer to Kieu.

ALIKAN
Wow, I've never heard you say so much! You look like a kid, but you speak like a gran'ma, eh?

Alikan slows his activities. Kieu takes the conical hat off and puts on a white veil.

ALIKAN
(continues)
Yeah. Never give yourself up. Never tell the whole story.
(pause)
Let's use the chair.

Alikan brings a wooden chair over. Kieu sits and arranges the veil.

TL

TL

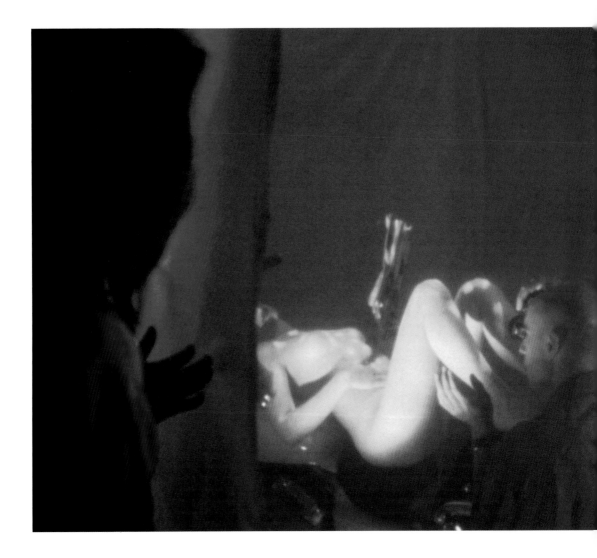

TL

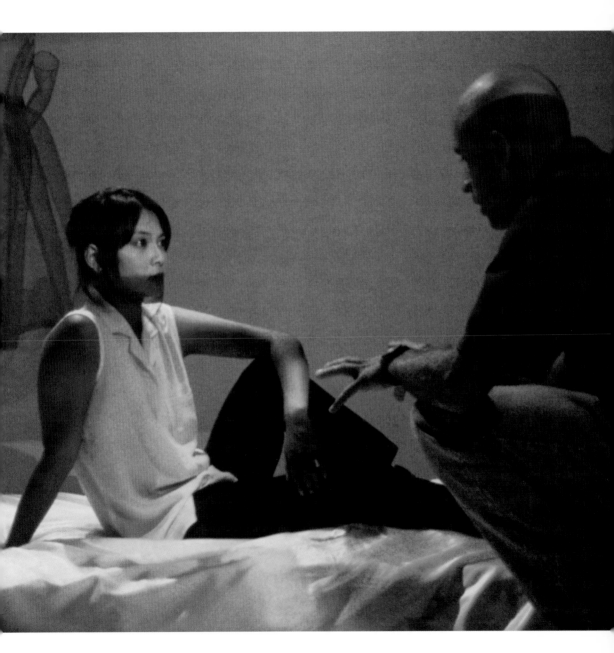

TL

TL

SC

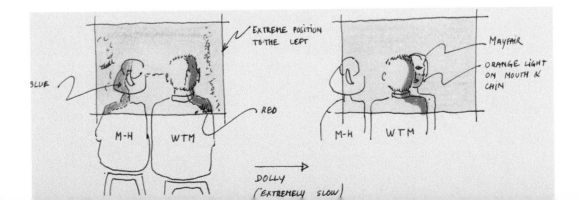

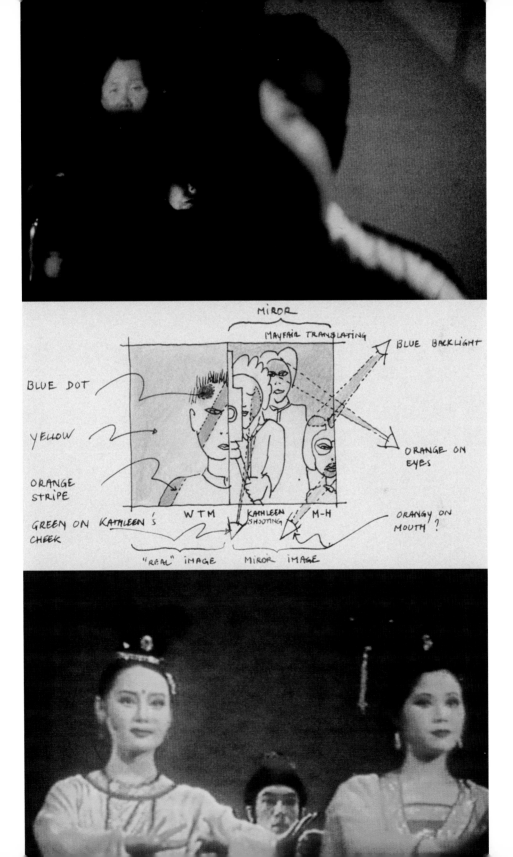

SC

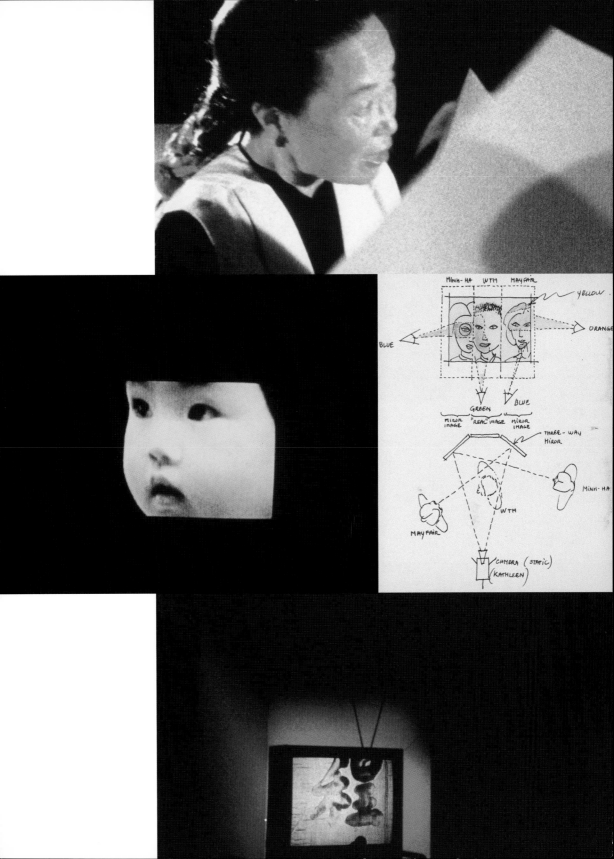

TL

ALIKAN
(continues)
Just don't forget *you* told me at the outset you don't really want people to recognize you, you don't want to show the whole of yourself, that's why I chose this as the most suitable format for your modeling.

KIEU
I know. I can't complain. But . . .

ALIKAN
But?

KIEU
Do you make male models sit in the same kind of poses?

Kieu drapes the veil over her face and turns toward Alikan.

ALIKAN
I used to work with male models. But of course they have different poses.

Kieu takes the veil off and rearranges it.

KIEU
(waiting)
Aren't you going to say why? In fact, I know what you're going to tell me. That the poses have to be different with every model. That's not enough though. There are always big holes in your answers.

Kieu holds a large leaf up to mask her face.

ALIKAN
(amused and interested)
You never give in! You really resist not having a head, don't you? Doesn't that give you a lot of headaches?

Kieu puts the leaf down, gets up, and drapes the white veil over Alikan's head.

KIEU
What a silly way out.

Alikan laughs. Kieu walks off screen.

Alikan pulls down a gauzy curtain in front of Kieu as she drops the sack dress and puts on a top made of metal pieces.

KIEU
Do you know that Chinese story about a king who wants to train his 100 wives in the arts of war?

Kieu pauses. Slightly surprised and amused, Alikan looks at her with curiosity and interest.

Crew members for A *Tale of Love*. From left to right: (*back row*) Lana Bernberg (key grip), Lisa Austin (2nd assistant camera), Angela D. Chou (art director), Trinh T. Minh-ha (director), Sofia Babiolakis (script supervisor), Lori Kay Wilson (assistant director), Kate Haug (assistant coordinator); (*front row*) Tracey Thompson (assistant camera); Kathleen Beeler (director of photography), Lauretta Molitor (sound recordist).

ALIKAN
No.

Kieu begins to pose a bit more extravagantly, composing dance gestures while telling the story.

KIEU
(continues)
Well, he ordered this well-known general of his to make soldiers out of them. The man thought it was going to be a piece of cake, but no matter how hard he tried, he couldn't get them to do it. The women fell about laughing every time he spoke, until the general decided to carry out the Absolute Law: with his own saber, he beheaded the king's favorite two wives, whom he had made commanders. So, in order to keep their heads, the other wives had no choice but to lose their heads on their own, by following his orders to the letter, like robots.

45. EXT   AUNT'S HOUSE   KIEU AND PHONE   SUNSET

Camera shows a beautiful view, with Kieu sitting outside. She has been scribbling. The phone rings. She quickly reaches for the phone. She picks it up, listens quietly for a few seconds, hangs up then starts drawing on a sheet of paper. Then she abruptly picks the telephone up again and starts dialing. After having dialed only part of the number, she hangs up, and makes a gesture of impatience. The conversation below is heard over the image, as in memory.

KIEU (VO)
Hello?

MAN (VO)
Kieu . . .

KIEU (VO)
(perplexed)
YYYes?

MAN (VO)
Remember the friend that you woke up over at Lynn's place? I haven't had a chance to introduce myself. This is Java.

KIEU (VO)
(surprised, short silence, then laughing lightly while speaking)
Did you say "Java"? . . . What a sunny name.

JAVA (VO)
What a voice . . . you've got such a voice! I miss it. (pause)

KIEU (VO)
Are you blind?

> JAVA (VO)
> *(laughs)*
> Not necessarily. But, it's true, I am not one of these aggressive eye people. I do think the world began with a sound.

> KIEU (VO)
> You listen very well, don't you? . . .

> JAVA (VO)
> Do you know that for some people living in the Philippines, love begins with touching, caressing, and kissing the ear, and not the mouth? They get really excited about ear contact and before doing anything else together, they listen to each other very carefully and very intimately.

46. CUT to CLOSE-UP of a creased bed sheet and a pillow.

> JAVA (VO)
> *(continues)*
> You can make love in speaking to one another.

> VERSE SINGER (VO)
> Oan kia theo mai voi tinh,
> mot minh minh biet mot minh minh hay.
> *(To passion sorrow clings and won't let go.)*

47. INT   JULIET'S HOUSE   KIEU AND JULIET   DAY

Juliet is busy writing when Kieu comes in with a tea tray. Juliet looks up and smiles to her, but continues to write. We HEAR the end of the verses sung in the previous scene.

> KIEU
> Do you want some tea?

Kieu puts down the tray, pours tea into cups and sits down at the table. Juliet smiles yes.

> KIEU
> Important letters?

> JULIET
> *(lightly ironic)*
> Important, yes. They're all important. Especially for lovers who are waiting for an answer to their burning problems. I've given myself a very suitable preoccupation; for sometime now, I've been helping the Juliet Club out during my spare time, and I enjoy it. It makes love at once so very important to our lives and so banal in its miseries.

KIEU
(almost laughing)
Did you say the "Juliet Club"?

JULIET
Yes. You might as well say, it's fate.
(pause)
Every year, over three thousand lovesick men and women from all over the world send their letters simply addressed to "Juliet, Verona, Italy." They know she doesn't exist, and they know that people like you and me are devoting our time to answering the letters, playing confessor, friend, or confidant to soothe their heartache, but they keep on sending letters to Juliet because they see her as the long-lasting symbol of true love.

KIEU
They think Juliet must know the answer to all love matters, don't they? And since one is never so lonely as when one's in love, she's probably the only one writing to some of them. But what kind of advice can you give a person in love?

JULIET
It's not easy. Prisoners of love often sing the same songs, and although I receive letters from all four corners of the world, I sometimes have the feeling that they are all one single long letter. Here. Listen to this woman's grief:
(picks up one of the letters nearby and reads)
"I grew up being taught that the only future I have is to get married and to make my husband happy. I piously followed the advice and got married at 17. I did everything I was told, and much more, but no matter how much I did, my husband wasn't happy. After twenty years of marriage, and having had three children, I started feeling bored with everything I did, like preparing a meal which routinely includes an entrance, a middle, and an exit—a bit like a three-act fairy tale."
(puts the letter down)
Where do you think that letter came from?

KIEU
It could be from anywhere, especially a Third World country; but the three-part meal tells me it must be from a Western country.

JULIET
(nodding)
Right. From France. This woman's at a loss now. At 50 years of age, she meets her first lover and again discovers the tremors of desire she'd forgotten about. But she doesn't want to leave her family, and she's writing to plead with her to tell her what to do.
(picks up and puts down another letter)
I get letters like this from all over, like this one from a young woman in Egypt who wonders if it's normal for her to find her Romeo so exasperatingly boring and really wants to know what true love actually feels like.

KIEU

Is that what most women say?

JULIET

Not all. But for many of them, especially for the ones who are better off financially, their disappointment with their partners usually has something to do with their lack of imagination and especially with romance.

48. EXT   BOARDWALK   KIEU AND DOG   SUNSET

Kieu is walking home. She runs into a stray dog and stops to talk to it. First we hear verses from *A Tale of Kieu*.

VERSE SINGER (VO)

Chung-quanh nhung nuoc-non nguoi,
dau long luu-lac nen vai bon cau.
*(Hemmed in by foreign streams and alien hills
the exile cried her grief in sad quatrains)*

KIEU

(petting it lovingly)

Come here, you little sweetie. . . . How come you're out here all by yourself? . . . Haven't you got a home to go to? Or are you all by yourself just like me? Where are you going? Do you know where you're going?. . . .Do you feel a bit lonely? *(caressing, recoiling when the dog jumps up)* Here, here, what a beautiful dog, with such sad eyes. . . why won't you speak to me? I wonder what language you speak. . . . I know, I know, they can't hear you, they can't understand you, can they? Can they? Good dog . . .

49. INT/EXT   KIEU'S ROOM   RAIN DAY

View from a room. SOUND OF RAIN. The rain is falling like a curtain over the landscape outside. CAMERA VERY SLOWLY COMES INTO FOCUS to reveal interior of room. STILL and QUIET. The silhouette of Kieu sitting still reading and silently staring out becomes more noticeable. Only the sound of the rain is distinctly heard.

KIEU (VO)

(heard in memory, coldly)

Chung minh se khong con gap duoc nhau nua.
(We can't see each other any more.)
(pause)
Thoi, anh dung bao gio tro lai day.
(Don't ever come back here.)
(then gentle)
Anh dung bao gio tro lai nua.
(Don't come back here.)

50. EXT OUTDOOR AUNT'S HOUSE KIEU AND MINH NIGHT

Kieu and Minh are sitting outside, contemplating the moon and listening to the sounds of the environment at night.

> MINH
> *(reciting a folksong)*
> Trang thanh trang doi them dinh
> Em xinh, em dung mot minh cung xinh.
> Trang thanh trang doi ngoai nuong,
> Den thanh, den doi tu phuong trong nha . . .
> *(With the bright moon lighting the courtyard*
> *Pretty you are, even standing alone.*
> *With the bright moon lighting the fields out there,*
> *And the bright lamp*
> *Lighting all the corners of the house.)*

> KIEU
> *(happily)*
> "Khoang vang dem truong,
> vi hoa nen phai danh duong tim hoa.
> Bay gio ro mat doi ta,
> biet dau roi nua chang la chiem bao."
> *(pause)* Anh con nho may cau tho nay trong *Truyen Kieu* khong?
> *("Along a lonesome darkened path*
> *for love of you I found my way to you.*
> *Now we stand face to face—but who can tell*
> *we shan't wake up and learn it was a dream?"*
> *Do you still remember these verses from* The Tale of Kieu?*)*

> MINH
> Nho chu.
> *(Of course I do.)*
> *(pause)*
> "Giai cau la duyen.
> Xua nay nhan dinh thang thien cung nhieu."
> *("That we have met means fate binds us.*
> *Man's will has often vanquished Heaven's whim.")*

Kieu makes an abrupt movement in throwing a stone into the water. Her hair, which is held back by a pin, spreads out as the pin falls out. Kieu reaches down to look for it, while Minh stares at her.

> MINH
> Em tim gi?
> *(What are you looking for?)*

> KIEU
> Tim cai cap toc.
> *(For my hair pin.)*

> MINH
> De anh tim cho.
> *(I'll find it for you.)*

They are now both looking for the pin in the dark, feeling with their hands the surfaces nearby. The search soon becomes a game, with the two hands looking frenetically for the missing pin. As their hands touch, they hit each other, laugh, and repeat the search again until their hands touch again and the game becomes a hand contest, hitting each other faster and faster. Their laughter resonates in the night.

51. INT   KIEU'S ROOM   RAIN   DAY

Kieu in her room, same as in scene 48. We HEAR Vietnamese verse singing.

> VERSE SINGER (VO)
> Nang tu chiec bong song the,
> duong kia noi no nhu chia moi sau;
> Bong dau da xe ngang dau,
> biet dau am-lanh biet dau ngot-bui?
> *(As Kieu sat by her window, all alone*
> *naked threads of gloom ran crisscross in her soul;*
> *Their sun is setting, hanging at head's height;*
> *Have they warm clothes, do they eat well or ill?)*

52. EXT   AUNT'S HOUSE   CHILD PLAYING WITH WATER   DAY

The same little girl playing with buckets and water. She is smiling at the camera.

53. EXT   STREETS   ALIKAN AND KIEU   SUNSET

Kieu closes the entrance door of Alikan's apartment behind her, and starts walking. A few seconds later, we see, in the background, Alikan also coming out of his apartment and silently following Kieu from a distance.

The CAMERA TRACKS Kieu as she seems to be wandering aimelessly. We see her walking through the streets and a park with Alikan still closely following her in the distance. She does not see him. He puts his sunglasses on while spying on her with great amusement. We see Kieu lingering in front of shop windows and fully absorbed in the movements around her. From time to time she makes a movement that compels Alikan to duck behind things in order to avoid being seen. Then, as Kieu hesitates before going into a store, she suddenly turns around

TL

and looks in Alikan's direction while he ducks away. She turns back again (we see her profile) and looks at the window displays. Then, as she realizes she's being followed, she looks in Alikan's direction again, then slowly smiles as she starts walking again.

Alikan puts on his sunglasses and walks in the direction of Kieu. The game of pursuit between Kieu and Alikan continues. In the end, Alikan loses track of Kieu. We see Kieu turning a corner and hiding behind a wall, looking at Alikan passing by. We see him taking off his glasses, looking around, and then leaving. We see her coming out from her hiding place, smiling triumphantly. Then, she takes a pair of sunglasses from her purse and puts them on while walking away.

54. EXT   AUNT'S HOUSE   KIEU'S DAYDREAMING   DAY

Kieu is writing at a low table outdoors. She stops writing and starts to daydream. We hear singing of verses from *The Tale of Kieu*.

> VERSE SINGER (VO)
> Thoi con con noi chi con?
> Song nho dat khach thac chon que nguoi!
> *(What else to say? Your daughter's doomed to live*
> *on foreign land and sleep in alien soil.)*
>
> Trong voi co-quoc biet dau la nha.
> *She peered far into space: Where was her home?)*

55. EXT   NEAR A LAKE   WOMAN AND CHILD   DAY

CLOSE-UP of a woman's body clad in *ao dai* (the Vietnamese dress) holding a little girl's hand. Camera shows the two hands, part of the woman's body, and part of the little girl's hair. The girl's hand tries to get free, but the woman's hand clasps it tightly, not letting it go. Both the woman's and the girl's heads are off-frame. CUT back to:

56. EXT   AUNT'S HOUSE   KIEU'S DAYDREAMING   DAY

Kieu, with an annoyed expression, mouths words almost inaudibly:

> KIEU
> Mother, get off my back.

57. INT   AUNT'S HOUSE   KIEU   NIGHT

Kieu is sleeping in her room. She's woken up by the distant sound of LOUD KNOCKS and VOICES. The voices are hardly audible.

VOICE (OS)

Mrs. Mai, Mrs. Mai. Emergency. There's an emergency. Please open up.

HURRIED FOOTSTEPS and sound of DOOR OPENING.

AUNT (OS)

Martha, what's happening? What's going on?

Kieu sits up in bed for a few seconds, then gets out.

VOICE (OS)

Please come right away. We need your help.

KIEU

(to the Aunt as she sees her leaving the house in a hurry)

Gi vay co?

(What's happening?)

58. EXT AUNT'S HOUSE KIEU AND AUNT DAWN

Kieu is waiting for her aunt, having prepared some tea. Aunt comes back, emotionally stressed out.

AUNT

(tired)

A, con. Sao con lai thuc doi co?

(Why are you waiting up for me?)

(taking tea from the teapot)

Toi nghiep cho Nancy, con ba Martha. Chong co ay ruou che di ve khuya roi lai danh dap co ta bam ca mat may than the. May ma da co nguoi can thiep. (pause) Chuyen nay chang co gi moi ca. Mac dau gap phai mot nguoi chong vu phu tan bao nhu the, nhung Nancy van khong muon ly di. Dem nao cung ngoi doi chong cho den gan sang.

(Poor Nancy, Martha's daughter. Her husband came back drunk and was beating her to a pulp. Fortunately, we intervened. This is nothing new. Although she fell for a brute, Nancy still doesn't want to get a divorce. Every night she waits for him until dawn.)

KIEU

(silence, then sadly)

Da, con cung thong cam cho co ay. Khong co gi buon kho bang khi phai doi nguoi than dem nay qua thang khac.

(I really feel for her. Nothing is more sad than having to wait for her loved one night after night.)

AUNT

Dung the. The nhung, con doi nghia la con co nguoi de mong nho. Co nguoi muon doi ma khong con ai de ma doi nua. Ngay thang troi qua lanh leo, dem nao cung giong nhu dem nao.

(Yes, but to wait means to still have someone to wait for. Some want to wait but have no one to wait for. The days go by in solitude, one night resembling another.)

Kieu looks at her aunt inquisitively in silence. Then, she lowers her eyes and nods sadly while staring in front of her.

> AUNT
> *(continues)*
> Nhieu canh gia dinh trong rat thuong. Co bao nhieu cap vo chong ly di tren giay to vi van de welfare, da di den cho tan vo. Mot phan cung vi phu nu minh qua day tim duoc viec lam, chang can chong de sinh song, cho nen khi bi danh dap doa nat, ho dau co cui dau chiu dung mai nhu vay duoc?
> *(Many family situations are very sad. How many welfare divorces have led to real divorce! Partly because our women can find work here and don't need a husband to survive. So when battered, they no longer lower their heads and endure.)*

Aunt and Kieu sip tea in silence.

> KIEU
> Thoi co vao nghi di, de con lo viec nha cho.
> *(Why don't you go and rest? I'll take care of the housework.)*

> AUNT
> U, co cung met.
> *(Yes, I'm quite tired.)*

Aunt goes inside to rest, while Kieu sweeps the courtyard. While she works, we hear:

> ALIKAN (VO)
> Every story of love is a story of voyeurism.

> JULIET (VO)
> Behind every perfume lies a love story . . .

> MINH (VO)
> Kieu!

59. EXT   AUNT'S HOUSE COURTYARD   KIEU   DAY

MEDIUM CLOSE-UP. Kieu is sitting under the mosquito net with the cricket box hanging in the bed. We see part of the mosquito net while Kieu looks at the crickets through the container and talks to them.

> KIEU
> *(intimately and affectionately)*
> Alright, since you're so sulky with me, I'll sing for you.

Kieu sings a few lines–instead of her voice, we hear loud music. She smiles happily.

> KIEU
> I can't remember. . . . Do you remember the song? Can you sing a song?

Slowly her face clouds over and tears flow from her eyes.

60. INT   WRITING INSERT   NIGHT

EXTREME CLOSE-UP on the tip of a pen and letters forming. Stay for a while with the rapid movement of the pen. Distinct SOUND OF PEN SCRATCHING on paper.

61. EXT   FIELD OF GRASS   KIEU   NIGHT

LONG SHOT of golden field of grass against night sky, with moon in view. Camera PANS slowly over still landscape. Kieu, wearing a long red dress, is running in the field, first one way, then another, appearing in unexpected places. CUT again to extreme CLOSE-UP of writing (same as scene 60).

62. EXT   FIELD OF GRASS   KIEU   NIGHT

MEDIUM SHOT of Kieu, wearing the same red dress, moving in circles in the field of grass, darting in and out of the frame.

63. EXT   INDUSTRIAL FACTORY   NIGHT

Kieu emerges from the dark, walking with hurried steps. She passes a stranger, and suddenly turns around, walks up to him, a man with a hat on, who is standing near a light source, but whose (backlit) face we cannot see.

> KIEU
> Excuse me, can you tell me what the four-letter word is today?

> MAN
> (indifferently)
> I wish I could, but I've not heard it all day.

> KIEU
> Are you sure you haven't heard it?

> MAN
> Well no, it may have passed me by, and I didn't recognize it.

> KIEU
> How can you not recognize it? You don't go looking for it. When it comes to you, it is always so glaring it makes you blind.

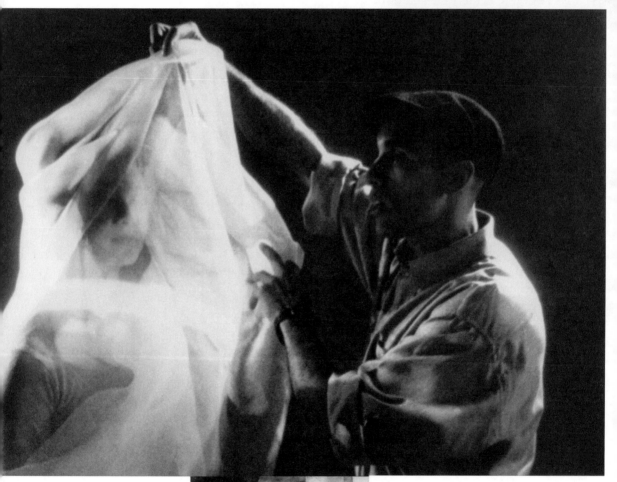

MAN
(voice suddenly changing, now helplessly)
But I'm never quite sure when it's come to me. Whenever I realize it's It, it's always either too early or too late.

KIEU
(slightly moved)
Have you lost your sight?

MAN
(still sounding helpless)
No. But I just can't see when the lights are too bright. I'm terribly afraid of disappointing.

KIEU
Of disappointing, or of being disappointed?

MAN
(hesitates)
Of . . . disappointing really. I always have the feeling that I'm lying, cheating, or betraying.

KIEU
Why do you feel like that?

MAN
(in a posture of withdrawal)
I can never tell for sure which four-letter word is blinding me.

He pulls a package of photographs from his pocket and gives it to Kieu.

MAN
(continues)
Can you tell me what you can see?

KIEU
(looking at him silently while holding the package, then, reading one by one, at irregular intervals)
HURT, HATE/LOVE/FACE, PAIN/BURN/BOND/FREE
(moving closer to him, exclaming)
They all come down to One Word. Can't you see ?
(looking closer at him)
What's wrong with your eyes? Let me see them. Maybe I can help.

MAN
(stepping back and abruptly,)

No, you can't. Don't do that or I'll *fire* you.

Kieu reaches out with her hand and the man stops her. In his move, we partly see his face — it's Alikan's.

>ALIKAN
>Kieu, don't do that, you're hurting the story!

CUT TO Kieu sleeping in Juliet's courtyard (as if she's just waking up from a short dream) exclaiming to herself aloud: "Alikan!"

64. EXT FACADE OF JULIET'S HOUSE KIEU DAY

FULL SHOT Kieu comes out of Juliet's house. Bright daylight, she seems to be blinded by the light, and raises her hand to protect her eyes. Leaning against the door, she starts crying. Looking helpless, she wipes the tears off with her hand.

65. EXT AUNT'S HOUSE KIEU MAGIC HOUR

Same setting as in scene 50 with Minh. This time Kieu is by herself, sitting in a meditation posture and looking at the same river/landscape. The CAMERA slowly PULLS BACK from a tight shot on the back of Kieu's head to a full shot that shows the river and a boat drifting by.

>KIEU (VO)
>I realize that Java is just a sound. A sound of love. Minh, a past fiction I can always return to, but whose ending I can not yet change. And Alikan. Once the veil is torn, what else remains but a solitary eye?
>*(pause)*
>Only Juliet will live forever. I will write her, I will fight her and no matter where she is, I know she will read, she will listen, she will write back, she will fight back.
>*(pause)*
>Narrative, in her world, is a track of scents passed on from lover to lover.

66. INT JULIET'S HOUSE KIEU AND JULIET DAY

Juliet is seen with her hair down, lost in thought (in reverie) with her bottles of perfumes and colognes spread out in front of her.

>JULIET
>*(softly to herself, almost in a murmur)*
>. . . a fruity blend of violet, pineapple, mimosa, and patchouli . . . following the passion . . . the fashion for all things green . . .

>KIEU (OS)
>And Juliet, thanks for having given me the opportunity to work on *The Tale*. I've learned a lot from the way people in the community see it and remember it.

(pause, on screen)
I feel like I'm living this *Tale* too. Perhaps not all of it—I'm a woman of the nineties, after all—but there are more and more Kieu stories being told by women themselves. Perhaps I'm somewhere in the beginning, or already in the ending?

JULIET
Kieu, have *you* got a love story to tell?

KIEU
I haven't. Not really.

JULIET
(smiling)
I'm sure you have. You can't hide it from me. That glow on you? It's been there for weeks. My little finger tells me this woman is in love.

KIEU
I didn't say I'm not. The problem is that I haven't got just one story. I've got several.
(pause)
All unfolding without a proper climax and ending.

JULIET
Then perhaps it's not a love story.

KIEU
Why not?

JULIET
Well, of course, the air we breathe is loaded with myriads of stories. But, if you just live one, and only one story with passion, then you tie all the loose threads together and make it into a single one. I believe only in great love, love that transcends every rule, even your own rules.

KIEU
What about betrayal? Is that part of it too?

JULIET
(slightly surprised, then nodding slowly while thinking)
That's a hard one. . . .

KIEU
So then, what does "great" mean? I may fall in love, I may be loved, but loving is different. It's not just a strong feeling. Blind passions can't last, no matter how strongly they start out.

JULIET

What some people say is that love doesn't just happen. It has to be created and nurtured. What I say is that love cannot be willed. It happens by accident, almost always through a mistake.

KIEU

Why do we have this need for an exceptional-individual kind of love story in our society? Is it because there's often no love in love stories?

Juliet gets up from her seat and moves away from Kieu. Camera slowly TRACKS with Juliet—

JULIET
(playfully parodying passion)
"If love be blind / It best agrees with night. . . .
Give me my Romeo: and, when he shall die,
Take him and cut him out in little stars,
And he will make the face of heaven so fine
That all the world will be in love with night,
And pay no worship to the garish sun." (Shakespeare)

KIEU (OS)
(with dry humor)
Please, no more Shakespeare! My ears are burning. Take him and cut him out in little stars, and see if they'll twinkle and laugh with every moon watcher.

JULIET
(continuing in the same mood)
"How silver-sweet sound lovers' tongues by night,
Like softest music to attending ears!"

Juliet slowly merges to a red background. When she turns around to look at Kieu again, she unexpectedly engages in a dance (resembling a martial-art dance) suggestive of Love and Death. The camera remains on Juliet dancing for the length of Kieu's off-screen comments.

KIEU (OS)
That's not music to me! The problem with your love story is that it invariably ends in *death*, or in marriage.
(pause)
You see, I prefer the less definite ending of *The Tale of Kieu,* which blends love and friendship, even in having Kieu marrying the first man she fell in love with, after fifteen years of separation . . . the happy ending. If I was going to tell it again, Love, Kieu's great love, wouldn't become a resting place. Kieu wouldn't turn into a proper wife at the end, but would be remembered for having made love a loyalty to more than one person. Loyalty *and* betrayal. She's in love with Love, not with a Prince Charming. Being loyal to Love, she continues to dwell in our hearts.

67. INT   KIEU'S BED ON THE DECK   KIEU WRITING   NIGHT

Kieu is writing, bent over a small table in her bed. She suddenly starts singing a series of high notes, sillily.

> AUNT (OS)
> Kieu, thoi du roi!
> *(Kieu, that's enough!)*

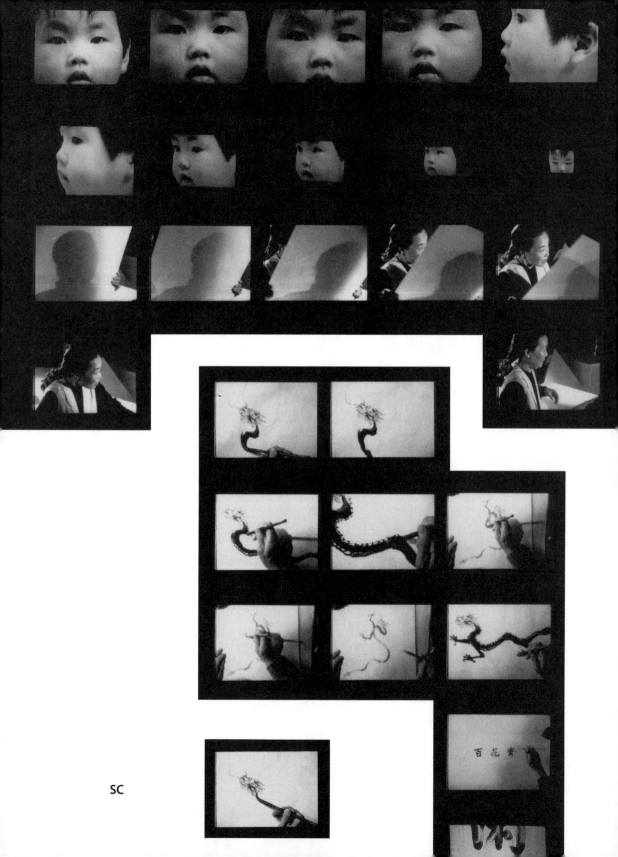

SC

SHOOT FOR THE CONTENTS[*]

filmscript

China–USA, 1991. 102 minute color film

Produced by: Jean-Paul Bourdier and Trinh T. Minh-ha
Directed, written, and edited by: Trinh T. Minh-ha
Mise-en-scene and Lighting Design: Jean-Paul Bourdier
Cinematography in the U.S.: Kathleen Beeler
Film and Video Camera in China: Trinh T. Minh-ha
Sound: Jim Kallett, Lynn Sachs, Dina Ciraulo
Narrators/performers: Ying Lee-Kelley as VOICE 1 and as Ying;
Dewi Yee as VOICE 2 and as Dewi
Interviewees/performers: Wu Tian Ming, with Mayfair Yang as
translator; Clairmonte Moore
Calligraphy and drawing: Fu Wen-Yan
Distributed by: Women Make Movies Inc., New York; Cinenova,
London (U.K.); Image Forum, Tokyo (Japan); Idera, Vancouver
(Canada). National Film & Video Lending Service, Melbourne
(Australia). International Sales: M&L Banks, New York

(*Note to the narrators:* The tone of Voices 1 and 2 should be
conversational; storytelling is what much of the text requires.
In the dynamics between the two women voices, there is a
slight competition—one that resembles the popular poetry
and proverb competition between several parties of men and
women in the countryside. Rhythm should be lively and constantly varied, especially in longer sections. Ad libs are welcome. Do not read aloud notes in parenthesis.)

· · ·

---

[*] First published in *Visual Anthropology Review* 8:1, Spring 1992. Also published in Germany in *Trinh T. Minh-ha. Texte, Filme, Gesprache*, ed. Hedwig Saxenhuber & Madeleine Bernstorff (Munchen, Wien und Berlin: Kunstverein Munchen, SYNEMA, Blickpilotin e. V., 1995).

1. (Wu Tian Ming sings and rehearses.)

2. VOICE 1: Any look at China is bound to be loaded with questions.

   VOICE 2: Her visible faces are minuscule compared to her unknown ones. Or is this true?

3. VOICE 2: The name for the game used to be "Shoot for the Contents."

   VOICE 1: Explain. What's your desire here?

   VOICE 2: I have heard that in ancient China, *fang-shih*, which refers to people, places, and cultures removed from the central court, dealt mostly with the areas of knowledge Confucius refused to discuss, namely, strange events, spirits, and fate. *Fang-shih* influence was significant in many areas of culture, including court social life. One of the games it offers as entertainment at the dinner parties of the rich and powerful is this game "Shoot for the Contents" or "Guessing the Contents."

   I used to be fascinated by the master of this art of divination, Kuan Lu. Not only because he could guess up to thirteen odd items placed inside a closed container with rarely a miss—naming them off one by one—but more so because he could spin so acutely and poetically such complex interpretations of the signs of the universe.

4. (We see the two women narrators—Women 1 with the same voice as VOICE 1 and Women 2 with the same voice as VOICE 2—working with large sheets of white paper, and we hear the sound of a printing press.)

   W1: This is but a shot in the dark.

   W2: There are three items. Make a guess at any one of them.

   W1: Let's see. . . . It is not quite an object

   W2: Right.

   W1: It begins with a B.

   W2: . . . Wrong . . .

   W1: It begins with a D.

   W1: (Searchingly.) Neither human nor quite animal, its miraculous changes are inscrutable. Comes from water and has five colors. Can be as small as a silkworm or as large as the world. It changes without fixed date and moves up or down without fixed time (according to Guan Xi).

   W2: When it is a He, he is "red as fire," when it is a She, she has a body "like flat waves."

W1: (In the *Book of Changes*) It is directly linked with the ruling class. It bears nine animal forms: the head of a camel, the horns of a deer, the ears of an ox, the eyes of a hare, the body of a snake covered with the scales of a carp, the belly of a frog, the claws of an eagle, and the paws of a tiger.

The beast . . . can be tamed and trained to the point where you may ride on its back. But on the underside of its throat it has scales a foot across that curl back from the body, and anyone who brushes against them is sure to die. This was Han-Fei's metaphor of the Chinese ruler who is to represent the Chinese people: a docile yet potentially dangerous dragon.

W2: A fabulous creation, *the dragon* expresses the idea of power and change.

5. VOICE 2: There is a thousand trillion Chinas as a Chinese storyteller would say: the China of people's imagining.

VOICE 1: Yes, The *Beijing Review* was quite vocal in condemning all this "talk about China being an enigma as it keeps on changing its policies." They said it is "quite off the mark" for observers abroad to think of changes in politics as an indication of instability.

VOICE 2: Well, in the art of reading mountains, it is said that "to find the dragon, one must first find its ancestors." Interpreting orientation and form is not without risk, because in Ancient books the beast exists in thousand forms; has ten thousand aspects; stands or crouches; is huge or tiny, unruly, or obedient, reserved or extravagant. Infinitely in metamorphosis, it dives deep, rises high, meanders, coils, leaps, and takes its flight.

6. VOICE 1: With Mao's suspicion of intellectuals, bookworms like yourself and your friends will fit right into one of the ten categories of "rightists." Yes, you would either be a revisionist, a right opportunist, or a rightist—in any case a "stinking No 9!"

VOICE 2: (Laughs.) What about the "two hundreds" policy that have survived Mao?

VOICE 1: Well, history seems to repeat itself. What happened more than thirty years ago? In 1956, Mao did initiate a period of public debate and Party rectification under the slogan, "Let a hundred flowers blossom, let a hundred schools of thought contend." His speech at first provoked no reaction. China's intellectuals had learned to distrust all official sugarcoated declarations of this kind. But in June 1957 the "hundred flowers" began to bloom furiously and the result was devastating for the regime.

The leaders responded to these unexpectedly virulent criticisms by lauching an immediate counteroffensive, thereby reopening a ruthless "weeding-out" campaign aimed at uncovering the "poisonous weeds" hidden among the "fragrant flowers." Mao's "hundred flowers" wilted in the heat of the short-lived but fiercely critical voices of students and intellectuals who opposed reciting blindly all the directives of the Party and questioned the Party's right to monopolize political power.

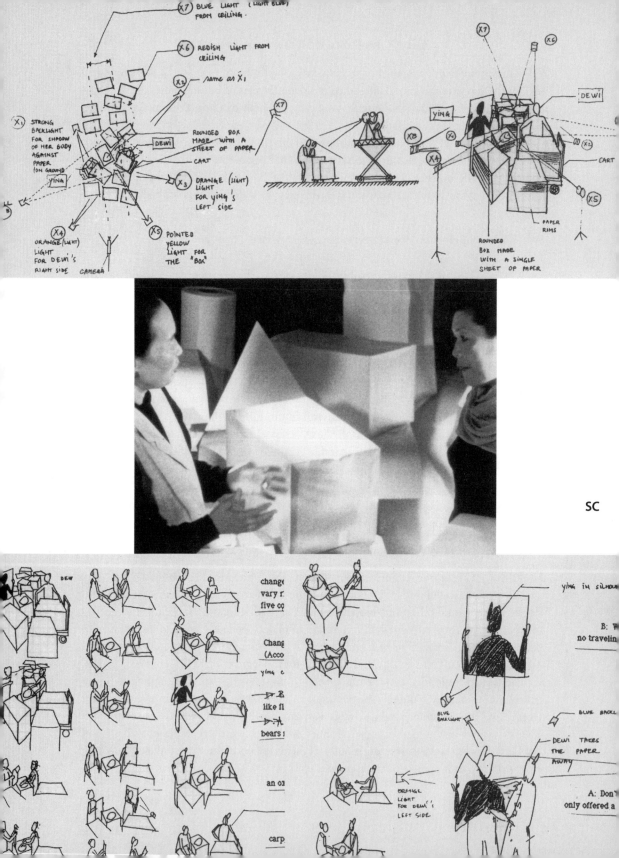

7.   (Transcribed from interview with Wu Tian Ming as translated by Mayfair Yang:) *"Right now in China there is no such thing as independent filmmaking, because there are two meanings to independent filmmaking: one, that it has independence in investment decisions; second, that it has independence in distribution. In the U.S. the decision to make what kind of film is really up to the situation of the market and so it is more free. However, in China, very often the kind of film that is going to be shown and going to be made is decided according to political needs of the moment, because in China, all filmmaking enterprises are in the hands of the State—although film studios can decide themselves what film they want to make. But afterward, it all has to pass through state censorship. So if you pass through state censorship and it's approved, then you can distribute the film. If it doesn't pass, then you can't.*

"The criteria for censorship: one of them is the political content. They want to make sure that it is politically correct, if you have made any political mistakes in your film. A second criterion is to look at whether there are any sex scenes or violent scenes.

"A few years ago some people tried to experiment in the direction of independent filmmaking. However, once they made the film, they had to deliver it over to the state film-distribution corporation, and as a result of that, they didn't make hardly any money at all.

"So there are two reasons for the difficulties of this kind of experiment: on the one hand, they have so little money that they can't really make a decent film, so they don't have an audience. The other reason is that no matter how good a film they make and no matter how welcome the film is in terms of the audience, how much the audience wants to see it, if it doesn't meet with the approval of the higher-ups then it won't be released at all, or will have limited release. So the few people who did experiment just gave up.

"Although American filmmaking can be considered all around independent, and there's a lot of freedom, at the same time there are aspects of the system that means that it doesn't really have freedom, it has limitations to its freedom, and that is because it is limited by the demands of the market. The boss of the film, his eyes always have to be focused on the expressions on the audience's face.

"So, although in China films are subject to all sorts of political censorship, however, at the same time you get the situation where you can point to the superiority of socialism, in that some film studios can support experimental films by young directors, which don't make any money. These experimental films, on the one hand they can be presented abroad in international festivals as films of high artistic value, and they can win great acclaim and recognition for the studio. At the same time, they also exert a tremendous influence in pushing forward the quality and form of other films produced by the studio. So in China, young directors don't have to worry about losing their jobs. If in the U.S. a young director makes two or three films that don't make any money, I think this director would lose his or her job."

8.   VOICE 1: The outsiders' journey is that of hit and miss. In-context subtleties are felt without being quite understood. But, important truths do intermittently burst forth without

warning; because it is easier to confide in foreigners whose short stay guarantees their discretion. Their being outsiders makes them at times strangely harmless.

VOICE 2: Think also of those of us here who do not speak all the Chinese languages; we are bound at some stage to hear through the translators' ears and to speak through their mouths—without them we would remain deaf and dumb. All depends on their finesse and their ability to mold our view. The political situation is such that actual situations necessarily require an indirect language; so there is always more to matters than meets the eye. Seeing through our own eyes does not guarantee any truth.

9. VOICE 1: Only in appearance does China offer an ever-changing face to the world. *(Silence.)* In fact, Mao always borrowed from traditional China, for the time when truly one thousands of flowers blossomed and a hundred schools contended was the 500 years before Confucianism was established as the state philosophy in the second century B.C. It was then, aside from Confucianism, that Taoism, Maoism, Legalism, Dialecticism, Agrarianism, and many others "isms" fully flowered.

VOICE 2: This was the time when it is said that "nothing is softer than water; yet water is stronger than anything else when it attacks the hardest and the most resistant." Gentleness always prevails over hardness *(Tao Te-Ching)*.

10. VOICE 1: Today coming back to Mao's persuasive speech, one cannot but read with some bewilderment the following affirmation: "We think that it is harmful to the growth of art and science if administrative measures are used to impose one particular style of art or school of thought and to ban another."

VOICE 2: This is close to "home." I mean, both homes. There are differences, but this is nothing specific to China.

VOICE 1: Don't shoot back at random. Here is what Mao also said in that speech: "Throughout history, new and correct things have often failed at the outset to win recognition from the majority of the people and have had to develop by twists and turns in struggle. It is therefore necessary to be careful about questions of right and wrong."

11. VOICE 1: "Man does not grind ink, but ink grinds men."

VOICE 2: Chuang Tzu once asked: "Where can I find a man who has forgotten words so I can talk to him?"

VOICE 1: It is said that "the five colors will blind a man's sight."

12. (Transcribed from interview with WTM) *"As a movie director, I personally would not wish my films to be transmitted or released as videos, because watching videos on a TV screen, the*

quality is very low compared to the full effect you get watching a film on a movie screen in a movie house. However, at the same time I understand that video distribution in the United States is quite large. I've heard that thirty to forty percent of its profits come from its release as a film in a movie house, and the rest of the profits come from its distribution as video. Therefore, I might have to dispense with my other concerns.

"The relationship between video and film is like this: in China, films have been made increasingly into videos, and at the same time, in recent years there have been fresh videos made, just as videos, not as films first."

13. VOICE 2: On the seventh day of the seventh moon, Hao Long chose to lie down in the sun. When someone asked what he was doing, he replied: "As with books, a man needs an occasional sunning to avoid mildew." (In *Wit and Humor From Old Cathay*, translated by J. Kowallis.)

14. VOICE 2: To the east was the azure dragon and the element of wood standing for spring and the rising sun. In the north was the black tortoise and the element of water indicating winter.

VOICE 1: With time and transformation, even the little red book was declared bad, since it had been compiled by that "traitor" Lin Biao who dared to criticize "the sun of our hearts." Today the Sun himself has been revised. The people are left with only some odds and ends of the holy words.

15. VOICE 1: Mao was a son of the earth. For ten years he lived in cave dwellings and immersed himself in manual labor. He cultivated many flowers and weeded out the poisonous ones.

VOICE 2: Mao was no peasant. Mao was a man of mind and a man of letters. During the Long March, it was said that he read most of the time and then he would sit and dream solitarily. When he immersed himself in manual labor, it wasn't forced labor. He was cultivating his own garden à la Voltaire.

VOICE 1: But there are further differences to be made. One of the tales spun in Yenan also relates how Mao used to be bored during the speeches made by party officials, although he himself was always fond of delivering long speeches. It was said that those who secretly collected his poems relied on the days of the Party's meetings, during which Mao would write a series of short, four-verses poems while the speeches went on, then he would throw them away, under the table, in crumpled paper balls.

VOICE 2: (Almost whispering:) "Dead at last! Without your death, China would have gone to pieces" (Liu Binyan).

VOICE 1: How dare you!

16. (Transcribed from interview with WTM) *"This is a popular song on the yellow loess soil in the high plateaus of Shaanxi province. As a child I was very familiar with these folk songs, and in my films you can often hear them. As a child I grew up in a very poor area. It is said that here you can dig really deep into the yellow loess soil, and all you'll find is just the same loess soil, no rocks, no stones.*

"I used to live in these cave dwellings in the hillsides. Between northern Shaanxi province and the middle plains, you can find these underground cave dwellings called Di Yao. They have a long gateway leading downward. They're very warm in winter because no wind comes in, and you also have a very hot kang, *which is an earthen raised bed, under which you burn firewood, and your whole body is nice and cosy. In the summer you feel very cool inside these dwellings. I think if the whole world lived in such dwellings, everyone would be very healthy.*

"As a child I used to accompany adults to the hills, and we used to herd sheep. We'd stand on the bare hillsides and yell out these folk songs, and our echos would just reverberate back and forth between the hillsides.

"Mixing together with the local people, I really developed deep feelings of attachment to them. So whenever I see these ordinary peasants from these areas, even though they may have dirty faces, and some of them may be very selfish, I still feel very close to them, and I still find them very endearing."

17. VOICE 1: "There cannot be two suns in one sky" Mao said when he assumed the position of the Son of Heaven.

VOICE 2: "If I conquer the mountain, then it is I who sits on the mountain." Only the leaders can issue orders. They monopolize the power to decree what is right and what is wrong. In every political or economic campaign launched, the people have been relegated to minor roles, forever "supporting enthusiastically," and "responding to the call" of the great man. Those who stray aside are labeled accordingly, for the rulers' authority encompasses every aspect of people's private lives.

18. VOICE 1: "When I have presented one corner of a subject to any one, and he cannot learn the other three from it," said Confucius, "I do not repeat my lesson."

VOICE 2: The Sage contributed to maintain a society rebellious to the state system, one based on a complex kinship system of loyalty and an intricate gift economy—but he died a pathetic old man who felt he had thrown it away on stony ground. His teachings have been twisted and he was made responsible for every aspect of China's backwardness.

VOICE 1: How could he not be made so on the women's question? "Woman is not the moon. She must rely on herself to shine." Chinese feminists are fond of these lines, and the Sage did nothing to unfossilize Chinese society when it comes to rebellion against gender inequality.

SC

19. VOICE 1:   Did you know Empress Wu reigned until the year 705, when she was 81 years old? No woman in Chinese history had claimed the official powers of Heaven and worn upon her back the imperial robes embroidered with the design of dragons and heavenly clouds.

    VOICE 2:   A woman on the Dragon Throne! What a miracle!

20. VOICE 2:   No, "a poet does not take an experience as the 'content' of his poem and pour it into a 'form.'" There is no poetry if there is no exploration of the language. "So the poet's task is not only to say something for the first time, but also to say for the thousand and first time, in a different way, what has been said a thousand times already" (James Liu).

    VOICE 1:   What is manifestly "real" to some eyes looks strangely stiff and conventional to others. You do not catch the vital spirit of things in formal likeness, said Chang Yen-Yuan of the T'ang period. What seems unrealistic may transmit the life force of things in ways that no mastery of their visible likeness can.

21. (Transcribed from interview with WTM) *"A good story must have lifelike characters, full of life and vitality, where each individual character has a unique personality, where the human relations constructed around each character develops and changes. A good story must have a moving content, its plot must be fresh, it mustn't repeat what others have already done, in other words, you don't chew over a steamed bun that somebody else has already chewed over.*
    "I think that art is always the discovery of the new, something that you discover yourself, something new in content and form. This is what makes a good film. Nowadays in many films you see the same old things done over and over again. You have the same old stories in new guises, and you have the same old styles. And the character images are traditional and the same, but put in new costumes and trotted forth. I think human beings are very rich and varigated, they have many aspects to them, and these new things must be discovered anew each time. I think this is the way to tell a good story, so that the audience will get much more out of it."

22. VOICE 2:   After all, Mao ruled through the power of rhymes and proverbs turned into snugly capsuled slogans.

    VOICE 1:   "You can't eat a steamed bun in one bite."

    VOICE 2:   Yes, he was accused of "formulating a system of indoctrination designed to turn all China into one chanting kindergarten" (D. Bloodworth).

    VOICE 1:   That could be worse!

23. VOICE 2:   A temple is said to be a landscape of the soul.

    VOICE 1:   "Be smooth, but be a square shooter." We seem to forget that it is in and through symbols that, consciously or unconsciously, we live, move and work.

24. VOICE 1:   The writings of the master contained the solutions to all problems, the answer to all questions. There was no situation in life that could not be settled with a quote from the great man.

    VOICE 2:   The great man? Which great man?

    (Handwritten on screen: CONFUCIUS OR MAO?)

25. VOICE 1:   Chou En-Lai's words: "When a wrong [political] tendency surges toward us like a rising tide, we must not fear isolation and must dare to go against the tide and brave it through." Mao's words were: "Going against the tide is a Marxist-Leninist principle."

    VOICE 2:   Confucius was condemned for having opposed social change. He was said to have had men arrested and executed for gathering a crowd to form an association, for spreading heretical views, and last but not least for confusing right and wrong.

26. VOICE 1:   The mother of Yongling was a devoted Buddhist, invoking the holy name of the Buddha all day long. Then one day, Yongling decided to call his mother on a pretext. The old lady answered. He then continued calling to her with great frequency. The mother grew annoyed and said: "What's this all about? Why all this yelling for me!" Yongling replied: "Aha! You become vexed when I call your name but three or four times. Yet the Buddha is beckoned to thousands of times a day. How angry he must be!" His mother was convinced by this logic to limit her daily chanting (*Wit and Humor From Old Cathay*, translated by Kowalis).

27. VOICE 1:   Mao used to compare revolutionaries who fought hard to overthrow feudal power but remained sceptical vis-à-vis his line of socialism, to the legendary Lord Shih, a dragon lover who collected pictures and statues of dragons with passion, but was said to have fled in a panic when a live dragon came down the road.

28. VOICE 1:   A peasant said it all: "Politics is just beating air with air."

    VOICE 2:   Confucius also knew what he did when he said, "I saw a dragon today. It condenses into an entity and disperses into nothing. It rides on cloud, appears and disappears."

29. (Transcribed from interview with Clairemonte Moore—synchronized voice and voice-over sometimes overlap:) "....*The people who were involved in the struggle there, as opposed to the Russian perception of things, that is all I can tell you. It didn't start with them, it started with the Cubans. . . . And it's also a Marxist tenet that each situation has its*

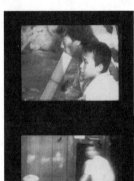

own social and historical dynamics, and you have to proceed from there. We know now that the Russian model has been a farce.

"I also find it very amusing that people can, thousands of miles away, situate themselves in a country that is one quarter of the world's population—a massive country just in terms of its land space—[and] attempt to become experts on another country, whether it's China, [or] the Caribbean. For me it's virtually impossible. I think the most interesting anecdote is that people don't even know themselves. These very experts have to go to a psychiatrist to tell them what's happened to them, what's the matter with them.

(Synchronized voice and voice-over woven together, with synch voice fading off while voice-over continues)

(Synch) ". . . . *For me, China is a place, someplace else, that has an enormous number of people, and it's virtually impossible for you to perceive of China other than this place far away. . . anti-colonialist . . . anti-imperialist . . .*

(Voice-over) "*. . . in that context, I think that for Deng Xiao Ping, to carry out his modernization program in alignment with America's wishes, which is to get free labor to produce certain things for the marketplace. The problem is that China has not yet decided whether it wants to go toward a free market, or whether it wants to have a dual economy. And, when the students and the automous workers came out, it became a serious threat to the present status quo, because they did not understand that . . . they never perceive of a situation in which the response to the modernization—we don't know what that represents.*

(Synch) "*I don't think that . . . I agree with Mao to the extent that, when intellectuals gather, they exchange ideas, and ideas are never limited or narrow. Intellecuals are involved in the whole spectrum of life—material life—that means from the ant to human beings. I use the ant as a microcosm, as a small epsilon, a small thing to a large thing, and the dichotomy, or apparent dichotomy between the two. . . . He's correct in that intellectuals express certain kinds of ideas, and people in power by definition see intellectuals as a threat to their status, or the status quo. So Mao was correct. I would like to take it a bit further by pointing out there, that intellectuals have a certain tradition—they're the people who have been taught with a certain kind of background—and within the context of modern society, they are the people who have been trained, they are the privileged people, whether you like it or not.*

"In any society, the state has to preserve itself. Tiananmen Square for me exemplifies the problem of non-organization to the extent that Mao's speech, "let a hundred . . . blossoms— let a hundred flowers blossom, let a hundred something contend" was another way in bringing the folks out of the closet, out of the holes, out of the various subterranean levels of Chinese society, only to wipe them out once again, because they pose a threat. They wanted to know what was going on, and the Tiananmen Square situation was one in which the Chinese again used after, I suppose fifteen years, to bring the intellectuals out so they'll expose themselves, and then move on them. The question is, it's a very dangerous situation for

China because if people can't express some kinds of ideas openly, and the State manipulates the manner in which they come out, then in my view, the State can't progress, can't make ammends or solve certain kinds of institutional problems."

30. VOICE 1: As a Chinese reporter noted, "It was inevitable either that economic reform would break through the old political order or that the old political order would act as a brake on economic reform" (L. Binyan).

   VOICE 2: And the truth about "China" is more often than not full of surprises, because ruptures and continuities occur side by side. And, as a saying goes, "We have lifted a rock only to drop it on our own feet."

31. (Wu Tian Ming's song)
   "You sitting on the mule up in front of the pack
   With the three lanterns glowing,
   On the mule hangs a bell, making that wong-wong sound
   If you're my lover, please wave your hand
   If you're not my lover, please just go on."

32. VOICE 1: The *Beijing Review* made it clear: Although China after Mao has made public the Chairman's mistakes, rectified so-called Left mistakes and adopted a correct line, there was no "de-Maofication."

   VOICE 2: (With a long sigh) A thousand-year sleep; a ten-day wake. It was a short Spring, but a memorable one, for the world wept at the sight of the massacre. Fear was the name of the wild shoot into the crowd. They couldn't distinguish all the different forms, so they were aiming blindly at the contents. That night, China's hundred flowers were, again, trampled ruthlessly.

33. VOICE 1: The "cultural revolution" was said to have confounded right and wrong. It made no distinction between the people and the enemy.

   VOICE 2: The Hundred Flowers episode revealed another dangerous source of opposition: the resurgent anti-Chinese nationalism of all the minorities. The government's propaganda attacked "Great Han chauvinism" but the minorities remain by and large the "barbarians." Their liberation can only be achieved with the intervention of the People's Liberation Army.

   VOICE 1: Writing on China's subtropical home of many nationalities, an officially assigned researcher from Northern China reported: "The poverty and primitiveness of Xishuangbana, apart from political causes, has been due to inaccessibility. . . . Though the changes has been great, this region is still backward compared with other parts of the country, and the People's Government is doing much to help bridge the gap."

VOICE 2: The same researcher also related that, "recalling the bad old days, the peasants say with deep feeling, 'Without the bright sunshine the lotus flowers could not bloom and without the golden bridge of socialism, how could we step from hell into heaven?' " (Zheng Lan).

34. (Transcribed from interview with CM, heard as voice-over) *"I jokingly refer to myself as a member of the residual class—an euphemism for living underground, for living outside the norms, for living outside the status quo. . . .*

    "This is important to me because, when I wake up in the morning, being a creature of habit, I either turn the radio on to NPR or KPFA. It's a very difficult task when one turns on the radio, because you feel you are being strangled, gradually asphyxiated, because of the way in which consciousness is produced."

35. VOICE 1: These private plots are called "the tails of capitalism." "For a long time, we did our best to cut them off. . . . Why should we go back to a less socialist organization now?"

    VOICE 2: While at sea, Master Ai anchored for the night in the cove of an island. At night he heard the sound of weeping coming from the water, coupled with humanlike voices. Listening more carefully, he overheard this conversation: "The Dragon King has issued a decree yesterday to the effect that all aquatic animals that have tails are to be beheaded. As I am an alligator, I weep because I am afraid of death. But thou art a frog and has no tail. Why weepest thou then?" Thereafter, he heard the plaintive reply: "I am indeed fortunate to have no tail at present, but the fact that I did once bear a tail as a tad-pole might be recalled" (*Wit and Humor From Old Cathay*, translated by Kowalis).

36. VOICE 1: Mao said it loud and clear, "Political power grows out of the barrel of a gun. . . . only with guns can the whole world be transformed."

    VOICE 2: Still, on the question of Tibet, Yin Fatan said: "One cannot comb different kinds of hair with the same brush."

37. (Transcribed from interview with CM, first heard as voice-over, then in synch) *"You ask me a question that arises out of the Sino-Soviet split, out of China's coming out of isolation. And the interesting thing about the Chinese model is first of all it's autonomous: We work side by side with you, the decision-making process was not left to the Chinese, it was left to the Tan-zanians, which meant that the Tanzanians can change the program, but kept the railroad going. The railroad has significant impact on that regional economic sphere because it allowed Zambia to transport its goods through to Tanzania—that had a port—but also enhanced Tanzania's position.*

    "The second thing they did was to introduce a health program based on the restoration of African medicine. What they did was to integrate Western medicine, Chinese medicine and

SC

African medicine, which allowed for the Africans to integrate all these various facets in the health system.

"The third and most important thing was the question of defense. The Chinese decided to (synch) teach the Tanzanians about guerilla warfare. They modernized their military system by teaching them guerilla warfare because they were surrounded by hostile nations. Largely, in view of the fact that they had built this railroad, Rhodesia didn't like it, South Africa didn't like, the Americans didn't like it, nobody liked the fact that this unfeasible thing was becoming a dream come true, a dream real. The military aspect of it was fundamental to the Tanzanian economy because they were able to engage in military combat at a level that the West was not able to confront, in my view. Because you're in your own back yard—I know of no country that engages in war that has lost the war, in modern times, based on guerilla warfare. So, in that sense, the Chinese model was in advance of the Soviet's, because the Chinese had a program in which they charged no interest on loan/aid: It was protracted over a long period of time and was paid.

"But then, the Chinese made another attempt to get into Africa, which was their moving into Mozambique, Angola. Savimbi—Running Dog. They went along, they supported Running Dog, largely because the Soviets supported MPLA. Now this has to be placed in the context. The Sino-Soviet split has to be seen as a crucial departure from the old solidarity, international solidarity with the Soviets, and all the anti-imperialists, anticolonization movement. And in that sense, one can say that the Chinese decided to support Savimbi without analyzing the destabilizing role that Savimbi would have played in that region. But they had to. It can be viewed as an independent position, but in terms of Africa it was a very retrograde position, in my view. That's why the question of 50–50, 50 percent failure, 50 percent success.

"I saw China as a very positive sign until Mao's death. And for me that's a very realistic position. I don't think . . . except for the people who make policy decisions, they have to situate themselves in China because they make policy; but for the average person, China is a place that is vast, and beautiful, and intriguing.

"I consider myself a member of the residual class largely because I am in-between it, I am not of it. By that I mean that people produce, there are people who appropriate people's labor, the ruling elite, they own the means of production. Then, there's the working class that doesn't have time to think about who it's giving its labor to, or to where. And me, who enjoys everything that both sides produce."

38. VOICE 1: China is an attractive piece of meat coveted by all. But this meat is very tough, and for years no one has been able to bite into it. These were Chou En-Lai's words.

VOICE 2: "Is eating and drinking a mere trifle? No. Class struggle exists even at the tips of one's chopsticks. Under the conditions of proletarian dictatorship the class enemy will attack us not only with steel bullets but more frequently with sugarcoated bullets. . . . As

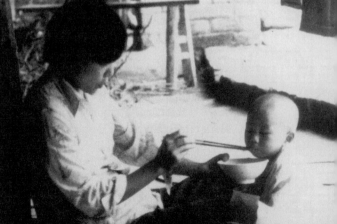

the saying goes, you can't lift your hand against them when you eat their food. This was Liu Yu Lang writing in *Red Flag*, the Party's journal.

39. VOICE 1:   No member of the May Fourth generation was more sensitive to the importance of words and the uses of language in politics than Mao.

VOICE 2:   His words were unconditionaly worshiped. But when words and acts no longer coincided, articles in the *People's Daily* did appear with headlines such as "Talking Nonsense" or "Great Empty Talk."

VOICE 1:   Every war waged for human rights is a war of meaning and of interpretation. The politics of the word is, as Mao put it, "a verbal struggle." And the struggle will never end. But Mao's word power prevails, even when Mao is denounced in the name of Mao.

40. VOICE 1:   When I came out of that bookstore, the young man in Shanghai asked with excitement, "What did you buy?" And I said, "Oh, well . . . a collection of essays on *China After Mao* by the *Beijing Review*." The young man looked at me with utter astonishment and exclaimed, "What did you buy that crap for?!" That's when I realized how good his English was.

VOICE 2:   What else do you remember of him?

VOICE 1:   Well, he was a former Red Guard. One day in the midst of a conversation, he asked me: "Do you know how we'll come to know whether or not we have succeeded in the Four Modernizations? . . . When each family in Shanghai will have a toilet of its own."

41. VOICE 1: "Now, how do we distinguish between 'right' and 'left' anyway? . . . Why are [those who support progress and oppose bureaucratism and conservatism] labeled 'rightist' while those who oppose reform and want to continue with the old ways are honored as 'leftist'? Why this strange inversion?" (L. Binyan) This was what a Chinese journalist asked a Party official forty years ago.

VOICE 2:   "Mountain and water are male and female. . . . If the dragon curls left, the water has to curl right; if the dragon curls right, the water has to curl left; the two embrace each other and only then does the site coalesce" (Ye, 1696). The system may be Right in its operative manners, but it situates itself on the Left.

42. VOICE 2:   A woman remarked that the rise of patriarchal society probably started when man began to accumulate personal, as over communal property. This change in secular power coincided with the rise of sun worship under a male priesthood. What was conceived as religious or spiritual values through the symbol of the moon, was transferred to the sun and came under masculine control (M. Esther Harding). Sun rationale and sun

cruelties hence reigned over moon thinking and moon madness. The sun hero was then a man who claimed to be the one and only son of Heaven.

VOICE 1:   As the dragon was appropriated as a symbol of the ruler, its use by ordinary people was considered an encroachment on the imperial authority. But, orders issued during the Yuan dynasty to prohibit dragon designs were ignored by the people. To compromise, imperial dragons were to have five claws while those used by ministers and lower ranks were to have only three or four claws. Later on, *names were rectified*, and the dragon with five claws remained a dragon, while one with four claws was called a python (Yang Xin).

43. VOICE 1:   The Dragon is said to have nine sons. The dragon of burden usually seen at the base of monuments; the dragon of fantasy standing on the roof with its head turned upward toward the sky; the loudmouth dragon frequently found on bells; the tiger-face dragon guarding the entrances of gaols; the food-lover dragon imprinted on rice bowls; the river-dragon adorning the parapets of bridges; the great-fighter dragon carved on the hilts of swords; the smoke-lover dragon decorating incense burners; and the recluse dragon appearing on closed doors.

44. VOICE 1:   China is red, yellow, and blue. Feared and hated, she used to be identified with the Red Menace, then she became the Golden Horde, the Yellow Peril, and finally, she drew both contempt and admiration for her "blue ants," as an American journalist once called her masses of workers uniformly clad in Mao outfits.

VOICE 2:   The story goes that Emperor Hui Tsung chose this line from a famous poem: "One speck of red among ten thousand of green." A candidate painted a stork in a group of pine trees, a speck of red on its head; a second showed the crimson sun setting over a welter of green waves; but the winning scene was that of a girl leaning pensively on a balcony with a cluster of willow trees below.

The word "red" is a symbol for woman.

45. (Transcribed from interview with WTM) *"The image of the dragon was created by our ancestors. It is said that the image came from the idea that there were two snakes in the sky, that the dragon is a composite of the horses head, the deer's antlers, the snake's body, and the chicken's claws. So the dragon symbolizes life itself, and to this day is a modern Chinese totem.*

"The dragon symbolizes power. For example, the emperor proclaimed himself a dragon; he was the true dragon's son of heaven. The Chinese also made the dragon into a kind of god. For example in times of drought, the people would beg for rain and they would go to the dragon king's temple. The dragon really reflects the complicated deep cultural attitudes of the Chinese people.

"The dragon is known in the Chinese tradition as something that controls the waters. I know of a story that goes back to about the early twentieth century, from the Tai Hang mountains in China. In this story, the villagers were having trouble getting rain, and they sent a representative to the dragon king, to his temple, to beg for sympathy. What they did was to attach very sharp knives to his arms. This method of begging for sympathy is called the vicious vapors. They would also attach four small knives to his neck so that whenever he moved he would cut himself. Then he would run at the head of the other villagers. They would run for more than twenty kilometers. This in the hot summer with no water to drink. And the knives would just cut into his arms and his body and his neck, and the blood would run out and would dry up and cake and clot, and then, when they got to the temple the whole village would kneel down and this man knelt there for one full day and one night. But the dragon king showed no mercy. No rain came down. This man died in the process.

"His son then went to the plains of Hubei province, to try to win this dragon king's mercy. All the villagers knelt down in front of this one for three days and three nights, but it still did not work. In despair and anger, the son just took this dragon king's image and hung him up from the ceiling and beat him very hard, and all of a sudden the heavens broke loose, and the rain just came pouring down. The dragon king was so angry that he just let loose his control over the water, and so the people had rain.

"This is a story that expresses a great deal the attitude that people have toward the dragon king."

46. VOICE 1: Here is another view of red from a Party official: "Ten or a hundred brainwashings are needed in the life of a man. Ten or a hundred Cultural Revolutions are needed in the life of China, if she is to remain Red for a thousand or ten thousand years. . . . Red doesn't last well; it fades" (Hsu Ching-hsien).

VOICE 2: Sure, "everything is possible," as a student in Chengdu said. "What was bad yesterday is good today but can be bad again tomorrow. One day we are told to adulate and worship a man, another day we are told to vilify and curse him. Then we are ordered again to glue back the shattered pieces of the same man we've damned. In the hand of our leaders we are mere puppets of the game of the day."

VOICE 2: The traditional opera retains its popularity with the masses down to the present day." Scholar Huang Shang compares it to the paintings of master Qi Baishi whose "depictions of grass, flowers, and landscapes are in simple, vigorous strokes that leave out many details, yet among the leaves and petals we often see such tiny insects as the dragonfly [or the] cricket painted in the *gongbi* style, the realistic method with such meticulous care that even the lines on their wings can be seen. . . . The performance of traditional opera artists vary from gross exaggeration to extreme precision." And restrictions of time and space are removed, giving the actors an extraordinary degree of freedom. Bold omissions and minute depictions become a perfectly harmonized entity in the whole performance.

VOICE 1:   As with Shen-Fu's garden, the joy is to see the small in the large and the large in the small; the real in the illusory, and the illusory in the real.

47. VOICE 2:   Dragon-head wall. Its workmanship may be very fine, and the head in its own way is splendid, but most garden lovers disapprove of such literal interpretations, for their lack of ambiguity can only limit the imagination.

VOICE 1:   China was called "The Mother of Gardens." Of the countries to which Western gardens are most deeply indebted she holds the highest place.

48. VOICE 2:   An inscription above one of the doorways of a garden reads, "The fragrance of antiquity lasts forever."

49. VOICE 2:   (Start as if already in the middle of a conversation.) Meticulous naturalist reconstructions of the landscape by painters of the past mainstream Northern School were disregarded by the Southern painters whose landscapes of the heart flowed freely with bold powerful lines and movements, stressing the oneness of the sensual, material, and spiritual worlds, thereby reproducing not the arrested forms of nature but its *vital spirit*.

VOICE 1:   Like the painter, the garden maker creates landscapes and is an interpreter, not a copyist. The true way has always been to capture the *ch'i yun*. In a successful garden, forms themselves are only starting points for the imagination to roam freely about.

50. (Interview with the calligrapher)
   —*You came from Shanghai?*
   —*Yes*
   —*Why did you immigrate to the United States?*
   —*(untranslated reply in Chinese)*

51. VOICE 1:   An old house is an intimate thing. Its walls, floors, windows, and doors bear the traces of human wear and tear.
   " . . . And we eye our painting like we sip our tea convinced that a hasty glance can only bring a superficial satisfaction, we look at them . . . until the inner significance sinks into our minds and the imagination is fed to the full." This is from painter Chiang Yee.

52. VOICE 1:   "The incense burner sits proudly by Buddha's hand on the temple altar, and the lowly night pot is hidden away under the bed; both are of clay, fired in one kiln; why then, is one so high, the other so low?" (Yunan folk poem, translated by R. Alley).

VOICE 2:   "the water will not be clear if there are too many fish in the river. Nothing can be accomplished if there are too many officials in government" (Yunan folk poem, translated by R. Alley).

53. (We SEE the two women narrators in the dark, next to stacks of large sheets of white paper, in the same setting as at the begining of the film)

W2: Wait here . . . another shot in the dark. There is almost no movement, no traveling, only a lousy head-on shot.

W1: Don't become infatuated with this machinery. . . . After all, you're only offered a guest shot on this show.

54. (Lights suddenly come on. We SEE the whole setting brightly lit. Transcribed from conversation between Dewi/W2 and Ying/W1:)

Dewi: Oh, Ying.

Ying: What do you do in real life?

Dewi: I'm supposed to be an actress [laughs]. I think.

Ying: I can believe that.

Dewi: Tell me, Ying, what do you do outside this show?

Ying: I think of myself—I like to think of myself as a political activist. It's not quite an occupation, but I manage to somehow make a living from it. No, this show has been interesting, because Mao is one of my heros.

Dewi: Really?

Ying: Most people in the United States don't know what China was like before the Revolution, before liberation. I used to go to school in the winter stepping over dead bodies, and it's hard to imagine a society where 98 percent of the people are poor with hardly a way to make a living and subject to famine and drought. And if you're in the city you just have to scrounge. And probably the worst thing was just the lack of value for human life, the lack of dignity, and that's something Mao, plus the people he was able to pull together and work with, was able to change in 5,000 years of history. There's never been a time when individual Chinese, now over a billion of them, have clothing, shelter, food, some dignity. That's the first time in history. I think it's been a miraculous . . . 50 years.

Dewi: So Mao was definitely the hope of China.

Ying: My relatives think of him as a wonderful revolutionary. Not so good as an administrator. And I suppose they're right. Even the cultural revolution had its problems.

Dewi: What's your feeling about China now?

Ying: I think that for all the deaths, Tiananmen was horrible, because here were television cameras watching the tanks, watching the troops come in. People tend to think of the thousands; I don't care how many thousands were killed. You have to think about the tens of thousands, the hundreds of thousands who were killed before the Revolution, the liberation, and they didn't die the heroic deaths that people did in Tiananmen Square. They died the deaths of misery of being a rickshaw coolie and dying when you're thirty-five because you don't have enough, you can't eat enough to get the calories to drag the rickshaw. . . . The indignity of being a prostitute when you're fourteen, fifteen, being a female in Confucius' China. It was disgusting. So I don't care how bad things are today, it's better than it was.

Dewi: We don't have a sense of the whole history of China.

Ying: Well, it is a dragon: all the incredible changes, and some of them miraculous—very, very powerful.

Dewi: I'm an American-born Chinese, and I find myself in a very fascinating position of trying to understand China, but being American. So, I have the pull: one hand on dryland over here, and one hand on dryland over there. (She unintentionally crushes an empty, fragile paper box) *And yes, my position is just as fragile, I feel sometimes. Because, with my hands spread out I find my feet wet.*

Ying: You're fourth generation, aren't you?

Dewi: Yes I am. I'm fourth generation, but both my parents were very steeped in Chinese culture.

Ying: How did they maintain that through three generations? And what does it mean being Chinese?

55. (Transcribed from CM's comments in an interval of rest, at the end of a take) *"I'm glad when this is going to be over. And I hope Minh-ha can do something with it; if she doesn't approve of what I say, do another thing. Just keep my mouth going.*

56. (Dewi powdering Ying's face in between two takes)

Ying: "Deep silence . . . "

Dewi: " . . . yeah"

57. (Transcribed from interview with CM, heard here as voice-over) *"The media in the United States had a function: to legitimize the modernization program. And to that extent, I'd say that the situation in Tiananmen Square was multifaceted, much more complex. It is clear that the materiality of the students was in question, as well as the workers—the workers wanted to preserve their privileges, as in any urban society. But the real problem is that, after the media shut off the Revolution by TV, the regime moved on the people—both the students and the workers; we couldn't distinguish who were students and who were workers! There's a famous song by Gil Scott-Heron, 'The Revolution Will Not Be Televised.'*

"The problem is that when you kill one person, it is justified for killing one hundred thousand. How long will we tolerate a situation in which the killing of one person can be justified in relation to those views that they do not espouse in relation to the ideological wishes of the

State. After the media projected the Tiananmen Square something, calling [it] demo-cratization and freedom—I don't think that has anything to do with it. Nobody knows. Only the people who speak the language of China understands that problem—what it is they were demonstrating, protesting against."

58. VOICE 2:   "It's not that I love these flowers more than life
                   Only when they're gone, life too may flee" (Tu Fu).

Hate, hurt, burn, bond. Which four-letter word had set me off? Pain? Fear or Free. Did I hear L . . . ? Or that other ill-famed, more trendy word? The one that sounds like dUCK, but is not Fully it, because of a typo error. One single consonant off and the word shifts radically to a different level of operation. Repeating it anew and stammering politely, let's say it's the one that sounds like Fowl, or rather, FoUl, no sorry, FUn and luCK put together. So goes the Way of music and meaning.

"It is in vain that we say what we see; what we see never resides in what we say. And it is vain that we attempt to show, by the use of images, metaphors, or similes, what we are saying; the space where they achieve their splendor is not that deployed by our eyes but that defined by the sequential elements of syntax."
—Michel Foucault

DOWNWARD

Surfacing, Non-Knowing

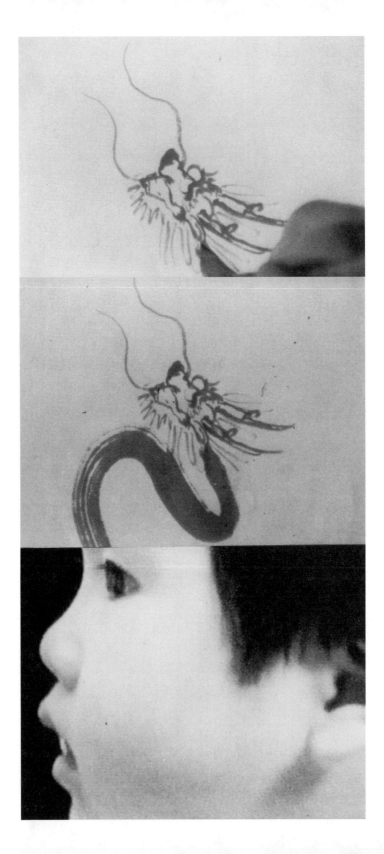

TWO SPIRALS

with Linda Tyler, Sarah Williams, Toroa Pohatu, and Tessa Barringer

Interview transcribed and edited by Tessa Barringer. First published as "Strategies of Displacement for Women, Natives and
Their Others: Intra-views with Trinh T. Minh-ha," in *Women's
Studies Journal* (New Zealand), Vol. 10, No. 1 (March 1994), with
the following introduction: *"These discussions with Trinh T.
Minh-ha were recorded when she visited Dunedin in August 1993
to screen her latest film* Shoot for the Contents. . . . *Participants
in this intra-view include: Linda Tyler, art history, School of Art,
Otago Polytechnic; Sarah Williams, women's studies, Toroa Pohatu,
Maori studies, Tessa Barringer, English, all at the University of
Otago. With each of us arriving literally and metaphorically from
a different place and with a different perspective, Minh-ha herself
became the center, the focal point that anchored and integrated
our diversity. As the discussion developed a wide variety of issues,
ranging from art and architecture to pedagogy, the politics of discourse, the politics of difference, questions of biculturalism, multiculturalism, and the problematics of anthropology. This movement
made of the discussion the kind of shifting, productive and 'impure' space that Minh-ha advocates in her work and which itself
describes her work. . . ."*

Tyler: *You seem also to be very interested in architecture. In particular, I've noticed in your work
that there's a lot of attention paid to interior spaces. Also you've worked with Jean-Paul Bourdier
on various collaborative projects on architecture. Is this a continuing interest of yours?*
T: Yes, that work was very much inspired by Jean-Paul because we work as a team on many projects, but I would say it also corresponds with my other interests as well. The word "dwelling,"
if one understand it as a verb and not a noun, involves everything in life; it's a mode of living.
The house in which, and with which, one lives, for example, or the house that one has built
tells us a lot about the cultural practices of the individual inhabitants as well as of their society.
A writer from Switzerland (F. Jotterand) once told me that the best way to learn about a culture
or a society was to look at its architecture. However, rather than focusing on monumental
architecture, we are more interested in what is known as "vernacular architecture," or in the
houses built outside of the market by the people for their own use.

T: *And it is also of interest to you how women create interior spaces, women as being more associated with houses or homes?*

T: It is dangerous to look at the home as mainly a concept associated with women. This is an issue the feminist struggle has clearly pointed out and we are still working with it critically. The question is not simply to reject it but perhaps to change the way we think about home. Home has always been opposed to abroad and traveling. It is the site of dwelling, the fixed or safe place to which one can always return. Because of such an opposition, cultural experts, for example, often conveniently treat the native cultures they study as dwelling sites; and while the traveling knower's subjectivity is considered to be shifting and mobile, that of the people studied tend to remain stable, therefore naturally retrievable and knowable. But the notion of home in itself involves the notion of traveling; because, existing only in relation to what has been defined as its opposites, "home" can never be the same. When those who leave—like myself—come back home, things have changed and so have I. Home is a site that is constantly shifting; it is only when it is opposed to everything outside, foreign, and abroad within a male economy of movement that it appears as something fixed or stable. When not subjected to such a dualism, home can be said to be also a site of change, whose movement often reflects a different pace and a different sense of time.

This being said, in the places we went to in Africa, for example, the houses and their interiors were usually considered to be the women's domain. They were the ones who created the living spaces and kept them alive. The men were active outside the house, in the domain of public relations. Here again, without careful negotiations, we may fall back into the public-and-private, home-and-abroad dichotomies. So the challenge is to deal with women and home, not in terms that oppose female to male but in terms that suggest different modes of dwelling and traveling. In all of the films I've made, I have stayed away from such dichotomies, and in *Naked Spaces—Living Is Round*, for example, I have dealt simultaneously with architecture, music, and film by looking at the way light determines or organizes women's daily activities as well as how these activities themselves structure the organization of space.

T: *In certain commentaries, people have used the metaphor of "weaving" to describe your work and have referred to elements within the work as being "interwoven." Do you, in your films for example, consciously strive for an effect where visual and audial information are interwoven? I'm particularly interested in this in relation to weaving when it is seen as a domestic art, an art associated with women, and an art that has traditionally been considered inferior to the fine arts. I wondered whether this was a deliberate strategy on your part?*

T: That is a nice way to approach it; I haven't thought of it in quite that way before. However, I can certainly make the connection here between the notion of "weaving" and that of impurity (which is another notion associated with women) or more generally, that of relationship. For example, a couple of readers have responded to *Woman, Native, Other* by arguing that such-and-such idea advanced here was not new, that it has already been put to use by others in the field challenged. But what is new? There are no new objects so to speak; rather, there are new relationships that one can draw from things, from the way people relate to one another, the way things communicate among themselves, and the way language reflects back on itself even when it is used to point to a reality outside itself.

What one has to work on is not simply the objects but the relationships generated by the coexistence of these objects in the very process of the work—in other words, the intervals between things, people, moments, events, and so on. For me, what is important is how one works on these relationships in order to bring out new forms of subjectivity, or new relationships between otherwise familiar things. My music, films, and books have all been explorations of subjectivities, or of relationships in their differences and multiplicities. There are many ways to discuss this question, but if I could focus on one example for the moment, it would be that of language (in the larger sense of the term). When I write a book or when I work on the text of a film, I am always looking for different ways of presenting "information," different ways of speaking and writing, even though these would have to be generated by the subject and the material themselves and cannot be imposed for the sake of new "forms."

One can use, for example, the kind of poetical, elliptical language that belongs to many cultures of marginalized peoples, or one can use a language that is very logical and rational as promoted by the mainstream media—in other words, a language subjected to linear reasoning and its classificatory power. It is this kind of explanatory language that I tend strongly to reject in *Reassemblage*, for example. Such a rejection was necessary for me at the time, since this was one of the first films I made in an attempt to unsay what has been said, or to say that one can communicate otherwise than through the language of linear reasoning and literal meaning. The issue is not, however, just one of opposing reason; if that was the case, then one would merely fall back into this dichotomy where reason belongs to the dominant culture—and to men—while intuition continues to be attributed to women and to other cultures.

What is at stake here is the problem of established power relationships. When this explanatory language becomes dominant, when it becomes so pervasive that the only way people can think about something is to think about it literally, then for me, that language also becomes dangerous, because its cultural centralization constitutes a form of impoverishment—the ways in which we think are reduced and homogenized—as it excludes or invalidates all other ways of communicating. So I had to say "no" to it in *Reassemblage*; but in the other films I've made since then, I've been using both kinds of language and more, in order to open up a different critical space. This leads us to a point I made earlier, if one does not censor oneself, if one fearlessly crosses boundaries—even those that one has made up for oneself on one's own terms—then one is bound to remain radically impure. But if one becomes too rigid in carrying out one's own rules, in an attempt to be pure, then one tends to close oneself off to other forms and other possibilities.

And, of course, this question of purity can be linked back to the notion of culture. Home, as we discussed earlier, has conventionally been considered to be the place of purity—you always return to Mother or to the site of authentic culture and language. The example of Native Americans in the States seems to be very relevant here. Historically, there has been an ongoing attempt to destroy the people and to erase their cultures; we have now come to a point where both the descendants of those who have destroyed and those who have been the victims mourn

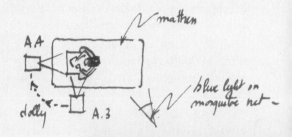

camera shoots
A.1 water

camera tilts
50 mm down in A2

camera lowered
in A.3

A.2

A.3

50 mm

crochet

petrol
or
gazoline lamp

mattress

mosquitoe net

mattress

A A

blue light on
mosquitoe net

dolly

A.3

the loss of an entire heritage. It's not just a question of losing a particular language or a particular set of cultural practices, but of losing a whole way of thinking and of living differently. However, even though I realize acutely how crucial the problem is, I also think that it's misleading to think of it only in terms of loss. What about all the Native Americans who are now living in "impurity," having to bridge several cultures to survive? When perceived as such, the place of impurity can become extremely enabling since one can draw from it unthought of relationships, and what one has then is a new, fresh reality that is not defined by a dualist shuttling between native and nonnative, but that is being created in the fearless crossing of the home-and-abroad or over here-and-over there boundaries.

Williams: *It seems to me that in this particular context [of New Zealand], the tensions between bicultural and multicultural perspectives are very much in the foreground, in ways that are perhaps different to that which we might experience in the United States. In terms of my own thinking, I've got to the point where I prefer to talk about post-culturalism and I'm beginning to suspect that perhaps the problem is with the very notion of culture itself as an organizing principle. It appears to create a form of categorization that leaves us only able to go back and forth between home and abroad, and as a consequence, we remain trapped in the kinds of binaries of which you've been so critical in your writing. In terms of a pedagogy, if minds aren't engaging in that kind of critical movement, if they are rejecting that potentially productive "impurity," what kind of languages are you finding most useful in your work for addressing questions of difference, and in particular, the tensions that arise between bicultural and multicultural perspectives?*
T: At first hearing, it may sound as if the problems here are unlike those in the States, but the more you speak about them, the more I realize that there are many similarities and there are many points common to both contexts. For me, it's not a question of choosing between biculturalism and multiculturalism but, rather, of dealing with what can be seen as the continuing inability to work with difference. If we talk about difference, then we are not talking about bi- or multi-; we are neither trying to polarize nor to add up safely without effecting change on the prevailing state of things.

In the United States, multiculturalism is a word that many people of color strongly reject. The only place where it appears as a positive catchword is in the mainstream media and that is a clear indication of how the word is being appropriated. The reason it is being rejected, in my view, is because it has become so unthreatening and depoliticized in its use; multiculturalism has almost the same liberal connotations as the word "pluralism." As you know, this has created a lot of problems for the struggles of marginalized people because it tends to obscure the issue of differences—ethnic, racial, sexual, gender, class, and others. Multiculturalism, understood as a bland melting pot, points back to the time in the States when the first European immigrants came to settle down and to appropriate the land. It was necessary for them then to form a white coalition and to promote unity of lifestyle and of values, and in order to achieve such a standardization, all differences were leveled out. "Multi-" here ultimately meant "uni-," or one-dimensional, and *the* way that had come to prevail in this multicultural advocacy was no other than the white man's way.

This perception of multiculturalism hasn't gone away yet, it is very much alive, especially in the mainstream media. That's why I think the use of such a word is dangerous. Co-opted in the context of liberal pluralism, it tends to dilute, suppress, and obscure a lot of issues; and in the end, what it denotes is a very uncommitted stance. Other terms have been put to use in today's context of cultural activity, such as "diversity," but even this word has become indicative of a form of safe appropriation and reductiveness—diversity for diversity's sake—since it tends to uphold culture as a commodifiable object of knowledge. Perhaps so far, the more effective term remains "cultural difference," a very old term, but one whose simplicity can lead to very complex forms of subjectivities (as seen in contemporary critical theories and practices); it implies the possibility of numerous processes of differentiation in dealing with the problem of cultural supremacy and cultural centralization.

The situation in New Zealand may be one in which the question of multiculturalism serves as a means of escapism for those who deny the urgency of the Maori struggle. So on the one hand you have people who try to dilute the issues of cultural difference by arguing that there are many cultures involved and not just two, and on the other hand, you have other people who, it seems, reactively or *strategically* push for biculturalism in order to prevent the liberal dispersal and dismissal of their cause. Multiculturalism has been used in many Western contexts to set marginalized people against each other and to avoid the specific issues of each group. But each situation has its own set of questions, and rather than trying to homogenize them, these have to be dealt with in their specificities and differences. The challenge is how to really deal with the difficulties and complexities of difference, not just the difference between cultures, but the difference that questions a whole system of truth and representation, and allows each case of marginalization to be dealt with as a unique case without losing sight of what it may share with other cases.

Barringer: *There's also the implication of difference within a culture, that no culture is in itself stable; it's a shifting space as well, isn't it, always moving always changing?*
T: The boundaries we are setting up are boundaries that are strategically important for political struggle. However, one should always remain open to the possible modification and transformation of these boundaries, otherwise we are unable to form any new alliances.

B: *You talk frequently in your work about the "strategies of displacement" that you use in order to prevent such boundaries from becoming fixed. In your films, you seem often to be entering other people's places. When you're approaching another's space (whether it be literal or metaphoric) with the intention of exploring it, what strategies of displacement do you find most useful in attempting to represent or theorize that space while, at the same time, respecting its difference and keeping it open and alive?*
T: The image I probably would have for such a process is the image of two spirals. As mentioned earlier, the place of the observer is always considered to be mobile and flexible, while the place of the observed is often thought of as unproblematically identifiable and hence static. Whereas in the process of displacement you've just described, there are at least two spiraling movements happening in the same space of exploration. You, as the onlooker, position yourself

differently according to different contexts and circumstances, but so does the "other" whom you're looking at. Each constitutes a site of subjectivities whose movement is neither simply linear nor circular. In the spiraling movement, you never come back to the same, and when two spirals move together in a space, there are moments when they meet and others when they do not. Trying to find a trajectory that allows the two movements to meet as much as possible without subsuming one to the other is how I also see the process of translation.

Many of the cultural translation works are carried out on the terms of the translator's culture, and so very little remains of that cultural encounter full of blanks—the spiraling movements where things come in contact with one another in ways that cannot entirely be measured. Often, all that you have is the translation, in your own terms, of what the other is. For me, that is where the danger lies, because we are not dealing with that double or multiple spiraling movement in which sometimes things meet and other times they don't. To bring that movement out is, of course, the challenge we constantly have to face with every single work we come up with.

B: *You talk of the gaps created by that kind of spiraling movement as being gifts, in that they give the signal for departure. It seems to me that these gifts are the challenge, and that the challenge lies in addressing your own process in its relation to the other subject, in recognizing that you are both moving, that you are both subjects in process. I'm interested in the way you deal with this in your work, in the way that you foreground your process, rather than yourself, as subject. And, of course, that then raises the question of who's in the frame. In framing the other are you not also framed yourself? Do you find it difficult to keep that movement going without getting caught up in a kind of endless self-reference, watching yourself watching yourself watching the other?*

T: I think that if that were the case, I would not be able to finalize any work; but I believe, and I think you put it very nicely, that what you encounter is the process itself or the processes in which subject and object are inseparable. The linearity and circularity of movement implied in "watching yourself watching yourself watching the other" is precisely what I have stayed away from when I chose the image of the two spirals. Here the point of reference is no longer "the self" but rather something more like the "interself." I also believe that the work in progress is not a work that awaits a better stage but rather something that is constantly on the move. Every work must have a beginning and an ending, just as every storyteller has a beginning and ending (and there is a beginning and an ending to every storyteller). And every work you come up with is a finished work because it is what you can do best at that moment, in a specific situation and circumstance. However, it is also a work in progress, because it partakes in a life process that links what you have done to what you will be doing, and each work materialized is simply a moment in the process, or a process within processes.

This notion of the moment is also very appropriate when applied to film. People often think that the film begins only when you start shooting, but shooting is just a moment in the process, a moment among many other moments. It is the moment in which the image takes shape, but what about all the other moments that make the moment of shooting what it is? What about everything that goes on before and after? If we see a film only in terms of that consecrated moment, then we are closing it off. How should I say this. . . . It's like reducing filmmaking to a question of finding solutions for a specific work, even though these solutions are unique to that work and cannot be repeated formulaically in any other. What is finalized in the film belongs to that very moment and circumstance. I consider my work to be radically inefficient when it comes to prescriptions. I cannot offer a model to follow. What I can offer lies not necessarily in the completed work itself, but rather in what one can find (or not find) in that place of film-making.

Pohatu: *This notion of a moment in time—a moment in a continuum in which the past and the future are happening in the present—that is very much the way in which a Maori mind works. I wondered if in coming to New Zealand you had some specific interest in Maori culture or is your interest more in terms of the difference of other people here?*

T: I do not wish to come in with a preconceived idea of what Maori culture is, and so I don't have any locked-in area of interest. I am, however, very interested in what you've just said, about the concept of time as the Maori people live it. For me, to discuss that continuum, one can look at the way education is being carried out. In the context of Western education, the process of learning and of transmitting knowledge is very much based on a linear notion of time.

For example, let's take a well-known philosopher like Jacques Derrida. I have been told that one cannot teach Derrida without also teaching the classical texts of Kant and Heidegger. But in order to understand Derrida, one does not necessarily need to go back to Kant and Heidegger (even when their texts are directly at stake), because in reading the latter two, one has to go further back yet to other classical and ancient works, and the process can go on forever. Not only the ideology of tracing the primary influences and returning to the so-called original texts is questionable because it is dependent on the more explicitly named and easily located references, but it also proves to be illusory in its claim to "deeper understanding." In other words, it has its own limits and is no more valid than any other approach. This being said, if one wishes to go back to Kant and Heidegger in order to read Derrida, that's fine, but when this linear approach is legitimized as the only valid way to teach or to learn, then we are again dealing with cultural authority and established power relationships.

Instead of going back to Kant and Heidegger, why not explore, for example, how Derrida's theories can meet Merce Cunningham's dances, or intersect with certain trends in contemporary performance arts? Why follow only the vertical and its hierarchies when the oblique and the horizontal in their multiplicities are no less relevant and no less fascinating for the quest of truth and knowledge? Why not explore first and foremost how any theory or any writing speaks specifically to us—to our situated social and individual selves—*from where we are*, in our actualities, our cultural differences, our circumstancial positionings and diversely mediated backgrounds? It has always been personally very important for me as a reader to inquire carefully into how a text engages and strikes me in a certain way, and what layers in the investigation of self and other it has opened up in me as I interact with it in my reading journey. In this continuum where the past and the future happen in the present, one should be able to come in at any point and reverberate accordingly. This is something that has always awakened my deepest curiosity when dealing with visual works. And I am very interested here in how Maori artists live and materialize this reverberation across time and space in the continuum.

B: *That notion of time also suggests the image you used earlier of the spirals that are interlaced with each other in a structure that collapses the notion of linearity. As they rotate the spirals touch at different places, setting up different relationships, perhaps unexpected relationships. I think that's one of the things I enjoy most about your work, the unexpected relationships, relationships that couldn't and wouldn't happen in a traditional context where those kinds of connections simply aren't made.*

W: *These ideas of plurality, of nonessentialist and multiple selves, obviously resonate for each of us here. Certainly, within the teaching situation, I've experienced a deep willingness on the part of students to question traditional and canonical values and practices. In your work, it seems to me that you are attempting to tap into another consciousness, another way of looking, that, by its very existence, unsettles those academic values and practices. Do you find that there is a deep hostility to other ways of knowing, an intense power structure (particularly in academia) that keeps, and has kept, the linear, rational way of knowing of the disembodied self in the dominant position for a number of years? Historically, how and why do you think that particular way of knowing has acquired such power?*

T: The question is a vast one and there are many ways to approach it, but perhaps I can suggest one here. One clearly recognizes the problem you describe in the prevailing systems of education, as discussed, and it is not only limited to the present or to the Western world. Students often find it very difficult to assume freedom; when you give them freedom, they experience it as chaos. It is very hard for many of them to accept that we can be confused together and, because of that strain of being confused together, we can move somewhere else, with and beyond the place in which we have been confined. The difficulty lies in accepting this moment of so-called confusion, the moment of blankness and of emptiness, through which one necessarily passes in order to have insight. In other words, confusion can be a mode of receptivity if one does not simply try to bypass it.

In considering the system of power to which you refer, one can go back to the sixteenth century; as you know, many theories have shown that the work done in the middle ages and those carried out today bear many similarities in the way they approach certain issues and certain questions. Looking at the history of Western thought, one can say that the period from the Renaissance to the beginning of the twentieth century is marked by a move constantly to affirm light over darkness, reason over intuition. In its attempt to overcome and suppress moments of confusion and darkness, this movement contributed to creating and establishing a situation in which light became opposed to dark.

A Japanese novelist (Jun'ichiro Tanizaki) writing on the perils of "excessive illumination" says that one cannot really appreciate the different qualities of light unless one understands how it is defined and revealed in its complexities by darkness. In other words, light is the inevitable product of darkness, and darkness, with its own range of colors and of visibility, is the indispensable element of life—the place of peace and repose, without whose recognition light becomes oppressive and self-destructive. However, during the period of Western thought mentioned, the drive for progress—progress viewed exclusively in terms of light and unity—could only deal with the coexistence of these two elements by setting them up against each other, until all that matters today for many people of this civilization is that which is most tangible and visible to them.

I think this privileging of the visible or the setting up of a mutually exclusive relationship between light and darkness, or between the civilized and the primitive has certainly participated in the process that has brought us to endorsing the comfortable, linear notion of history and linear mode of knowing, to the detriment of other ways of thinking and exploring. But as you've noted, once these different ways are brought out in practice, one really pays dearly for it; at least, that has always been my experience in the academic world, whether this occasional, deep hostility is directed to my written or filmic work. But such a task has to be carried on anyway, it's a way of surviving. If I did not take up the challenge and persist in the struggle, I would be closing myself up in places that were preassigned for me. The only way to get out, or rather to resist such ready-made slots is to keep on doing this kind of critical and creative work. Hopefully it will open up doors for other people, but first of all, it opens doors for yourself.

W: *There has been a suggestion recently, in anthropological circles, that indigenous filmmaking is nothing more than a fad, that cultural studies needs an "other" and that you happen to be a very convenient other for us at this moment. The implication being that the fad will pass and then real anthropologists will get back to doing real ethnographies about how we see real other peoples. I wonder if you have any response to that?*
T: Any one of us working in a struggle knows that we adapt our positions to the circumstances and use certain terms for tactical and strategical reasons, but this does not mean we're submitted to any of them. I have discussed elsewhere the necessity for marginalized people to say two or three things at a time. This does not imply the absence of a position or the incapacity to take up a position; instead, it suggests that positioning oneself is always tactical and political. For example, I may, if I am in Vietnam, be very hostile toward China, because in its historical relation to Vietnam, China represents the imperialist force and the centralized culture. But, if I am outside of Vietnam, in the States for example, I would generally speak on the side of China because, from this position, China represents a certain Third World "visibility." It is the site for possible Third World alliances. From each place then, I would speak differently about China, but that does not mean that my position in the States is contradictory to the one I take on in Vietnam. They are both based on the same principle, on whether we are going to let ourselves be subjected to the dominant culture without challenging it while problematizing our own involvement in it.

The suggestion that such positionings are in fashion right now and that they will eventually die away denotes an inability to recognize the strategical nature of their adoption. The critical stances at work won't just die away; instead, they will take on other forms and other names, and other people will carry on the struggle. What one can never escape is the way relationships, as I discussed earlier, define you and your activities. In any encounter with the "other," what you face is also yourself and your set of practices, and as long as you continue to indulge in a position where you can point at someone else and speak safely, then you are simply buying time, trying to bypass the very issue of subject and power or of cultural supremacy, whose negation has precisely contributed to the instability of anthropology as a discipline. If one does not critically address one's relation to knowledge, then one constantly finds oneself in a position of having to reconfirm one's authority through the setting up of fences and of all kinds of disciplinary rules.

W: *Some of your work has been very critical of anthropology. Do you feel that it is the discipline itself that creates a way of knowing that should not be, or is not, tenable? What is your reaction to the individual transformations of the discipline into something like cultural studies, Maori studies, women's studies? Is this a cultural phenomenon that you find to be hopeful?*

T: The criticism I made of anthropology does not only concern anthropology, although as a discipline that seeks to "reveal" one culture to another, it has certainly been discussed at length in my work. But I have carried out critical work in other areas as well. My first published book, *Un art sans oeuvre* (loosely translated as *An Art Without Masterpiece*) already problematized the notion of "art," of philosophy and literature. So anthropology is not the only field in trouble, as contemporary theories have amply shown.

I wouldn't say, for example, that anthropology has to disappear, and that in place of it we should have something like cultural studies, because as I've suggested earlier, cultural studies is now also being colonized. In its attempts to open up the notion of "culture," it rarely asks the question of whose culture and which culture (on the international map) is being studied. Its rise in the academic world can work against other marginalized fields such as women's studies, ethnic studies, for example. In other words, cultural studies tends to subsume all other studies programs into one. So while I think it is extremely stimulating to have such a thing as cultural studies—a field or a project that remains open-ended and has the potential to politicize our everyday, mundane activities—I also think that one should challenge it in its ethnohistorical perspective and prevent its recuperation in the academic world. The problem of ethnocentrism is still very much present here, and to further what I said earlier, it may take on new forms and new names, but it has not died away, and the fight will have to go on.

The fight must be carried on simultaneously in at least two directions. Women's studies, for example, has had to struggle in the past with its being stabilized as a program or a department of its own in academic institutions. As such, it became a women's thing in the midst of the university. But without having a "home" of its own, it's difficult for it to effect change on university curricula, and hence, at the same time as texts written by women or focusing on gender issues should be taught in all fields, it is also necessary that women's studies has a base from which it can make its demands and to which it can return to refocus its energy. The same may apply to cultural studies. We have to open the notion of cultural studies, so that the emphasis is not merely laid on a contestation of the opposition between low and high cultures in the U.K. and the U.S., but also on the different existing cultures in the world, whether low or high. Cultural studies should then meet intercultural studies, acknowledging that there are many contexts, many cultures involved in such a project.

P: *Isn't it the notion then of keeping an insider's and an outsider's view? It seems to me that what you're saying is, let us keep the position of insider, be it of anthropology or whatever, because that position offers a perspective that has value. For native persons, or for people of difference, it is as if* *you have a mirror image of yourself, as well as a window looking out on the world. In Maori studies, we try to teach our students that you must look through that window at society, but, at the same time, you must look also at your own reflection so that you are moving backward and forward, aware of both the insider's and the outsider's view. And that it is important to keep both views because each offers something that the other cannot see.*

T: That's a wonderful image. And one that is most relevant to my work because I would say that all my films are about this positioning of outsider and insider, and each one of them is a different attempt to address the multiple degrees of insideness and outsideness involved. It has been very important for marginalized people to claim the right to self-representation; needless to say, this is an absolutely necessary fight. But, what we need now is to carry out work that offers at least two movements at the same time: one claiming the right to self-representation, and the other dealing with the politics of representation, thereby refusing the boundaries or the limits that are being imposed on our activities. For example, let's consider the idea that Maori people must do work on Maori people, that you must mind your own business, stay in your own territory, and not try to move out of it. The people who are marked by their skin color, their gender, their class, their sexuality are conveniently supposed to limit their activities to areas pre-marked for them, whereas the non-marked, the white people, the dominant self or the "flexible I" can deploy its activities across all boundaries and document the world. We should be careful not to contribute to such a confining state of things and be prepared to fight on both fronts at the same time.

THE OFF-SCREEN VOYEUR

with Kim Hawkins

First published as "Trinh T. Minh-ha's Fiction Within a Fiction,"
in *Film/Tape World*, Vol. 8, No. 8 (September 1995).

Hawkins: *What was it about* The Tale of Kieu *that helped inspire you to make this film?*
Trinh: On the one hand, it is the national love poem of Vietnam whose story every Vietnamese remembers, whether they are in Vietnam or spread around the globe in the Vietnamese communities of the diaspora. On the other hand, it's remarkable that a people identifies the destiny of their country with the fate of a woman, Kieu. Why? Perhaps because she's a controversial character who personifies Love. Her prostitution for survival in patriarchal society raises tensions similar to those resulting from Vietnam's difficult processes of assimilation and rejection under foreign dominations and oppressive regimes. But above all, I would say, because Kieu's story was told in verse (3,254 verses) whose poetry and rhythms were drawn from the songs and proverbs of folk tradition. It was through its rhythms that *The Tale* became popular among the people and was remembered by all classes of society.

H: *One character, Juliet, says "I believe only in great love, love that transcends every rule, even your own rules." What do you think is a "love story" if the "rules" are to be broken and it is to be reinvented?*
T: One of the questions raised by the film is, as a character puts it: "Why do we have this need for an exceptional-individual kind of love story in our society? Is it because there is often no love in love stories?" So to introduce a break in such a habit, one has to expose the fiction of love in the making of a love story. Rather than merely focusing on the content and trying to sell or consume it as "a love story," I have, for example, worked on the experience of film as being a sensuous exploration of both body and mind. This does not only involve the showing of sensuality on screen or the discussion of it among the characters, but also the way one works with the verbal, the visual, and the musical elements of film—let's say, how in a scene, the tension created by a camera movement, between several primary colors, or between image and sound is as important, as telling as what is happening between the actors, their dialogues and body movements. There is a silent conversation between the graphic, the plastic, and the linguistic elements of the film, and none of these elements is there simply to serve "the story." There are

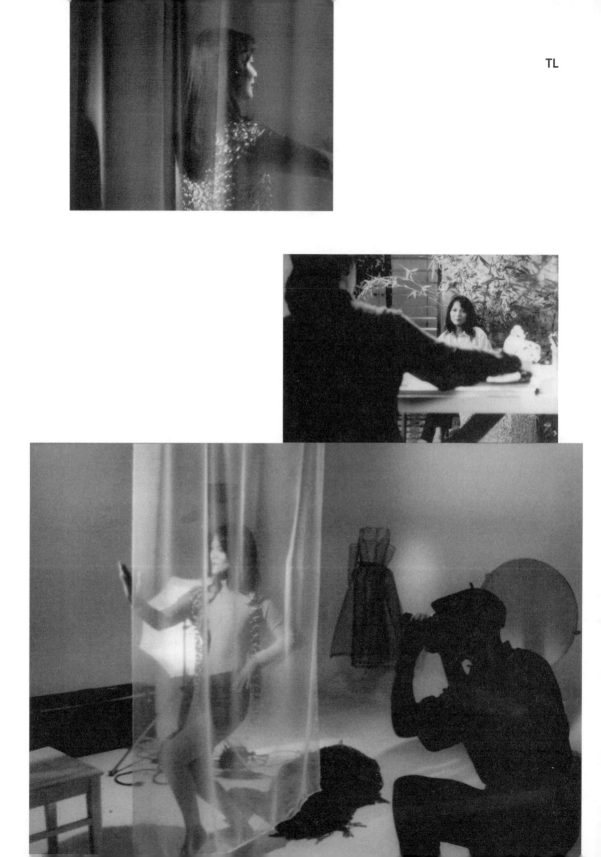

many ways to enter the film or to experience love: through the many senses and many reasonings. No matter how much we may thread the same beaten paths, each love story we live remains unique to us, so how you enter (or don't enter) this love-on-film story is for you to decide.

H: *As I was watching some of the more intimate scenes, I felt uncomfortable at times, like I was spying on someone . . . almost like a voyeur.*

T: It's an important remark. Unlike in other films where you can safely indulge in voyeurism, being a voyeur here is acknowledged and even given a prominent part in the film. Your feeling uncomfortable is probably due to the many levels of voyeurism that you are being exposed to in the film. One can say that behind every love story on screen is a story of voyeurism on and off screen. By making you aware of your being a voyeur while watching the actors acting self-consciously, the film induces reflections on the makers' and viewers' consumption of love stories. When your looking at a scene raises questions, then something interesting is happening . . . at least your position as spectator is at issue.

H: *It was interesting how you had Alikan and a woman touching one another while both wearing blindfolds. . . . It gives the viewer a heightened awareness of watching them both because there is no one in the scene watching one another.*

T: The scene plays on both the look and on the touch. It's the one scene in which Alikan is precisely not looking, and touching seems most effective when you can't see. I would also situate this scene in relation to the decapitation of women, which I've dealt with all throughout the film. For me the relationship between Alikan and Kieu should not merely be a relation of conflict—between man and woman, or between the all-powerful look of the photographer and the submissive look-at-ness of the model. Although she's idealized as a headless female body, Kieu is actually not quite headless because she reflects aloud on her role, thereby opening up a space where the question "who's looking at whom?" is always at play. As viewers, we often find it more exciting when we can indulge in looking at intimate pictures without being looked at. In other words, we are constantly veiling the female body as we look, for things that are not all too obvious to our eyes can speak volumes to our imagination. Here, the tension between wanting the veil and rejecting it necessarily remains unresolved. And filmmaking is a complex form of veiling. So rather than simply condemning the veil, we also have to deal with the power of its attraction as with desire in love relationships.

H: *In* The Tale of Kieu, *the poem says* "Along a lonesome darkened path, for love of you I found my way to you. Now we stand face to face, but who can say we shan't wake up to find it was a dream?" *Reality, memory, and dreams are woven throughout the film and in your words* "open up a space allowing them to unfold in linear and nonlinear time and [the film] can be viewed as a symphony of colors, sounds and reflections." *The opening scene is charged with the passion of a young woman crisscrossing a field in what appears to be a dream . . . or a memory. Images of water and rain appear in rhythms. Can you talk about your use of dreams, and the dualism of the dreamlike images in contrast with the crisp, bright daytime shots?*

T: The dream reality acts on many levels in the film. Our love relationships often begin, end, and unfold like a dream. Film reality is as evanescent as dream reality. In producing love stories, makers and actors often function in dreamlike situations where one is intensely involved in a scene and then suddenly as one turns around, one realizes the whole crew is also watching. Dreams bring us both closer to and farther from reality. I love this accurate concept of being a dream within a dream often encountered in non-Western thinking such as among the Arborigial peoples of Australia whose traditions are translated as The Law or The Dreaming. Buddhist teachings have also always pointed to the transient nature of desire, of the senses, of life itself, and hence of what we hold on to as "life reality." So I don't see things in terms of dualisms, and in the film it's not a question of contrasting dream and reality or of saying that images are fictional, but rather, that we are a fiction within a fiction. Linear and nonlinear time unfold simultaneously and neither the characters nor the mise-en-scène are entirely "realist."

H: *Can you also talk a little more about the rhythm of the film?*

T: To give the viewer more than just a story or a message, one has to deal with the tools that define one's activity. In filmmaking, these tools are precisely the sound images and their relationships. But drawing relationships is working with rhythms. Whether one is conscious of it or not, rhythm marks one's experience of film and allows one to remember it, even if one cannot articulate it in the immediate present. People talk about plot, action, story line, acting, and message when they consume a narrative, but what about the whole rhythm of the film and how it affects the viewer? Rhythm is here not synonymous with action, speed, or editing, and it is not just an aesthetic device. It determines nonverbally the quality of a relationship—between people, events, elements of cinema, or again, between the sensual and the intellectual. It determines the way the viewer responds to, disengages from, or tunes in with the film. Unfortunately, mainstream media have desensitized us to the many ways of receiving stories and information other than those they have normalized. What about action, what about plot, when, for example, the action is in the rhythm itself, or when what's at stake is not merely "the action" but the equal, multiple *inter*actions of diverse presences on film (such as the moves of lighting, camera, bodies, and thoughts within and between frames)?

H: *Can you describe Jean-Paul Bourdier's role in working on* A Tale of Love *and how that partnership works for you?*

T: As you know, Jean-Paul is not only the coproducer, codirector, and production designer of the film, but he's also responsible for all the lighting design of the scenes. We have collaborated on many projects, so Jean-Paul understands very well how I operate with the camera in my previous films. He describes such camera work as one that is not subjected to representation and does not fix, "capture," objectify, or center. It does not simply follow "the action," but caresses, passes by things, and has its own independence. This is what you largely find in the camera work of *A Tale of Love*, on which Jean-Paul has also shared responsibility. We work extremely well together because we have very different strengths and it's interesting for me to see what we come up with in our differences.

H: *It was noticeably peaceful on the set throughout production, and I wanted to ask about your experience of shooting the film?*

T: I think many people on the crew knew my work and this really helped. Those who did not might have had a hard time with the whole process. Most crew members were very competent and ethical, so although we went through some very hard days, with fourteen to sixteen hours work and a night shooting schedule, the crew remained very committed. Some might have found in me a rather quiet director, not projecting the usual image of "the director" they expected, but as I had worked out with Jean-Paul, he was to lead the action so I could have the perspective and the space to reflect on what was going on.

H: *In making* A Tale of Love, *are you venturing into the personal and if so can you explain what it means for a filmmaker to face one's own subjectivity within a narrative film?*

T: I've always worked with the intimate personal in my films. But let me give you an example of what "facing one's own subjectivity in narrative film" can mean. In some of the initial responses to the film I've had so far, people may watch critically how voyeurism and the decapitation of women are exposed in the story between Alikan and Kieu. And they may see the filmmaker reflected in Alikan's role. But the "missing link" here is how the on screen also points back to their position as spectators, or how we all participate in voyeurism and the decapitation of women in the way we consume narrative films. So when I raise the question of the headless female body, I can say [*laughs*] that I'm facing a very personal and yet collective situation. One I've been coping and dealing with everyday in every realm of my activities, for it has to do with people's expectations (as discussed earlier) of how I should speak, write, make film, teach, or simply behave according to the norms of patriarchal society.

TL

FLOWERS REPRESSION

with Paul Kalina

Edited from the interview conducted when *Shoot for the Contents* showed at the 1992 Rotterdam Film Festival. A shortened version of it was first published as "The Importance of the Place Where You Stand," in *Filmnews*, June 1992, with the following introduction by Paul Kalina: "Shoot For the Contents, *the latest film by Trinh T. Minh-ha, will be screening at both the Sydney and Melbourne film festivals. The new film is an organic extension of Trinh's previous* Surname Viet, Given Name Nam *(seen at the 1990 festivals). This time she examines the culture and identity of China, poignantly raising the issue of the 'outsider'—both as a filmmaker in the dubious business of "representing truth" and as a Vietnamese coming to terms with a culture that has dominated her own. The film questions the very fundamentals of the documentary form and presents a perspective on contemporary China that is challenging, fascinating, and highly emotive."*

Trinh: I can situate the film (*Shoot for the Contents*) both in a historical and a personal context, because the two are very linked here. Historically speaking, the situation between China and Vietnam has always been very difficult. China has dominated Vietnam for a thousand years, so Vietnamese identity has often been reactively defined by insiders in opposition to everything thought to be valued by the Chinese. But of course it's impossible for us to deny our strong ties to Chinese culture. We share a whole background, in lifestyle and customs, including numerous sayings and proverbs—not to mention Confucius' profound influence—and yet we try to reject each other all the time. On my own itinerary, Vietnam is the site where Indian and Chinese cultures meet. The project I started out with was indeed on both China and India. I had already shot footage in both countries, but I decided to focus first on the China footage, and since there was so much material gathered in the process, this material grew into a film of its own. The film on India will be done in the near future, and the two can be shown separately or together.

Personally, making a film on China helped to change my consciousness. While I was in China, because of the tension between the two nations, because of what had been officially written in Chinese journals and newspapers, I noticed how very surprised people often are to encounter a Vietnamese—that is, an "enemy"or an uninvited guest—traveling independently in their territory. You can feel the tension between the two nations from their reactions, and today following the very recent normalization between China and Vietnam, I think the gap might be bridged—no matter how imperfectly—and the relationship might change for the better. But as for me, thanks to the making of the film, I was able to reenter China differently as I was moving away from what I already knew of Her, from both an outsider and insider's point of view. The film was shot before the events of Tiananmen Square. I was to go back that very month, but I decided not to, because I had enough material. The political connotations and dimensions of that event then had to be conveyed indirectly in the film because of the people involved in my research for it. You can't jeopardize a person's future just for the sake of a message or a story for your film.

Kalina: *The film uses a high level of stylization; the alternation of film and video, the framing, lighting, and so on. Can you explain a bit about why you assembled it this way?*
T: There are many things to be said about any of the decisions in the film, they are all related. Of course, in terms of location and subjectivity I am the site (rather than the source of) where all these decisions meet. Like in all my other films, the strategies I use usually point back to the making and the viewing of the work. The way you conceive and receive the material can tell you a lot about your intimate and social or political self. For example, I would say there are at least three endings to the film, and depending on which one stands out as "the conclusive message," viewers have been "exiting" or leaving the film quite differently. The three endings are also indicative of the way the film is structured, and of the kind of material involved in it. To begin with, the very last statement of the film is a quote from a poem by Tu Fu, which says, "It's not that I love these flowers more than life / Only when they're gone life too may flee." The verses refer back to a saying frequently heard in the film, which Mao's regime had turned into a slogan, "Let a hundred flowers bloom, let a hundred schools of thought contend." In spite of this slogan the blooming of the flowers was, as is well known, immediately repressed. As the quoted verses suggest, the repression of China's flowers can be dealt with either in its limited or in its full scope, or in both. It's not that we love, in their diversity, the flowers (opinions, cultivated realms of knowledge, modes of being) more than life itself; after all life is more important, and perhaps it is to protect that life that certain repressive political decisions were made. But when you smother the flower, life too may flee. A flower (or a work of life and art) can be seen merely as an object, a passing beauty with a decorative function, or it can, as it commonly does in Asian thoughts, refer to an inner or outer movement—the opening, growing, and maturing of a collective and of an individual state of awareness. In other words, the film ends with something that opens up, it doesn't simply judge the regime or the government for doing something against "democracy," but asks questions that allow us to widen our field of activity.

For me, to take on a political stance is to never be content with anything that is packaged for you. The political mind always pushes further, as it raises questions there where things seem evident and remains skeptical about reductive solutions too easily arrived at. Before Tu Fu's poem, however, you hear the statement by the African-American man about how the killing of one person would serve as a pretext to kill one hundred thousand. He also talks about the role of the media, the way it paints the world and produces knowledge. You have to raise questions about what sort of information we receive in the news and what interest these serve rather than just accept what is given as fact or historical data. Further back, before that statement, one of the women narrators voices her own opinion, saying something extreme, like "I don't care how many thousands of people die, it's still better than before." This comment has upset a lot of people, and I knew it would, but I don't mind making room in the film for it because otherwise I would be censoring the film's or my own hundred flowers. The woman situated herself as a political activist and gave the context as to why she thought that way, so why suppress that view? The viewers can decide for themselves; if they are bothered by this emphatic statement, they still have the rest of the film.

The text of the film is extremely skeptical about Mao, skeptical to the point of relating him to Confucius—you cannot have a more ironic insight into Mao than that. So when the viewer gets stuck on one statement (singling it out from the general context of the film), that reaction tells us something about the political positioning of the person. This is just one example of how in the film I use a strategy. The same thing could be said about the aesthetic choices. I will mention only one: In the very first interview, there are three colors, green, red, and blue. Color in the film has partly to do with the relationship being drawn between film and video. Image resolution is not really at issue here, because if one compares the two media in those terms, film always seems to be on top. One has to take video for what it has to offer, for its unique properties. The first thing that strikes my eye when using both film and video images is precisely the distinctive qualities of their colors. The kind of saturated artificiality obtained in video is inimitable. And the way one holds a video camera is very different from the way one handles a film camera. So what became, among others, two structural elements in the film are color and gesture. The cameras' gestures are part of the film's calligraphy, as is the Chinese calligrapher's brushwork—a work in the tradition of Chinese arts, whose inseparable visual and verbal dimension has made of poetry and painting a single activity. One paints because one is a writer and one writes because one is a painter. Whereas in Western arts there is a tendency to privilege either the image or the word, or else to set up an opposition between the plastic and the linguistic sytems.

In that first interview you see blue, red, and green. Red runs through the entirety of the film. It is not only a symbol of life and of revolution, but as the story about the painting contest makes clear, it is also the color of femininity, and hence the symbol of woman. In the mise-en-scène of the interview you see the translator, who is a woman, lit in red and it is through her that we hear the thoughts of the Chinese filmmaker. We do not really see this filmmaker's face until much further into the film, when he speaks about story making and later tells the story of the Dragon King. What is offered to the viewer is first and foremost the mediation of the translator (that is, the translator for the interviewee *in* the film as well as the translators *of* the film—the makers and the viewers). Everything is mediated, whether it is through verbal language or through the production of images: the setting, shooting, and, cutting of the film, and so on.

K: *There seems to be more than one dialogue taking place in that scene. The questions and answers are almost at cross-purposes to one another.*

T: The idea of dialogue also brings in the role of the viewer, because if you just see the face of the man and hear a voice translating over his words, there is no third presence, no third eye looking. But in that mise-en-scène you have a third person who is sitting there listening silently, and, of course, you only see the backs of the interviewer and interviewee. So it's set up as if there's an intimate dialogue between a man and a woman, but actually it's not, it's a translation.

K: *There's a wonderful moment in the film where calligraphy text is translated. The word "Right" appears, followed by "Left." Then, below that another symbol is translated as "Right" and next to that is "Wrong." Is there a greater level of meaning-making, of trust, for you, in words or images?*

T: I don't think there's more meaning in one or the other; even a silent image speaks volumes. Each one of us sees images so differently. To assume, as many people do, that there's an audience out there that is quite homogeneous in the way it looks at images, for me is quite self-deluding. People's responses to images vary widely, especially when you start soliciting their creative participation. I don't think the filmmaker can ever be dogmatic about what he or she tries to show. If you do, meaning becomes a pawn in the game of power. And that's what has caused wars and the senseless killings that ensue. The English word for the two "Rights" is exactly the same, it is only by their juxtaposition with other words—Left, in one case, and Wrong, in the other—that their difference in meaning emerges. In the context of the film and among the many readings possible, you can humorously translate that vertically, "Right" always looks "Right," whereas horizontally, it is bound to face "Left" or "Wrong." To point to the absurdity of the war of words, or of judgments of right and wrong, is to expose all wars as wars between fictions. Words and images are tools among many others, tools not to fix and close down, but to clear and open up the ground for new possibilities. It sounds a bit negative, but actually it's not a question of having faith or not in them. It's rooted in the nature of language and image for meanings always to shift. This is why we go on innovating and creating.

K: *Rather than debate whether your films are documentaries or fictions, do you think they can be discussed within a tradition of radical first-person experimental filmmaking?*

T: Not quite, because while most of my films give you an impression of first-person filmmaking, there's also a deep questioning of the first-person. I have done this differently in each of my works. For example, in the films on Africa, you hear a voice-over that can be identified as the filmmaker's, and it's my own voice, but actually what is said is not only about myself. Every time I use "I," it's just a site for other "I"s to crisscross, and it doesn't have this personal-story quality. Not everything personal is political, but if you can politicize or socialize something personal, then the personal is not merely personal. In other words, my films deal with the vicissitudes, or the difficulties, of representation, it's delusive to think that one can present a true self or a pure vision.

百花齊放

Let a hundred flowers bloom

ma

SC

K: *You mentioned earlier that your perspective of China was altered by making this film. Can you explain a bit more about that?*

T: Mainly of what we assume China to be. The film disturbs binary oppositions by using humor to display their "Great Emptiness." We discussed earlier about "Right" and "Left," "Right" and "Wrong." As with my previous films, the question of (depositioning) the insider and the outsider is always at work. There is such a large range of positions in between, let's say, someone who is really an insider-insider and yet an outsider at the time of filming, like the Chinese filmmaker (Wu Tian-Ming) who is temporarily residing in the U.S.; and someone like the African-American man, who is an outsider-insider-outsider, intimately part of Third World politics but clearly foreign to the culture. The two Chinese-American women narrators can be said to be insiders-outsiders, while I myself, whose voice they also perform (since I wrote a large part of the narration), would be something like an outsider-insider. The difference in degrees and nuances is subtle and complex. A way of simplifying all this for foreigners is, very often, to say that China is impossible to understand. As the film goes on, you see that even Mao, the person who wanted to do away radically with everything he considered to be feudalistic customs and practices, is the very person who not only made use of oral traditions, with great eloquence and success, but also carried on himself the tradition among men of letters, of writing poetry. He ruled the country because he knew how to tap and to turn to advantage what through their traditions has been dear to the Chinese. There's a very strong sense of continuity despite all the changes. One can talk about China as *The Beijing Review* did, saying that it's absolutely off the mark to think that changes in policy are indicative of instability. For them they are a form of stability. These two oppositional aspects of a reality coexist; they are, in political matter, accordingly confounded, inverted, and can even become interchangeable.

What changed for me coming from Vietnam were all the prejudices I had about China; the more I went into the culture the more these prejudices just crumbled down. For example, having started work on the film, I did not merely make a one-way judgment when I saw the Tiananmen Square event on the media. Of course, you cannot help being extremely emotional about the killing and massacre, but I realized more acutely in making the film that there are a lot of questions that have not been asked about the role of the media in the production of meaning and knowledge. Which does not mean that I am not siding with the students, it just means that you need also to really question the place where you stand as a media person. Every time you give information, that information should reflect more than itself—its condition, your own location, for example—so that you are not just standing in a safe place and pointing your finger at others.

K: *You use the term "fossilized" to describe gender inequality in China.*

T: In China, as in other socialist contexts, the question of women's rights has to be dealt with in a much more visible and official way, at least this is what every official document related to this matter shows. But that doesn't mean that the struggle of women ends with the advent of a socialist regime. Far from it. Burgeoning right in the midst of other revolutionary movements, the struggle being carried on by women is, as feminists have analyzed, the longest revolution — one that has no definite limit in history. No matter what women have achieved and how long they have fought alongside their male comrades, the question of gender difference and inequality always comes up at a certain point, since it is rather common to see a revolutionary man turn around and oppress the women of his entourage. Often, it is through gender that one realizes the question of oppression is not quite understood among one's coworkers. In the case of China, who speaks on behalf of women? Who writes that feminism cannot exist outside of the official network? How is it that the voices that get to be heard and endorsed have always been exclusively those of official women delegates? It seems as if one simply goes from a system of deeply rooted sexist and paternalistic Confucian values to one of loudly officialized equality, in which what women are granted is the right to exceed men in becoming a loyal and efficacious servant of statism. The struggle certainly continues.

K: *What will your next project be?*
T: I don't usually start a film with a preconceived plan or schema. I may choose a point or rather a field of departure, but it's just that.

K: *I imagine it must be difficult to raise money for projects that have only a point of departure.*
T: It is extremely difficult, but I usually start making a film without any budget. It has constantly been a struggle. It's very difficult in the States to find support for the filmmaker or the "artist." Funding is always for a salable idea, or for a project; in some you are funded, in others not, or never. In my case it takes at least four or five sources of funding to allow me to complete a film, and the time I put into raising funds is often three or four times more than the time it takes me to make the film. Perhaps rather than thinking of projects, one can simply think in terms of image making. "Documentary" so far has been where the "battleground" is situated for me. I have been struggling with the question of truth and information, and that's where a critical space can be opened up in a most challenging manner. But I may go more into this other area, dear to the commercial world of entertainment—I would like to see what one can do critically and differently in terms of narrative. I am talking here about this category called fiction, but actually the issues are so related, we are probably just dealing here with different sets of problems, different types of fiction, different ways of fictionalizing, or different experiences of truth in the fictions of life.

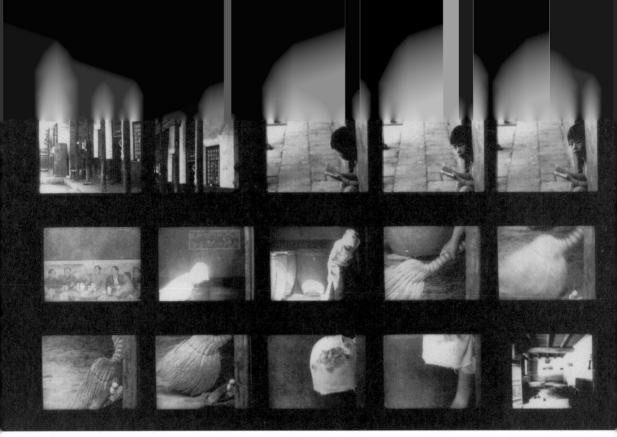

SPEAKING NEARBY

with Nancy Chen

Previously published in *Visualizing Theory. Selected Essays From V.A.R. 1990–1994*, ed. L. Taylor, New York: Routledge, 1994.

Chen: *One of the most important questions for myself deals with the personal. In your latest film* Shoot for the Contents *Clairmonte Moore refers to himself as "a member of the residual class," which is a euphemism for "living underground, for living outside the norm, and for living outside of the status quo." Then another character Dewi refers to having the "pull" of being here and there. I think that this reflects on the personal, and I would like to ask how your family background or personal experience has influenced your work.*

Trinh: Although the ideology of "starting from the source" has always proved to be very limiting, I would take that question into consideration since the speaking or interviewing subject is never apolitical, and such a question coming from you may be quite differently nuanced. There is not much, in the kind of education we receive here in the West, that emphasizes or even recognizes the importance of constantly having contact with what is actually within ourselves, or of understanding a structure from within ourselves out. The tendency is always to relate to a situation or to an object as if it is only outside of oneself. Whereas elsewhere, in Vietnam, or in other Asian and African cultures, for example, one often learns to "know the world inwardly," so that the deeper we go into ourselves, the wider we go into society. For me, this is where the challenge lies in terms of materializing a reality, because the personal is not naturally political, and every personal story is not necessarily political.

In talking about the personal, it is always difficult to draw that fine line between what is merely individualistic and what may be relevant to a wider number of people. Nothing is *given* in the process of understanding the "social" of our daily lives. So every single work I come up with is yet another attempt to inscribe this constant flow from the inside out and outside in. The interview with Clairmonte in *Shoot for the Contents* is certainly a good example to start with. His role in the film is both politically and personally significant. In locating himself, Clairmonte has partly contributed to situating the place from which the film speaks. The way a number of viewers reacted to his presence in the film has confirmed what I thought might happen when I was working on it. Usually in a work on China, people do not expect the voice of knowledge to be other than that of an insider—here a Chinese—or that of an institutionalized authority—a scholar whose expertise on China would immediately give him or her the license to speak about such and such culture, and whose superimposed name and title on the screen serve to validate what he or she has to say. No such signpost is used in *Shoot*, Clairmonte, who among all the interviewees discusses Chinese politics most directly, is of African rather than Chinese descent; and furthermore, there is no immediate urge to present him as someone who "speaks as . . . " What you have is the voice of a person who little by little comes to situate himself through the diverse social and political positions he assumes, as well as through his analysis of himself and of the media in the States. So when Clairmonte designates himself literally and figuratively as being from a residual class, this not only refers to the place from which he analyzes China—which is not that of an expert about whom he has spoken jokingly, but more let's say that of an ordinary person who is well versed in politics. The designation, as you've pointed out, also reflects back on my own situation: I have been making films on Africa from a hybrid site where the meeting of several cultures (on non-Western ground) and the notions of outsider and insider (Asian and Third World in the context of Africa) need to be reread.

C: *This is where you talk about the intersubjective situation in your writings.*

T: Right. I have dealt with this hybridity in my previous films quite differently, but the place from which Clairmonte speaks in *Shoot* is indirectly linked to the place from which I spoke in relation to Africa. Just as it is bothersome to see a member of the Third World talking about (the representation of) another Third World culture—instead of minding our own business [*both laugh*] as we have been herded to—it is also bothersome for a number of viewers who had seen *Shoot*, to have to deal with Clairmonte's presence in it. And of course, the question never comes out straight, it always comes out obliquely like: "Why the black man in the film? Has this been thought out?" Or, in the form of assumptions such as: "Is he a professor at Berkeley?" "Is he teaching African studies or sociology?"

C: *In some ways those questions indicate there's a need for authenticity. My question about Clairmonte concerns what he said about identity, and I think that the issue of identity runs throughout all of your work. You've often talked about hyphenated people, and I'm interested if in any way that notion stems from your personal experience. Have you felt that people have tried to push you, of being a Vietnamese-American or Asian-American, or woman-filmmaker? All of these different categories is what Clairmonte points out to. In your works and writings you distinctly push away that tendency.*

I think you are quite right in pointing out earlier that there is a very strong tendency to begin with a psychological sketch like "What are your primary influences. . . ." [laugh] I would be very interested in learning about your particular experiences in Vietnam. Could you talk more about that?

T: I will. But again, for having been asked this question many times, especially in interviews for newspapers, I would link here the problematization of identity in my work with what the first chapter of *Woman, Native, Other* opened on: the dilemma, especially in the context of women, of having one's work explained (or brought to closure) through one's personality and particular attributes. In such a highly individualistic society as the one we belong to here, it is very comforting for a reader to consume difference as a commodity by starting with the difference in culture or background, which is the best way to escape the issues of power, knowledge, and subjectivity raised.

My past in Vietnam does not just belong to me. And since the Vietnamese communities, whether here in the U.S. or there in Vietnam, are not abstract entities, I can only speak while learning to keep silent, for the risk of jeopardizing someone's reputation and right to speech is always present. Suffice it to say that I come from a large family, in which three different political factions existed. These political tendencies were not always freely assumed, they were bound to circumstances as in the case of the family members who remained in Hanoi (where I was born) and those who were compelled to move to Saigon (where I grew up). The third faction comprised those involved with the National Liberation Front in the South. This is why the dualistic divide between pro- and anticommunists has always appeared to me as a simplistic product of the rivalry between (what once were) the two superpowers. It can never even come close to the complexity of the Vietnam reality. All three factions had suffered under the regime to which they belonged, and all three had, at one time or another, been the scapegoat of specific political moments. As a family, however, we love each other dearly despite the absurd situations in which we found ourselves divided. This is a stance that many viewers have recognized in *Surname Viet Given Name Nam*, but hopefully it is one that they will also see in the treatment of Mao as a figure and in the multiple play between Left and Right, or Right and Wrong in *Shoot.*

How I came to study in the States still strikes me today as a miracle. The dozen of letters I blindly sent out to a number of universities to seek admission into work-study programs . . . it was like throwing a bottle to the sea. But, fortunately enough, a small school in Ohio (Wilmington College) of no more than a thousand and some students wanted a representative of Vietnam. And so there I was, studying three days of the week and working the other three days at a hospital, in addition to some other small odd jobs that helped me to get through financially. As an "international student," I was put in contact with all other foreign students, as well as with "minority" students who were often isolated from the mainstream of Euro-American students. It was hardly surprising then that the works of African-American poets and playwrights should be the first to really move and impress me. By the sheer fact that I was with an international community, I was introduced to a range of diverse cultures. So the kind of education I got in such an environment (more from outside than inside the classroom) cannot be as rich as what it had been if I had stayed in Vietnam or if I were born in the States. Some of my best friends there, and later on at the University of Illinois were Haitians, Senegaleses, and Kenyans. Thanks to these encounters, I subsequently decided to go to Senegal to live and teach.

When I planned for university education abroad, I could have tried France (where financially speaking, education is free) instead of the United States. I decided on the United States mainly because I wanted a rupture [*laugh*] with the educational background in Vietnam that was based on a Vietnamized model of the old, pre-1968 French system. Later on, I did go to France after I came to the States, in a mere university exchange program. It was one of these phenomena of colonialism: I was sent there to teach English to French students [*laugh*].

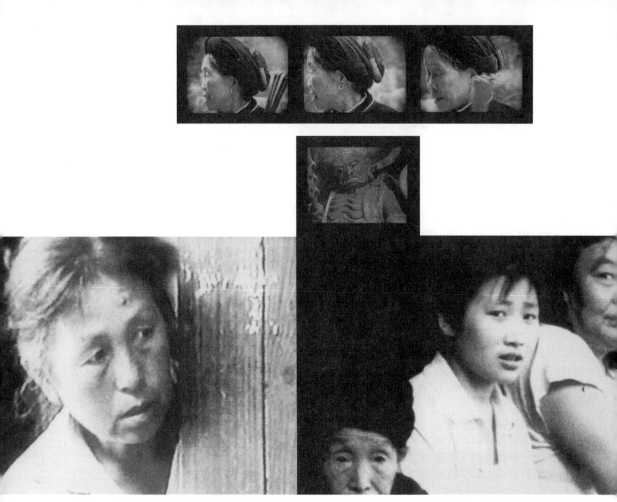

During this year in France I didn't study with any of the writers whose works I appreciate. Everything that I have done has always been a leap away from what I have learned, and nothing in my work directly reflects the education I have had except through a relation of displacement and rupture as mentioned. While in Paris, I studied at the Sorbonne Paris-IV. It was *the* most conservative school of the Sorbonne. But one of the happy encounters I made was with noted Vietnamese scholar and musician Tran Van Khe, who continues until today to shuttle to and fro between France and Vietnam for his research, and with whom I studied ethnomusicology. That's the part that I got the most out of in Paris. So you go to Paris, finally to learn ethnomusicology with a Vietnamese [*both laugh*].

C: *This throws my question about intellectual influences or ruptures the question [laugh]. In your works particularly your writings on anthropology, ethnography, and ethnographic films there's a critique of the standard, the center of rationality, the center of TRUTH. I think that critique is also shared by many anthropologists particularly in the post-structuralist tradition. Do you think that there is more possibility in ethnography if people use these tools? What do you think would be possible with reflexivity or with multi-vocality?*

T: Anthropology is just one site of discussion among others in my work. I know that a number of people tend to focus obsessively on this site. But such a focus on anthropology despite the fact that the arguments advanced involve more than one occupied territory, discipline, profession, and culture seems above all to tell us where the stakes are the highest. Although angry responses from professionals and academics of other fields to my films and books are intermittently expected, most of the masked outraged reactions do tend to come from Euro-American anthropologists and cultural experts. This, of course, is hardly surprising. They are so busy defending the discipline, the institution, and the specialized knowledge it produces that what they have to say on works like mine only tells us about themselves and the interests at issue. I am reminded here of a conference panel years ago in which the discussion on one of my previous films was carried out with the participation of three Euro-American anthropologists. Time and again they tried to wrap up the session with dismissive judgments, but the audience would not let go of the discussion. After more than an hour of intense arguments, during which a number of people in the audience voiced their disapproval of the anthropologists' responses, one woman was so exasperated and distressed, that she simply said to them: "The more you speak, the further you dig your own grave."

If we take the critical work in *Reassemblage*, for example, it is quite clear that it is not simply aimed at the anthropologist, but also at the missionary, the Peace Corps volunteer, the tourist, and last but not least at myself as onlooker. In my writing and filmmaking, it has always been important for me to carry out critical work in such a way that there is room for people to reflect on their own struggle and to use the tools offered so as to further it on their own terms. Such a work is radically incapable of prescription. Hence, these tools are sometimes also appropriated and turned against the very filmmaker or writer, which is a risk I am willing to take. I have, indeed, put myself in a situation where I cannot criticize without taking away the secure ground on which I stand. All this is being said because your question, although steered in a slightly different direction, does remind me indirectly of another question, which I often get

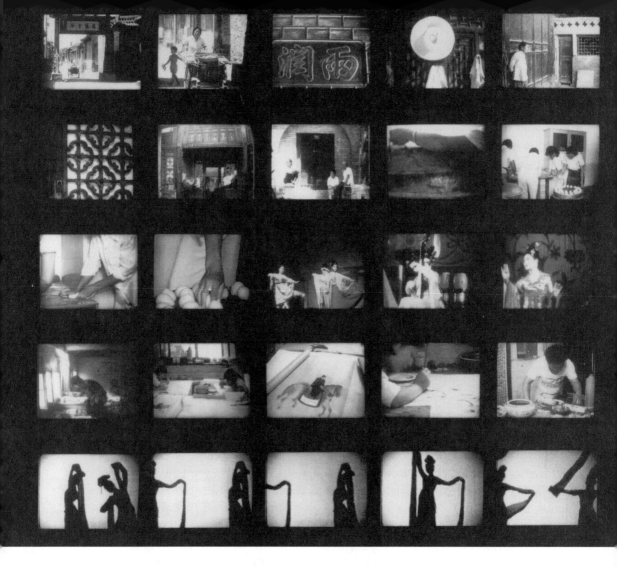

under varying forms: at a panel discussion in Edinburgh on Third cinema, for example, after two hours of interaction with the audience, and of lecture by panelists, including myself, someone came to me and said in response to my paper: "Oh, but then anthropology is still possible!" I took it both as a constructive statement and a misinterpretation. A constructive statement, because only a critical work developed to the limits or effected on the limits (here, of anthropology) has the potential to trigger such a question as: "Is anthropology still a possible project?" And a misinterpretation, because this is not just a question geared toward anthropology, but one that involves all of us from the diverse fields of social sciences, humanities, and arts.

Whether reflexivity and multi-vocality contributes anything to ethnography or not would have to depend on the way they are practiced. It seems quite evident that the critique I made of anthropology is not new—many have done it before and many are doing it now. But what remains unique to each enterprise are not so much the objects as the relationships drawn between them. So the question remains: how? How is reflexivity understood and materialized? If it is reduced to a form of mere breast beating or of self-criticism for further improvement, it certainly does not lead us very far. I have written more at length on this question elsewhere ["Documentary Is/Not a Name," October, No. 52, 1990] and to simplify a complex issue, I would just say here that if the tools are dealt with only so as to further the production of anthropological knowledge, or to find a better solution for anthropology as a discipline, then what is achieved is either a refinement in the pseudoscience of appropriating Otherness or a mere stir within the same frame. But if the project is carried out precisely at that limit where anthropology could be abolished in what it tries to institutionalize, then nobody here is on safe ground. Multi-vocality, for example, is not necessarily a solution to the problems of centralized and hierarchical knowledge when it is practiced accumulatively—by juxtaposing voices that continue to speak within identified boundaries. Like the much abused concept of multiculturalism, multi-vocality here could also lead to the bland "melting-pot" type of attitude, in which "multi" means "no"—no voice—or is used only to better mask the Voice, that very place from where meaning is put together. On the other hand, multi-vocality can open up to a non-identifiable ground where boundaries are always undone, at the same time as they are accordingly assumed. Working at the borderline of what is and what no longer is anthropology one also knows that if one crosses that border, if one can depart from where one is, one can also return to it more freely, without attachment to the norms generated on one side or the other. So the work effected would constantly question both its interiority and its exteriority to the frame of anthropology.

C: *This goes back to your previous point that being within is also being without, being inside and outside. I think this answers my next question, which is about how if naming, identifying, and defining are problematic, how does one go about practicing? I think that you are saying that it also opens up a space being right on that boundary.*

My next question turns from theory to practice now in filmmaking. Your writing has often been compared to performance art. Could you say that this is also true of your filmmaking as well in the four films that you have made so far?

T: I like the thought that my texts are being viewed as performance art [*laugh*]. I think it is very adequate. Viewers have varied widely in their approaches to my films. Again, because of the way these films are made, how the viewers enter them tells us acutely how they situate themselves. The films have often been compared to musical compositions and appreciated by people in performance, architecture, dance, or poetry, for example. So I think there is something to be said about the filmmaking process. Although I have never consciously taken inspiration from any specific art while I write, shoot, or edit a film, for me, the process of making a film comes very close to those of composing music and of writing poetry. When one is not *just* trying to capture an object, to explain a cultural event, or to inform for the sake of information; when one refuses to commodify knowledge, one necessarily disengages oneself from the mainstream ideology of communication, whose linear and transparent use of language and the media reduces these to a mere vehicle of ideas. Thus, every time one puts forth an image, a word, a sound, or a silence, these are never instruments simply called upon to serve a story or a message. They have a set of meanings, a function, and a rhythm of their own within the world that each film builds anew. This can be viewed as being characteristic of the way poets use words and composers use sounds.

Here I'll have to make clear that through the notion of "poetic language," I am certainly not referring to the poetic as the site for the constitution of a subjectivity, or as an estheticized practice of language. Rather, I am referring to the fact that language is fundamentally reflexive, and only in poetic language can one deal with meaning in a revolutionary way. For the nature of poetry is to offer meaning in such a way that it can never end with what is said or shown, destabilizing thereby the speaking subject and exposing the fiction of all rationalization. Roland Barthes astutely summed up this situation when he remarked that "the real antonym of the 'poetic' is not the prosaic, but the stereotyped." Such a statement is all the more perceptive as the stereotyped is not a false representation, but rather, an arrested representation of a changing reality. So to avoid merely falling into this pervasive world of the stereotyped and the clichéd, filmmaking has all to gain when conceived as a performance that engages as well as questions (its own) language. However, since the ideology of what constitutes "clarity" and "accessibility" continues to be largely taken for granted, poetic practice can be "difficult" to a number of viewers, because our ability in mainstream films and media to play with meanings other than the literal ones that pervade our visual and aural environment is rarely solicited. Everything has to be packaged for consumption.

C: *With regard to your films you've always been able to show that even what one sees with one's eyes, as you say in your books, is not necessarily the truth. My next question concerns Laura Mulvey's comment on language where any tool can be used for dominance as well as empowerment. Do you think that this is also true of poetic approaches to film?*
T: Oh, yes. This is what I have just tried to say in clarifying what is meant by the "poetic" in a context that does not lend itself easily to classification. As numerous feminists works of the last two decades have shown, it is illusory to think that women can remain outside of the patriarcal system of language. The question is, as I mentioned earlier, how to engage poetical language without simply turning it into an estheticized, subjectivist product, hence allowing it to be classified. Language is at the same time a site for empowerment and a site for enslavement. And it is particularly enslaving when its workings remain invisible. Now, how one does bring that out

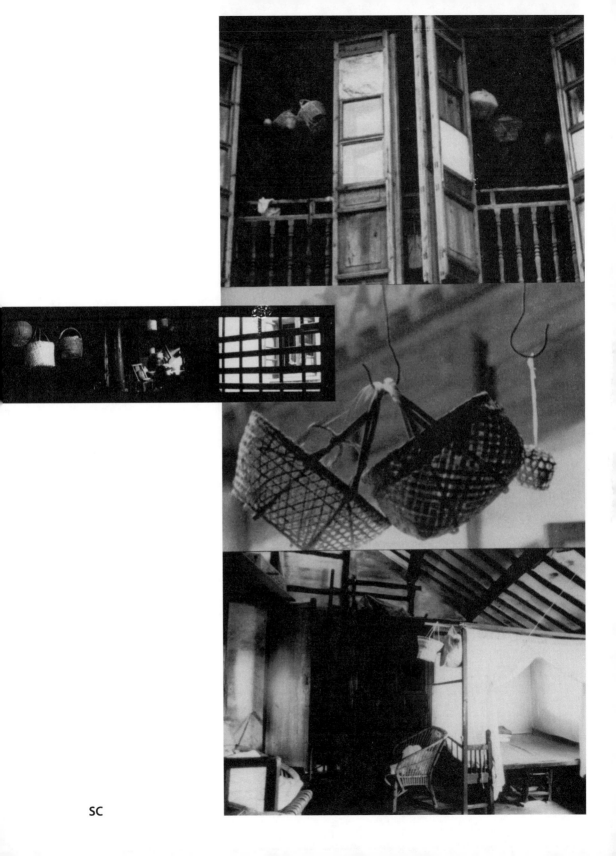

in a film, for example, is precisely what I have tried to do in *Surname Viet Given Name Nam*. This is an aspect of the film that highly differentiates it, let's say from *Reassemblage*. If, in the latter the space of language and meaning is constantly interrupted or effaced by the gaps of non-senses, absences, and silences; in *Surname Viet*, this space is featured manifestly as presences—albeit presences positioned in the context of a critical politics of interview and translation.

Viewers who take for granted the workings of language and remain insensitive to their very visible treatment in *Surname Viet*, also tend to obscure the struggle of women and their difficult relation to the symbolic contract. Hence, as expected, these viewers' readings are likely to fall within the dualist confine of a pro- or anticommunist rationale. Whereas, what is important is not only what the women say but what site of language they occupy (or do not occupy) in their struggle. With this also comes the play between the oral and the written, the sung and the said, the rehearsed and the non-rehearsed, and the different uses of English as well as of Vietnamese. So, if instead of reading the film conventionally from the point of view of content and subject matter, one reads it in terms of language plurality, comparing the diverse speeches—including those translated and reenacted from the reponses by women in Vietnam, and those retrieved "authentically" on the site from the women in the States about their own lives—then one may find oneself radically shifting ground in one's reading. The play effected between literal and nonliteral languages can be infinite and the two should not be mutually exclusive of each other. Everything I criticize in one film can be taken up again and used *differently* in another film. There is no need to censor ourselves in what we can do.

C: *I'm also intrigued by your works where you mention "talking nearby instead of talking about," this is one of the techniques you mention to "make visible the invisible." How might indirect language do precisely that (make visible the invisible)?*
T: The link is nicely done, especially between "speaking nearby" and indirect language. In other words, a speaking that does not objectify does not point to an object as if it is distant from the speaking subject or absent from the speaking place. A speaking that reflects on itself and can come very close to a subject without, however, seizing or claiming it. A speaking in brief, whose closures are only moments of transition opening up to other possible moments of transition—these are forms of indirectness well understood by anyone in tune with poetic language. Every element constructed in a film refers to the world around it, while having at the same time a life of its own. And this life is precisely what is lacking when one uses word, image, or sound just as an instrument of thought. To say therefore that one prefers not to speak about but rather to speak nearby is a great challenge. Because actually, this is not just a technique or a statement to be made verbally. It is an attitude in life, a way of positioning oneself in relation to the world. Thus, the challenge is to materialize it in all aspects of the film: verbally, musically, visually. That challenge is renewed with every work I realize, whether filmic or written.

The term of the issue raised is, of course, much broader than the questions generated by any of the specific work I've completed (such as *Reassemblage*, in which the speaking about and speaking nearby serve as a point of departure for a cultural and cinematic reflection). Truth never yields itself in anything said or shown. One cannot just point a camera at it to catch it, the very effort to do so will kill it. It is worth quoting here again Walter Benjamin for whom, "nothing is poorer than a truth expressed as it was thought." Truth can only be approached indirectly if one does not want to lose it and find oneself hanging on to a dead, empty skin. Even when the indirect has to take refuge in the very figures of the direct, it continues to defy the closure of a direct reading. This is a form of indirectness that I have to deal with in *Surname Viet*, but even more so in *Shoot*. Because here, there is necessarily, among others, a layered play between political discourse and poetical language, or between the direct role of men and the indirect role of women.

C: *That leads me to some questions that I had about your latest film because you choose Mao as a political figure and he is also one who uses language to play with. There is a direct quote in the film "Mao ruled through the power of rhymes and proverbs." I think this is a very apt and appropriate statement about the scope of the film. I'm curious as to "Why China?" You mentioned before about how your next project or your next film is a rupture from the previous one. So was going to China just a complete change from* Surname Viet?

T: It's not quite a rupture. I don't see it that way. Nor do I see one film as being better than another, there is no linear progress in my filmic work. There is probably only a way of raising questions differently from different angles in different contexts. The rupture I mentioned earlier has more to do with my general education background. So why China? One can say that there is no more an answer to this question than to: "Why Africa?" which I often get, and "Why Vietnam?" [*laugh*], which I like to also ask in return. Indeed, when people inquire matter-of-factly about my next film in Vietnam, I cannot help but ask "Why Vietnam?" Why do I have to focus on Vietnam? And this leads us back to a statement I made earlier, concerning the way marginalized peoples are herded to mind their own business. So that the area, the "homeland" in which they are allowed to work remains heavily marked, whereas the areas in which Euro-Americans' activities are deployed can go on unmarked. One is here confined to one's own culture, ethnicity, sexuality, and gender. And that's often the only way for insiders within the marked boundaries to make themselves heard or to gain approval.

This being said, China is a very important step in my personal itinerary, even though the quest into Chinese culture has, in fact, more to do with the relation between the two cultures—Vietnamese and Chinese—than with anything strictly personal. The Vietnamese people are no exception when it comes to nationalism. Our language is equiped with numerous daily expressions that are extremely pejorative toward our neighbors, especially toward Chinese people. But Vietnam was the site where precisely the Chinese and Indian cultures met, hence what is known as the Vietnamese culture certainly owes much from the crossing of these two ancient civilizations.

Every work I realized, has been realized to transform my own consciousness. If I went to Africa to dive into a culture that was mostly unknown to me then, I went to China mainly because I was curious as to how I could depart from what I knew of Her. The prejudices that the Vietnamese carry vis-à-vis the Chinese are certainly historical and political. The past domination of Vietnam by China and the antagonistic relationship nurtured between the two nations (this relationship has only been normalized some months ago) have been weighing so heavily on the Vietnamese pysche that very often Vietnamese identity would be defined in

SC

counteraction to everything thought to be Chinese. And yet it suffices to look a bit harder at the Vietnamese culture—at its music, to mention a most explicit example—to realize how much it has inherited from both China and India. It is not an easy task to deny their influences, even when people need to reject them in order to move on. An anecdote whose humor proved to be double-edged was that during my stay in China, I quickly learned to restrain myself from telling people that I was originally from Vietnam—unless someone really wanted to know (precisely because of the high tension between the two countries at the time). The local intellectuals, however, seemed to be much more open vis-à-vis Vietnam as they did not think of Her as an enemy country but rather, as a neighbor or "a brother." This, to the point that one of them even told me reassuringly in a conversation: "Well, you know it's alright that you are from Vietnam; after all, She is a province of China." [*Laughs*]

C: *So it reifies that power relationship. . . .*
T: Yes, right. . . . [*laughter*] On a personal level, I did want to go further than the facades of such a power relationship and to understand China differently. But the task was not all easy because to go further here also meant to go back to an ancestral heritage of the Vietnamese culture. I've tried to bring this out in the film through a look at politics via the arts.

C: *I think Wu Tian Ming's commentary in the film gives a very good description of the present state of the arts in China. I have another question. In your book* When the Moon Waxes Red *there is a chapter on Barthes and Asia. This is where you talk about his notion of the void and how it is important not to have any fixed notions of what Asia is supposed to be about. Previously you've just stated that this film* Shoot for the Contents *is precisely about that void, but one of the difficulties about creating a space where there can be a void is the fact that some people are unnerved by it, but [there is] also the possibility of reifying stereotypes, of reifying the notion of Asia as other or as exotic, or feminine, or mysterious. Do you think that this was something you had thought about carefully in making your film or in the process of making your film did this issue come up?*
T: It always does, with every single film that I have made. And the risk of having viewers misread one's films through their own closures is always there. The only consistent signs that tell me how my films may have avoided falling into these ready-made slots is the controversial and at times contradictory nature of the readings they have suscitated. But to say the space of the Void can reify stereotypes is already to reify the Void. Perhaps before I go any further here with *Shoot*, I should ask you what in the film makes you think that people could fall right back on a stereotyped image of China?

C: *Possibly when there are different scenes of China. In the film one cuts from one location to another, so you see scenes that are in northern China and then the next few frames you see Xishuanbana from southern China and they are all conflated as one image or representation of China. I saw this film with several China scholars and they were very concerned with the image of China as being enigmatic, as a space that is a void that cannot be defined, and the possible reification of China as a mystery.*
T: Are these scholars from here in the States or from China?

C: *These aren't Chinese friends.*

T: Maybe that is one difference worth noting, because as I mentioned earlier, there is no speaking subject that is apolitical, and sometimes I have had very different readings of my earlier films from Africans than from African Americans, for example, not to mention Euro-Americans. . . . Although generalizations are never adequate, and you will always have people who cross the lines. First of all, to take up the point you make about conflating the images from different cultures across China: The film has a structure that momentarily calls for this deliberate violation of internal borders, but other than that, this structure is devised precisely so as to emphasize the heterogeneity of Chinese society and the profound differences within it—hence the impossibility to simply treat China as a known Other. If you remember, it is at the beginning of the film, when Mao's concept of the Hundred Flowers is being introduced that you see a succession of images from different places in China. This is the very idea of the hundred flowers, which the visuals indirectly evoke. But as the film progresses, the cultural differences that successively demarcate one region from another is sensually and politically set into relief and never do any of these places really mix. The necessary transgression and the careful differentiation of cultural groupings have always been both structurally very important in my films, in *Shoot* as well as in the three previous ones.

As far as the Void is concerned, the comment certainly reveals how people understand and receive the Void in their lives. For some, "void" is apparently only the opposite of "full." As absence to a presence or as lack to a center, it obviously raises a lot of anxieties and frustrations because all that is read into it is a form of negation. But I would make the difference between that negative notion of the void, which is so typical of the kind of dualist thinking pervasively encountered in the West, and the spiritual Void thanks to which possibilities keep on renewing, hence nothing can be simply classified, arrested, and reified. There is this incredible fear of nonaction in modern society, and every empty space has to be filled up, blocked, occupied, talked about. It is precisely the whole of such an economy of *suture* [*laughs*], as film theorists calls it, that is at stake in this context of the Void.

Nobody, who understands the necessity of the Void and the vital open space it offers in terms of creativity, would ever make that comment (which is mystifying in itself as it equates void with enigma and mystery), because the existence of everything around us is due to the Void. So why all this anxiety? What's the problem with presenting life in all its complexities? And, as we have discussed earlier, isn't such a reaction expected after all when the authority of specialized or packageable knowledge is at stake? Among other possible examples, I would also like to remind here, that when the film opens with a remark such as "Any look at China is bound to be loaded with questions," that remark is both supported and countered by the next statement, which begins affirming "Her visible faces are minuscule compared to her unknown ones," but ends with the question: *"Or is this true?"* As in a throw of the dice, this casual question is precisely a point of departure for the film and the reflection on the arts and politics of China. It is later on followed by another statement that says "Only in appearance does China offer an ever-changing face to the world." So the knowable and unknowable are never presented as being mutually exclusive of one another.

A distinction that may be useful here is the one theorists have made between a "radical negativity" and a negation. The negation is what the negative, dualistic reading of the void points to, while a radical negativity entails a constant questioning of arrested representations—here, of China. This is where Barthes' statement on the stereotyped being the antonym of the poetic, is most relevant. There are a few immediate examples that I can mention (although specific examples never cover the scope of the issue raised, they just tell you about the single problem involved in each case) in terms of the choices I made in the film to prevent its readings from closing off neatly within the knowable or unknowable categories. Again, the question of language: The dialogue between the two women narrators features not only a difference in ideology but also a difference in the modes of speaking. Both modes can easily be mis/identified: one as the illogical, elliptical, and metaphorical language of poetry, and the other as the logical, linear, and dogmatic language of political discourse. If the film is entirely done with only one of these two languages, then the risk of it falling into the confines of one camp or the other is very high. But in *Shoot* you have both, and the narrators' dialogue is also punctured all along by the direct speeches of the interviews, or else by songs, which offer a link between the verbal and the nonverbal.

C: *Also by the text itself where you have English and Chinese characters as well as Confucius and Mao . . .*
T: Exactly. Sometimes, it is strategically important to reappropriate the stereotypes and to juxtapose them next to one another so that they may cancel each other out. For example, the fact that in the film the "Great Man" can be both Confucius and Mao makes these two giants' teachings at times sillily interchangeable. Such a merging is both amusing and extremely ironical for those of us who are familiar with China's history and the relentless campaigns Mao launched against all vestiges of Confucianism in Chinese society. The merging therefore also exposes all wars fought in the name of human rights as being first and foremost a war of language and meaning. In other words, what Mao called "the verbal struggle" is a fight between "fictions." The coexistence of opposite realities and the possible interchangeability of their fictions is precisely what I have attempted to bring out on all levels of the film, verbally as well as cinematically. If the only feeling the viewer retains of *Shoot* is that of a negative void, then I think the film would just be falling flat on what it tries to do; it would be incapable of provoking the kind of vexed, as well as elated and excited, reactions it did so far with its reception.

C: *You mention the viewer quite often and in another interview you once said that audience making is the responsibility of the filmmaker. Can you talk about who your viewers are, what audience, and for whom are you making a film if such a purpose exists?*
T: There are many ways to approach this question and there are many languages that have been circulated in relation to the concept of audience. You have the dated notion of mass audience, which can no longer go unquestioned in today's critical context, because mass implies first and foremost active commodification, passive consumption. Mass production, in other words, is production by the fewest possible number, as Gandhi would say *[laughs]*. And here you have this other notion of the audience, which refuses to let itself be degraded through

standardization. For, as Lenin would also say, and I quote by memory, "One does not bring art *down* to the people, one raises art *up* to the people." Such an approach would avoid the leveling out of differences implied in the concept of the "mass," which defines the people as an anonymous aggregate of individuals incapable of really thinking for themselves, incapable of being challenged in their frame of thought, and hence incapable of understanding the product if information is not packaged for effortless and immediate consumption. They are the ones who are easily "spoken for" as being also smart consumers whose growing sophisticated needs requires that the entertainment market produce yet faster goods and more effectual throwaways in the name of better service. Here, the problem is not that such a description of the audience is false, but that its reductive rationale reinforces the ideology in power.

The question "for whom does one write?" or "for whom does one make a film?" was extremely useful some thirty years ago, in the sixties. It has had its historical moment, as it was then linked to the compelling notion of "engaged art." Thanks to it, the demystification of the creative act has almost become an accepted fact: The writer or the artist is bound to look critically at the relations of production and can no longer indulge in the notion of "pure creativity." But thanks to it also, the notion of audience today has been pushed much further in its complexities, so that simply knowing for whom you make a film is no longer sufficient. Such a targeting of audience, which has the potential to change radically the way one writes or makes a film, often proves to be no more than a common marketing tool in the process of commodification. Hence, instead of talking about "the audience," theorists would generally rather talk about "the spectator" or "the viewer." Today also, many of us have come to realize that power relationships are not simply to be found in the evident locations of power—here, in the establishments that hold the means of production—but that they also circulate among and within ourselves, because the way we write and make films is the way we position ourselves socially and politically. Form and content cannot be separated.

Furthermore, in the context of "alternative," "experimental" films, to know or *not* to know whom you are making a film for can both leave you trapped in a form of escapism: You declare that you don't care about audience; you are simply content with the circulation of your work among friends and a number of marginalized workers like yourself; and you continue to protect yourself by remaining safely within identified limits. Whereas I think each film one makes is a bottle thrown into the sea. The fact that you always work on the very limits of the known and unknown audiences, you are bound to modify these limits whose demarcation changes each time and remains unpredictable to you. This is the context in which I said that the filmmaker is responsible for building his or her audience.

So of importance today is to make a film in which the viewer—whether visually present or not—is inscribed in the way the film is scripted and shot. Through a number of creative strategies, this process is made visible and audible to the audience, who is thus solicited to interact and to retrace it in viewing the film. Anybody can make *Reassemblage*, for example. The part that cannot be imitated, taught, or repeated is the relationship one develops with the tools that define one's activities and oneself as filmmaker. That part is irreducible and unique to each worker, but the part that could be opened up to the viewer is the "unsutured" process of meaning production. With this, we'll need to ask what accessibility means: a work in which the creative process is offered to the viewer? Or a work in which high-production values see to it that the packaging of information and of fiction stories remain mystifying to the non-connoisseur audience—many of whom still believe that you have to hold several millions in your hand in order to make a feature of real appeal to the wide number?

C: *You've answered on many levels but your last point draws attention to the state of independent art and experimental film here in the U.S. Could you comment on your experience with or inter- actions with those who try to categorize your work as documentary, as ethnographic, as avant- garde feminist, as independent. Could you talk about the process of independent filmmaking instead of more mainstream films?*

T: Independent filmmaking for me is not simply a question of producing so-called "low- budget" films outside the funding networks of Hollywood. It has more to do with a radical dif- ference in understanding filmmaking. Here, once a film is completed, you're not really done with it, rather, you're starting another journey with it. You cannot focus solely on the creative process and leave the responsibilities of fund-raising and distribution to someone else (even if you work with a producer and a distributor). You are as much involved in the pre- and the post- than in the production stage itself. Once your film is released you may have to travel with it and the direct contact you have with the public does impact the way you'll be making your next film. Not at all in the sense that you serve the needs of the audience, which is what the mainstream has always claimed to do, but rather in the sense of a mutual challenge: You chal- lenge each other in your assumptions and expectations. So for example, the fact that a number of viewers react negatively to certain choices you have made or to the direction you have taken does not necessarily lead you to renounce them for the next time. On the contrary, precisely because of such reactions you may want to persist and come back to them yet in different ways.

In my case, the contact also allows me to live out the demystification of *intention* in film- making. With the kind of interaction I solicit from the viewers—asking each of them actually to put together "their own film" from the film they have seen—the filmmaker's intention can- not account for all the readings that they have mediated to their realities. Thereby, the process of independent filmmaking entails a different relationship of creating and receiving, hence of production and exhibition. Since it is no easy task to build one's audiences, the process remains a constant struggle, albeit one that I am quite happy to carry on. Viewers also need to assume their responsibilities by looking critically at the representative place from which they voice their opinions on the film. Ironically enough, those who inquire about the audience of my films often seem to think that they and their immediate peers are the only people who get to see the film and can understand it. What their questions say in essence is: We are your audience. Is that all that you have as an audience? [*laugh*]. If that is the case, then I think that none of us independent filmmakers would continue to make films. For me, interacting with the viewers of our films is part of independent filmmaking. The more acutely we feel the changes in our audi- ences, the more it demands from us as filmmakers. Therefore, while our close involvement in the processes of fund-raising and distribution often proves to be frustrating, we also realize that this mutual challenge between the work and the film public, or between the creative gesture and the cinematic apparatus, is precisely what keeps independent filmmaking alive.

CHARACTER ZONE

with Gwendolyn Foster

A shortened version of this interview was first published as "A Tale of Love: A Dialogue With Trinh T. Minh-ha," in *Film Criticism*, Vol. XXI, No. 3 (Spring 1997) with the following introduction: *"Film and video artist Trinh T. Minh-ha has revolutionized narrative and post-narrative filmmaking with her films and videos, which displace the voyeuristic gaze of the traditional Western viewer and re-theorize the relationship between spectator, filmmaker, and performer. In her work, she has emerged as one of the most influential theorists, filmmakers, and composers of the postcolonial late-twentieth century. Trinh T. Minh-ha's works have been widely screened in the United States and abroad, and her writings have been published in several collections of critical essays and several volumes devoted to her work alone. . . . After Trinh T. Minh-ha released her most recent film,* A Tale of Love, *I interviewed Minh-ha in the spring of 199[6] on her work as an artist and critical theoretician, and more specifically on* A Tale of Love, *which is her first 35 mm narrative feature, although it remains, in many respects, as unconventional and uncompromising as her earlier works."*

Foster: A Tale of Love *transgresses the borders between narrative film and experimental film. I read it as a postmodern performative enunciation of a nineteenth-century Vietnamese poem,* The Tale of Kieu. *I was wondering how you might classify the film, if it even needed classification, and how those people who have seen the film are classifying it. It's been positioned as your "first narrative film." I am wondering how you feel about that.*

Trinh: Yes, no doubt, the term is not mine and I don't consider *A Tale of Love* my first narrative film. One can see it as a natural extension of my previous work or one can see it as a different kind of performance, a new trajectory in directions similar to those taken by my earlier films. These have always resisted the reductive binaries set up between "fiction" and "documentary" films.

F: *Exactly. This brings up the issue of categorization.*

T: I've made it quite clear, in the writings and interviews published, that "experimental" is not a genre and "documentary" does not really exist since everything goes through fictional devices in film. Rather than reverting endlessly to these established categories, I would prefer to speak about different degrees of staged and unstaged material, or about different spaces of resistance—such as that of enriching meaning while divesting it of its power to order images and sound. I work with the tension these differences raise and the way they creatively or critically contaminate each other. This largely accounts for the difficulties my films kept on encountering in many exhibition venues, including those that claimed to support multicultural, independent or alternative work. The films I've been making confront people in their normalized need to categorize, to make sense and to know all. It is in this vein that A *Tale* also continue to frustrate easy consumption, although it certainly differs from the earlier films in its work process. For example, none of my previous films was scripted before the shooting, while in this film almost everything was scripted ahead of time, albeit in a form that was unusual for the actors and the crew.

F: *What was different about the way you worked with the actors and the crew on this film?*
T: The script I gave them had all the scenes, with storyboards that showed all the camera positions and movements, the framings, as well as the lighting designs for each scene. But there was no set order to these scenes. I wrote them both as a director and as an editor, so I was leaving room for the scenes to build on one another during the shooting and to find their own order in the editing phase. Since I did away with sequential order, the planning was at times very frustrating for the key organizing members, including the script supervisor, who is traditionally the continuity person. Working with a large crew in a limited time frame makes it almost impossible to improvise and to operate outside of the framework of traditional narrative filmmaking, in which the specific division of labor tends to become at times too rigid and constraining. However, most of the "department heads" of our crew had more than one role to fulfill, and I can't complain, for everyone did their best. The actors, for example, tried very hard to make their lines, their roles and their precisely blocked movements all seem natural despite the quite "unnatural" nature of the script. I myself had to shift ground radically and to conceive of the space of 'improvisation' other than as a space of spontaneous formation. The openings offered should then be found elsewhere than in the dichotomy of unscripted versus scripted work.

F: *I could feel there was a real tension there between performative forms and for you I was wondering how it felt to be directing in a different genre even though I know it is a genre coming out of your own tradition. I wonder whether you felt in some ways more free and in some ways more restricted in the making of* A Tale of Love? *I'm also very interested in the spare acting style of the film.*
T: In some ways it was certainly more restrictive. I used to have a crew of three to six people maximum, and I was doing most of the work myself, including the camera and sound recording in remote rural contexts. Of course, the time was then my own. I shot whatever I saw or whenever the moment was ripe for shooting, and I shot it the way I looked at it through the lens. The indeterminate waiting and looking without using the camera was always part of the shooting. As soon as you start working with a crew of seventeen to twenty-five people, the space

for improvisation is extremely limited. Because of budgetary constraints, I cannot afford, for example, what Godard can sometimes afford; which is to keep the actors for a certain length of time (he mentioned three to six months) so that he can experiment and write his script from day to day as he works with them. Or, for example, the case of Robert Bresson, who asks his "models" (or nonactors) to perform their actions mechanically and exactly as he wants them, and then to repeat them until they no longer notice what they are doing. It is in this mechanical precision that he feels he can capture something "raw" (*matiere brut*) of his models. These are two examples of ways of reconceiving acting which I love, but I had a different situation and very different constraints. These constraints actually added to the film because I learned to work with them and use them to my advantage.

Since experimentation cannot be equated with improvisation in this film, I was compelled to come up with a space of acting whose slightly denaturalized performance would hit on very different sensitive chords in our reception of narrative film. It was more a question, let's say, of performing with the unknown (what is veiled to our ear and eye) within the appearance of the known. As Alikan, the photographer, states in the film, here everything is performed for and nothing is really unforeseen. Freedom in a highly constructed space is a different kind of freedom, much less obvious and hence more easily mistakable for its absence. Yet it is in this space that elements unknown to myself, to the actors, and to the end product emerge in the moments of production and reception. Performing here is not simply evaluated according to how well an actor can portray the psychology and behavior of a given character. The intent is not to capture "natural" or naturalistic acting, but rather what remains unforeseeable, for example, when one works with precision on duration. The overall choreography of the camera movement in the film is both exact and exacting. There is not a single shot-reverse-shot in the entirety of this feature-length film, and what may become perceptible when the camera stays fixed on two actors in dialogue, or when it passes by them in a mercilessly slow movement, is the very space of viewing and of performing. When the actors' slightest self-consciousness becomes visible to the spectators, the latter may also become conscious of their own moment of consumption of the "spectacle" or of the "scene" acted on screen for them, and hence the general discomfort that some of them have voiced.

F: *That seems to me to have an added resonance within the context of this film because it is about a woman who is a model who, of course, makes her living performing for the camera. This film is a meditation on performance and dramatic narrative and I think it breaks open the boundaries of what we think of as performing, especially in performing a poem, and in a sense re/performing the poem* The Tale of Kieu.

T: Right . . . yes, exactly.

F: *One could read the film in the traditional linear narrative fashion in the sense that it centers on a heroine, Kieu, who is in love with writing. She's investigating* The Tale of Kieu *and working as a model. But as the film unfolds I see her as a figure who moves across narrative zones. I notice she often gazes at the viewer and speaks to us as she actively deconstructs the very narrative that she embodies. Towards the middle of the film, the narrative drive of the film becomes, I think, less*

and less linear. I'm referring to those sections of the film in which we watch her writing and day-dreaming, thinking about writing and fantasizing. She makes me think of a "character zone," a very fluid zone in the sense that Bakhtin used that phrase. Do you see her that way?

T: To some extent, yes. Most of the experimentation done in narrative film focuses on the structure of the narrative. Very few filmmakers have worked on the space of acting to stretch the dimension of the narrative. Marguerite Duras certainly contributed to calling into question narrative form by doing away with acting as impersonifying and representing. Her complex use of the voice (voice-over, voice off screen; external, nonpsychological, non-interiorized voices) in relation to blank spaces, love, death, desire, and their absence-presence through the actors' bodies is unique. It is more common among experimental filmmakers to rupture the narrative by using nonlinear time and space, for example. But for me, since I've always worked at the limits of several categories, several narrative realms at once, it was not a question of simply rejecting linearity or doing away with the story.

F: *Yes, here we have many stories, many Kieus, many levels of narrative and at the same time there really is no unified narrative. It's very pleasurable to experience.*

T: You start out with a story and you realize, as it unfolds, that there's not really a story in the film. The thread created moves forward crisscrossed and interlaced by other threads until it breaks with its own linearity; and hence, a story is told mainly to say that there is no story—only a complex, tightly knit tissue of activities and events that have no single explanation, as in life. Of course, a number of viewers tend to catch immediately onto the relationship between Kieu, the protagonist, and Alikan, the photographer, because what they see above all is a conflict between genders, cultures, economical and political positions (boss/employee, subject/object). The ideology of conventional narrative is, as Raul Ruiz puts it, based on the globalized central conflict theory; a theory that rules over both the film industries of the world, and the political system of the U.S. as a dominant model nation. Fortunately, however, for other viewers and myself, there is no real conflict in *A Tale*. Not only is the relationship with Alikan merely one among the three visualized in the film, but there are also many relationships other than the ones people tend to follow, especially those not dependent on actors and dialogues. These dialogues are further not real dialogues; they are written as story spaces that are peculiar to each role designed, and despite their close interactions, they maintain their independent logic—not good versus bad logic, but only *different* ones.

Here the notion of fluid "character zone" raised in your earlier question is very relevant. I am thinking more specifically of the movements of the characters across dream states and reality on film. I could talk in dichotomies and say they are the landscapes of a person in love: internal and external, past and present, mythical and historical, literary and filmic. I could also see these movements as inscribing a multiplicity of narrative threads and narrative interfaces. An example is the night scene (in an industrial setting) toward the end of the film when Kieu is speaking to a man wearing a raincoat and a hat, whom we do not recognize as Alikan until either the last line of the scene or until we see Kieu, in the next day shot, waking up (in Juliet's court) and uttering his name with surprise. The same day shot with Kieu drowsing off (in Juliet's court) is seen somewhere toward the beginning of the film. So many things have happened in the film during this lapse of time that a multitude of questions may be raised as to both the nature of that night scene (is it a nightmare? a fantasy? a memory?), and the nature of the events that came before it (Was she telling herself stories all this time? Or was the daydream dreaming her?). No single linear explanation can account for these narrative interfaces in which performer and performance, dreamer and dream are constituted like the two sides of a coin. One cannot say that she's simply moving in and out of fantasy and reality, but rather, that it's a different zone we are experiencing.

F: *I really like that sense, as a viewer, of falling into that zone because it's undescribable and it makes you want to see the film again and reexperience the cracks and fissures in narrative and character. One thing I was really interested in was the implications you make between writing and loving and the connection to the rhetoric around women as writers. In particular, I was thinking of some the writing that's been done on women writing such as Cixous' "The Laugh of the Medusa." But it also made me rethink Plato's* Phaedrus. *Both speak specifically about writing, creativity and romantic love and how they're very much tied to the body. I was struck by the ways in which you embodied and enacted these ideas in the film.*

T: Well, I'm certainly glad to hear that because although I do not expect viewers to be receptive to all the layers involved (I myself am still learning to articulate them), the fact that some viewers, yourself included, may be familiar with feminist writing would make all the difference. If we don't center our attention on this so-called conflict in the film, then there's a whole other narrative layer that may come to the front. This is the realm in which Kieu as a character shuttles between more than one identity and contributes to the afterlives of *The Tale*. No matter how non-illustrative the relation is, the film's present-day Kieu who lives as an immigrant in the States and does research on the *Tale of Kieu* is also embodying the poem's nineteenth-century Kieu who sacrifices herself for love; and in that sense, she partakes in the life experiences of the thousands of all-time Kieus whom her Aunt mentioned in the film. As with my other films, there are many forms of reflexivity in *A Tale*. And working with them means opening up to the possibility of engaging with infinity within the very finiteness of a constructed film space. Kieu's self-reflectivity and reflexivity constantly shift; the question is not simply that of doubling—one looks into the mirror and sees a reflection or a double of oneself—but that of one reflection reflecting another reflection to infinity. Kieu's reality here is in tune both with the boundless (or bounding) reality of love, and with the radically reflexive nature of cinema and writing. It is this notion of shifting interface and reflection, with no side passing for the original, that really interests me, especially in working with voyeurism in this film.

F: *Exactly. Another aspect that I really liked about the film is that it obviously is a meditation on the discourse around the politics of women and objectification and voyeurism. I felt engaged in a performance that was voyeuristic and at the same time it made me critique that place of voyeurism. This must be provoking all sorts of responses from audience members. Can you talk about that?*

T: Yes, I think the film can offer the viewer a unique entryway when it is placed in the context of feminism; but if you miss that entryway, there are other possible ways to enter *A Tale*, because the voyeur has appeared quite prominently in a number of writers', filmmakers', and artists' works. One can look at the entire history of narrative in terms of voyeurism—how different forms of voyeurism are deployed in order to sustain narrative power, and how they are made to go unnoticed, especially among spectators who, unaware of their complicity as screen voyeurs, want to be "convinced" of what they see. In other words, the production of (unacknowledged) voyeurism and the consumption of realist narrative continue to feed on each other. It's difficult for me to tell right now how audiences are viewing the film because it has just been released. From the screenings I attended, its reception already oscillates between a very high discomfort and a very intense, enthusiastic response.

F: *Maybe even a bit of both. I do remember being a bit shocked that you were taking on what can be shown and what cannot be shown. I mean, we're looking at women being looked at and with all the discourse around women being reduced to their object status of to-be-looked-at-ness, this is transgressive space that you're moving into. And it is clearly an important counterstrategy. It made me constantly ask myself questions such as, how is Trinh, as a woman filmmaker, different in her representation of voyeurism? How can I negotiate the many different narrative strands of the film with relation to the questions of voyeurism and spectatorship? How is this moving the discourse of pornography further beyond rigid moralistically defined ideals?*

T: Right. Actually the film does not really show nudity in a pornographic way and it doesn't have any lovemaking scenes, for example. As a filmmaker has said it before, when it comes to lovemaking, all actors just start looking like all other actors. The way lovemaking scenes are realized on film remains quite homogenous throughout the history of commercial narrative. Knowing my background, it was perhaps unavoidable that you would ask how a feminist treatment of voyeurism could be different, but this is one way of approaching A *Tale*. I would say that the viewers' discomfort with it so far seem to be less easily locatable, perhaps because it takes time to articulate this discomfort, and there is no consensus among them as to where or what disturbs them. Some think it's the script; some, the lack of plot and unified storyline; others, the acting and the actors; and others yet, the explicit recognition of themselves being voyeurs.

A number of comments did focus on the acting, which some spectators find "hard to look at," "self-conscious," "distant," "odd," or they simply "didn't like the style." Informed viewers have invoked similarities with the films of Straub and Huillet or of Duras. What seems striking in the more negative comments is the fact that viewers differ markedly in their opinions about the specific actors: the one they really have problem with is definitely not always the same (and this applies 'democratically' to all five main actors of the film), and yet each sees in *one* and only one particular actor the unequivocal source of their discomfort. Several viewers have also divided the acting, in accordance with the setting and the characters, into three levels: more natural, more stylized, and in between the two, mid-stylized. By these comments, it seems likely to me that the viewer is uncomfortable, because she or he feels some of the acute moments when the actors themselves are self-conscious. This is exactly what I was aiming for, although I was not sure what the exact outcome would be. A *Tale* does not fall squarely into the kind of film whose actors' deliveries sound deliberately *read* or monotonously flat because the artifice is clearly exposed as such. There are a number of films that work in that direction, Yvonne Rainer's films, for example. In my case, I was experimenting with different effects in a slightly different space, and I didn't want the scripted lines to sound distinctly "read." I would let the actors try to make their deliveries as naturalistic as possible because I knew that the "dialogues" I wrote could not be entirely naturalized, although what ultimately resists being naturalized remains undefined, and hence fascinating to me.

F: *So, in a sense, you're acting as an ethnographer of performance itself. You are problematizing acting styles in ways that, I think, are questioning naturalistic expression. I'm thinking particularly of moments such as the moment when Kieu tells the photographer, Alikan, that what he really wants is a headless body. There's a sense, as a viewer, that she may not have said that (in any sort of reality or narrative construct that we're used to) but she's saying it in this film and there's something disconcerting and abstract about the way she says it. I was wondering how the actors felt about delivering these lines. It must have been discomforting or maybe funny at points.*
T: Actually, it seemed that what bothered them, or at least in the case of Dominic Overstreet, the actor who played Alikan, was not so much the lines themselves as the way they were written. He would repeatedly try to change the sentence slightly to make it more colloquial. At one point, I asked him to tell me on camera the problems he was having with the script. And he said that, for him, it's not really written in American English, the kind of English he's used to, it's written in British English. I was tickled to hear that because there is some truth to such a remark; I was taught English in Vietnam by British or British-educated teachers, and furthermore, both my personal assistant and the script supervisor speak British English. Yet I know the problem is not only to be found there; it also has to do with how, when and where (in what situations) the lines are supposed to be delivered. Alikan is working with a model who "resists not having a head" and whose uncommon lines can leave both actors slightly at a loss as to finding the right tone and reaction for them.

F: *It's very active and self-reflective in a wonderful way. I was astounded and found great visual pleasure watching the scene in which the male photographer is blinded. I don't know if that was an allusion or not but it reminded me of something that nineteenth-century women writers do to heroes in Gothic romances. I was particularly thinking of* Wuthering Heights. *I wondered if you were making an allusion or if I was just looking for connections to women writers?*
T: This is a wonderful reading. But for me, this was not a direct allusion because when I was creating it, I was doing it quite intuitively in relation to the whole context of voyeurism. It is important to note that in the scene you mentioned, both the man and the woman are blindfolded. The people working with me and some of the viewers who have seen the film have been really struck by the fact that for the first time neither can *see* each other.

F: *Yes, that scene is certainly one of the most transgressive images. It certainly destroys subject-object positionality as we know it. It is a staggering image. To look as a voyeur at both male and female who are bound with the veil feels oddly powerful yet self-conscious because we find ourselves surprised in our active gaze.*

T: On the one hand, it is a rupture with domination by eye because only touching prevails here in the relationship between the man and the woman. And the sense of touch is all the more heightened when sight is hindered. Vision and visuality have long been the domain in which male mastery is exerted, while the eroticism of the female body through touch is an area some feminists have reappropriated and theorized at length. On the other hand, one can say that the film is a trap for the gaze, and the gender line is not so clear-cut. Except for Alikan, the other voyeurs in the film are women, and as you mention, the scene we discuss is one among those designed to call attention to the viewing space or to the spectator's own voyeurism. (If the actors can't see each other then, who's looking at them?) Finally, it is not just looking at the scene, but being put on the spot—the voyeur's encounter with his or her own gaze—that has the potential to make the viewers most uncomfortable, even though they may not recognize this and would rather find fault elsewhere.

F: *Perhaps because it's a new experience. We have not really seen images like this before, images that place us in a different kind of subjectivity with relation to our sense of voyeuristic pleasure. There are other scenes that have a resonance in their ability to render pleasure and discomfort in the viewer. I'm thinking of the scene in which Kieu takes the veil and puts it on herself. That was something that seemed out of the ordinary.*
T: Which one was that?

F: *At one point Kieu seems to be taking a lot more control of her situation. She goes to work at the photo studio and there she takes the veil and places it on herself. I think this happens immediately before she gets verbally assertive towards Alikan. She tells him he really only wants a headless body. This is interesting because immediately before this, when she entered the studio, she was flipping through a book of pornographic images of women. She's taking more and more of her body back, of her subjectivity back. I was very drawn to those scenes and also to the scenes between Juliet and Kieu in which they discuss the history of fragrances and love. I know there's some critical writing about fragrance and film and eroticism. For me, this is wrapped into the idea of writing and performing and romance.*
T: In filmmaking the two senses that are most privileged are the visual and the auditive. The other senses, like touch, taste, and smell, are extremely difficult to solicit without falling into the order of meaning. One hears or looks at a film; but one can only literally touch, taste, and smell a piece of celluloid. Perhaps it is necessary to return here to the notion of film as event rather than as mere spectacle; instead of centering on the screen, the viewer's experience of film is also engaged in the extra-screen space—that is, the movie-house space or the immediate environment. I am reminded here of a practice, in Japanese Kabuki theater, devised to heighten the audience's sensual experience of the play: with the extended notion of the stage and the many uses made of the passageway(s) *(hanamichi)* that runs through the audience, a play can, for example, have its "fragrant stamp," or its performance can be intensified at specific moments—such as at the last rites of a funeral, when the body of a beloved character is placed in a palanquin with a bowl of incense, and as the palanquin is carried through the audience, the theater is slowly filled with the mournful fragrance.

This is quite a challenge for a filmmaker to convey through film, and unfortunately, one cannot aim for similar effects with today's movie-theater audiences (a public, for example, largely not initiated to the language of fragrance and its precise use in different rites and ceremonies), since most of us tend to minimize the sense of smell as well as the tools to qualify it. However, it seems that the time when, despite oneself, one becomes oversensitive and one's senses are wildly awoken, is when one is in the state of being in love. Since the film enacts this state, with all of its lucidity and its silliness, it is important to dedicate a large part of the film to the importance of smell. Andy Warhol wrote a whole chapter on smell and perfume. What interests me is that you find perfume in all women's magazines. So in the film it is through Juliet, who is the editor of a women's magazine, that one hears about how stories and fragrances can be created. When you see how inventively the creation of perfume in these women's magazines is written about, it's just really amazing. It's a whole unexplored area, for me, of creativity.

F: *It is. It's another area where women have had a voice. Something that's very powerful that maybe we haven't recognized as such. It was really funny that immediately after seeing your film I just happened to be flipping through* Interview *and there was an ad that said "green is now," and, of course, it reminded me of the section of the film when Juliet talks about green and how green is sexy right now.*
T: Yes, very much [*laughs*].

F: *Another thing I am really interested in is the use of multiple voice-overs in the film. In the context of the discussion of disembodied knowledge and embodied knowledge, Kieu has a number of very active voice-overs presented within the context of the discourse of eroticism of headless women. I thought that was really funny and poetic. The film repositions the voice-over in search of a multiplicity of subject positions for Kieu. Was this choice made as you edited the film or had you had those sort of ideas in your mind before you wrote it?*
T: The lines Kieu read in voice-over were written with the script from the start (albeit on separate sheets to be recorded at the postproduction phase), but I only decided on how and where they came in when I built the soundtrack. As I've mentioned earlier, the order of these lines was not set in advance; the film took form during the shooting and changed again during the editing. It was in the process of going from one form to another that the different designations of the voice-overs (the verse singing can be another indirect voice) emerged.

F: *One thing that should be noted is how the character Kieu stresses that the importance of Kieu (of the poem) lies in her resistance. Kieu forces us to think about the daily acts of resistance that so many women, particularly women who are read as "victims," perform. I find it significant that Kieu is walking along in front of stripclubs when we hear her voice-over reflecting on the morality of Kieu. What she says in her voice-over is as important as her actions. By walking along beside the sex workers she gestures toward a rereading of sex worker as "non-victim," and she claims space in a transgressive performative act. It makes us uncomfortable, yet it is also pleasurable. The film reminds the viewer that both are subject to a duality in terms of norms of proper female*

behavior. Within the context of the film, I get a sense that The Tale of Kieu *is one of the most culturally significant poems of the Vietnamese diaspora. Why did you choose this poem?*

T: It is a very important poem for the Vietnamese. I already touched on the figure of Kieu in one of my previous films, *Surname Viet Given Name Nam.* It was then placed in the context of mythical, historical and current women of resistance of Vietnam. Kieu's passion-driven life, marked by unremitting misfortunes and sustained by her sacrifice, endurance, and loyalty, has become the allegory for Vietnam's destiny. But if in *Surname Viet* the film's reflexive dimension is gradually brought out through a number of devices and more explicitly toward the end in the comments of a voice-over, in A *Tale of Love* you don't have the explicit staging of any voice that stands outside "the story" to comment on it; in other words, there's no visible metadiscourse. That is discomforting for viewers who expect, as with my other films, to be informed more directly of the moves involved by a voice that pulls out from the film to reflect on it. I decided in this film that I would have none of that, so meaning, form, and structure evolve out of the tension between the filmmaker, the subject and the viewer. As we've discussed, the reflexive dimension is both diffused in every narrative layer and concentrated in the treatment of voyeurism. This seems to have made filmviewers even more uncomfortable.

Voyeurism is here further coupled with the aesthetics and politics of the veil. Of course, the veil and the headless female body are reflected in many ways in the film, both literally and metaphorically. Linked to voyeurism, it is framed in a whole fabric of relations. First, Alikan's love for everything that is veiled, including the *look* of the model. That the model should not "look back" while he shoots is certainly nothing new in photography (the naturalistic formula we all abide by when shooting on location is: "Don't look at the camera, just go on with your activities as if I'm not there"). Looking back is also commonly experienced as an act of defiance, a perilous act that is historically feared for its ability to divest the Master of his power to possess and control. In many parts of the world, the unveiled woman is still the one who moves about "undressed." She who looks back rather than hide or be oblivious to her body and her sensuality is bound to provoke. And here we paradoxically link up with the other dimension of the veil: if Alikan uses all kinds of veiling devices, it is both to dispossess the model of her power to gaze and to prevent the image from falling into the realm of pornography (in pornography, the nude often looks straight—provocatively and invitingly—at the camera). The veil is oppressive, but it can also become a form of resistance—hence the importance of the scene in which both man and woman are blindfolded, and the necessity of also having women voyeurs in the film, as mentioned. The way we all partake in the politics and aesthetics of veiling is complex and often paradoxical.

The scene that you mentioned, having Kieu walking outdoors, is therefore very important for me personally. I've noticed, for example, how in certain Middle Eastern cultures—this should apply to other contexts across nations as well—the streets continue to belong to men while the domestic realm remains women's domain. But this being said, I don't want to reiterate that binary opposition between public and private space as developed in certain feminists's work. Let's just say that since the street belongs to men, women have a different space. Whenever they go out into the street, for example, they only go out at certain hours of the day. The unspoken rule is that they shouldn't be seen too much in daylight and they shouldn't be seen at night, it should be somewhere in between. This is what I've noticed in Yemen. Between 4 and 6 p.m. the women come out in the street completely veiled. This is the time of the day when their veiled silhouettes are seen moving outside against the walls of the houses. So, for me, the scenes of women walking outdoors at night, the scene of Kieu walking by herself and a later scene in which the camera pans along with women outside on the street, is also a way of gesturing toward the whole history of veiling. The dark of night itself is a veil. Even in progressive societies, a woman is not supposed to be alone, outside in the street if she comes, let's say, from a well-to-do family or if she has been "properly educated." The night belongs, actually, to those of the margins: sex workers, drug users, secret lovers, and so on. So the scenes of women walking outdoors can be liberatory, but they also remind us of the values of society and the restraints it puts on women in their movement. For how is a woman walking aimlessly alone at night looked at?

F: *Even up until very recently Western women weren't allowed to travel without a chaperone with them. That brings me back to the issue of the veil. In this way, the veil is actually someone who travels with you. The idea of taking back space is something that's important to me in a feminist performative context. I read Kieu as* devenir femme *or "becoming woman" in the sense that French feminists use this term. Kieu has flashbacks or fantasy sequences in which she sees herself as a child. I was wondering if you were staging a primal fantasy of mother/daughter recovery or if you were doing something different here?*

T: No, actually, I was thinking more in the context of the tale or the poem itself. This poem opens with a very famous scene in which Kieu goes to a temple. There she suddenly sees a desolated tomb and weeps over it, moved by the fact that nobody's really tending this tomb. At night, the woman who was buried there comes back to her. It is through this woman that Kieu becomes very conscious of the fact that she's a talented woman and that women with many talents are bound in life to suffer. She begins remembering signs from her childhood that foretold how she was going to suffer in life because of her beauty and her talent. The scene where you first see Kieu as a child, precisely alludes to that part of the poem. But it can also work on another level, especially for people who are not familiar with the poem. For example, it can evoke a physical and psychological response. In these memory scenes, the child is seen near a body of water. The element of water which runs through the film is very important; here, it is visually tied to the image of Kieu playing naked freely and to her memories of home. This is again an intervention of women's space. Another device that I use here is the voice-over, the brief voice of memory. Instead of using a standard device such as a dissolve, or a color change to signal the passage to fantasy or memory, I simply have her name being called by an offscreen voice. To hear one's name called by an ex-lover or by a relative can trigger unexpected memories or it can lead one to an immediate change of zone. One can enter and exit a zone by a smell, a sight or a sound. So, yes, the scenes with the little girl introduce the viewer to the relation between mother and daughter. This is tied to another thematic thread in the film between tradition and modernity; between the Vietnamese in the diaspora and the Vietnamese "at home" in Vietnam. The link between the two can be both moving, warm, affectionate, and tense, burdensome, problematic, but either way, one cannot simply dispense with it. The mother figure is always present.

F: *This is a little bit off the topic but I feel like you're maybe making a connection in this film between how people of the supposed "Third World" are lumped together in a space called "the Other" and the way in which romantic narratives break down our notions of an undifferentiated Other. Kieu is very much like Kieu of the poem and yet unlike her. And Juliet is also like and unlike Juliet of* Romeo and Juliet. *I like the way that you challenge categorizations. You challenge the notion of the Other just as you challenge our notion of self. This revolves around a questioning of the constructions of our essential love tales.*

T: This is your own reading of the film. The film is made to invite such readings so I'm very happy to hear them. But, I would rather say that I was working with multiplicity. The letters Juliet receives indicate, for example, that even though people know Juliet does not exist, they still address their letters to "Juliet, Verona, Italy." The same can be said of *The Tale of Kieu*, which every Vietnamese remembers, whether it serves the official narrative of the Vietnamese government or whether it is carried on by the people who have exiled themselves from Vietnam. The verses have long become part of our daily expressions. Instead of saying how bad a person is or of describing what kind of a person one is dealing with, for example, one just invokes the name of one of the typical characters in *The Tale* to communicate precisely what one means. It happens with all classes of people. Because the poem is written in a rhythm taken from Vietnamese proverbs and folksongs, people remember it very easily and they quote its verses as popular sayings. But, for me, what remains most amazing is the fact that a whole people identify the destiny of their country with the love story of a woman. Kieu personifies Love. This is the link to Juliet and Romeo, for Kieu is not one heroine, not one character but, as it is stated in the film, she's numberless. There are as many Kieus as there are talented women across generations whose destinies Kieu's story has typified. Kieu is a multiplicity, just as Juliet is a multiplicity. So, for me, it's not so much a question of opposing the West to its Other or of correcting the gap between the self and the other. "Juliet" is a name that stands for a person, at the same time, she's a character in the film whose fiction evolves from another fiction, she's a symbol for love and a love site that is radically a multiplicity.

F: *I guess what I was speaking of was the whole discourse of the essentialized notion of woman. Which would mean that "Third World" stories cannot be spoken of in context of "First World" stories. And you really break that down by aligning* Romeo and Juliet *with* The Tale of Kieu. *I mean not in distinct categorizations, but in ways that you can, at least, see parallels because, of course, people always quote* Romeo and Juliet. *People constantly refer to that love story, which, of course, has such a tragic ending. I'm drawn to the scene in which Kieu questions Juliet about her conception of romance. She says to her, "The problem with your love story is that it invariably ends in death or in marriage. You see, I prefer the less definite ending of* The Tale of Kieu *which ends in love and friendship." I was very interested in the idea of female love and friendship in the film. The friendship between Kieu and Juliet is foregrounded. Their relationship is just as important, if not more important, than the relationship between Kieu and Alikan.*

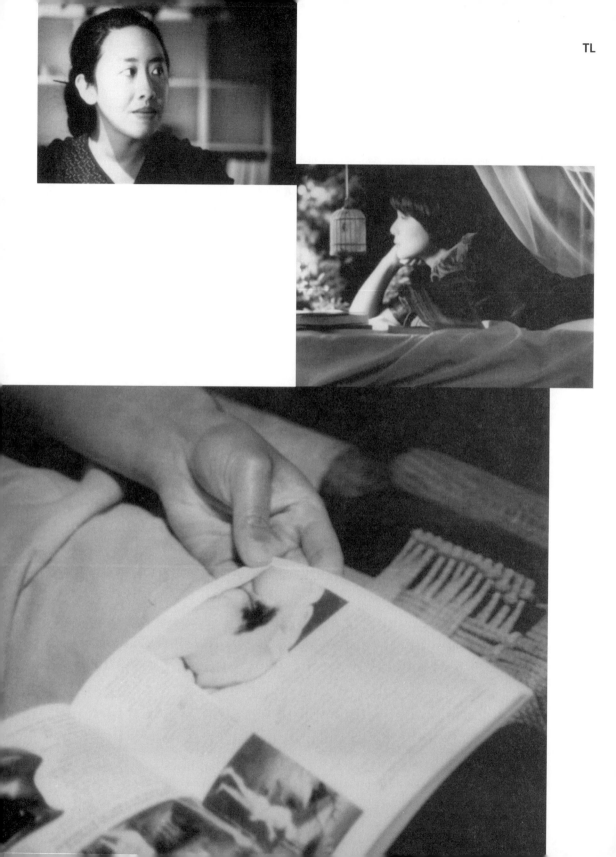

T: Yes. I am happy you noticed that because, for me, the relationship between Juliet and Kieu is decisive. They move through different levels. At the beginning it might seem as if it their friendship is based on an editor-writer relationship, which is usually inequitable. Some viewers have rightly seen Juliet as a mentor or elder sister in relation to Kieu, who is younger and an emergent writer. But, for me, I think they are equals in the sense that the performance space and the acting trajectory allow them to develop as equals.

F: *It's a relationship usually based to some extent on money and privilege, but in the film, it's a more even exchange; it is a fantasy relationship. The two women spend great amounts of time together and Juliet speaks from her heart in ways that are really interesting to me. In other words, she says the unexpected. Going back to what you were talking about, in reference to new ways of looking at acting, I'd like you to talk about that section of the film in which Juliet does a performative dance. It was very funny and unusual and self-reflective. It is during the scene when they're talking about* Romeo and Juliet. *Juliet stares directly at the camera and begins dancing. Her dance seems to be out of context. I was wondering why she suddenly begins doing those dance moves?*

T: Yes, there's one aspect of my film work which comes out very strongly with certain audiences and totally gets lost on other audiences. And that's the whole dimension of humor. To some extent it may be because of cultural difference. When *Surname Viet Given Name Nam* was premiered in San Francisco, half of the audience, the Vietnamese-speaking audience were laughing at certain parts while the English-speaking audience laughed at other parts. They were almost never in synch, and some of the viewers were disoriented by that because they had the feeling they had missed out on something. Language seemed to have played a role here. But then the reception of *Shoot for the Contents* [a film in which English is heard but no subtitles are used because a translator speaks and appears on screen for most of the Chinese interactions] was similarly disparate; it varied from audiences that were extremely serious and totally silent throughout the film to audiences in which people were laughing and giggling all along. The same thing seems to be happening with *A Tale of Love*. The very first small audience I showed it to—mostly programmers—were deadly serious with it, but when *A Tale* had a sneak preview with hundreds of people, they were largely laughing and giggling throughout the film. Many media makers and consumers tend to reduce humor to its most evidently comical connotation (the sitcom kind of jokes), but humor can be subtle, barely present, yet disturbing, tragic, anarchic, dissociative, moving and deconstructive, and so on. Humor is not only in what makes one laugh, but it also lies in one's ability to respond (with humor). With humor, things always leak, and as you've seen, there is definitely a dimension to my films that is quite silly and that has no logical explanation.

F: *And that's part of our whole notion of romance. There's a whole playful, illogical part of it that we can't quite explain.*

T: Exactly. Many aspects of the film invite immediate experience and exceed rational interpretations. The dance sequence to which you refer is one of these nonrational events. In addition to the mental relations woven in the film, there is this other dimension that is extremely important for me—in this film more than any other film—because I know the difficulty that I'm creating for the viewer. It is this dimension, especially when it clicks with the conceptual dimension, which I find most stimulating to work with—I don't have an adequate name for it; we can call it plastic, sensual, nonverbal; something that involves the poetry of the stage image, the language of color and space, or the sense of painted rhythm. It is mind-boggling to note how certain audiences are highly sensitive to it while others are totally oblivious to it. In the scene you mention, in response to Kieu's speculation on love, death, friendship and happy ending, Juliet makes up a dance. Here, I asked Juliet to come up with a mixture of different kinds of dances, and to improvise on her own. It's not simply a dance that fits in one of the known categories that people usually have in mind. It may look like It, but it's not quite It. . . . Rather, it's a dance that comes out as a physical response to what she's hearing, that is, an intellectual reflection. It's a form of resisting the closure of meaning, whether in movements of the body or of the mind.

F: *Another thing I wanted to talk to you about was something I'm interested in because I'm a filmmaker and so is my husband. We have collaborated both in film and performance art, so I'm always interested in the nature of collaborative partnerships. Also, I have written a great deal on women filmmakers, many of whom worked with their husbands in collaborative partnerships. Often one or the other tends to get sole credit for a project because when one codirects, when you give credit to both partners, often someone chooses who'll get the credit. Usually it is a film historian, curator, or archivist. Usually they'll choose the male partner. For example, Elizaveta Svilova codirected many of the Vertov films, and there are many, many other examples. I want to make sure that it is known that Jean-Paul Bourdier codirected this film with you and that you often codirect. In Western culture, we tend to see the artist as an individual and we have trouble with the notion of any kind of collaborative art. I wonder if you would talk a little about the nature of collaboration and your experience of collaboration?*

T: "Collaboration" is a term that is highly esteemed among marginalized groups because there is a tendency to value collaborative work over individual work in contexts where it is almost impossible to escape the burden of representation. There is a number of film collectives (of which the more successful ones are Sankofa, or the Black Audio Film and Video Collective in the U.K., for example), through which a certain rejection of individual authorship may thrive. I think it's a wonderful concept but most of the time what happens in collaborative situations is that you end up having one person who directs and then the other people work with the director. Some of the solutions that collectives have come up with is to have different members direct different films. But in the process, it usually becomes clear that you only have one or two directors on whom the members of the collective rely to "give direction" to a project. So, unless one works with someone on equal ground, but whose areas of strength are radically different from one's own (even when situated in the same field), one cannot really talk about collaboration. Collaboration happens not when something common is shared between the collaborators, but when something that belongs to neither of them comes to pass between them. This is what happens between Jean-Paul and I when we work together.

Not only did Jean-Paul take part in all of my previous films—he was consistently the co-producer, production designer or art director—but we have also written two books on African architecture together. For the films shot in Africa, even though he didn't have to design any specific setting, we selected all the sites together. He did research for all the locations and had a major role in deciding at which site we would choose to film. He really has an eye for that. We have different strengths, though. Every time we encounter the same experience, we have totally different approaches to that experience. For example, during the shooting of *Naked Spaces* or of *Shoot for the Contents*, Jean-Paul's relation to movement and space was certainly that of a passionate "eye feeler" that sees and feels almost everything at once. As an architect, he apprehends space in its overall expanse and potential; receives it instantaneously in form, volume, plan, and structural capacities; and visualizes it effortlessly from a bird's-eye view. A building is immediately envisioned as time, age, trace. My relation to space and the built environment is almost the opposite—blind, fragmented, temporal, circumstancial—I don't see through walls and roofs, so I move around unknowingly, and I'm always at a loss. Both relations are necessary in filmmaking. So in A *Tale of Love*, which Jean-Paul codirected, in addition to fulfilling all the other tasks mentioned, we decided to divide our roles accordingly: Jean-Paul would direct according to the script. Being the one who actually facilitated all the action during the shooting, he was the "true director." I was a very quiet director because I needed the space both to take in and to pull out from the whole process. The execution of ideas is not all that there is, of course, to filmmaking; but one easily forgets that, especially when one is working with some twenty-five people and everybody wants the director's attention. The fact that we codirected the film really allowed me to have that space, to reflect on what was going on in the production process and how that might act on the editing and postproduction of the material. More than with my previous films, Jean-Paul's production design and lighting design in A *Tale* play a decisive role in bringing out what I've discussed earlier as being most stimulating: the sensual, nonverbal, unmeasurable dimension of the film.

TL

SCENT, SOUND, AND CINEMA

with Mary Zournazi

Interview conducted by Mary Zournazi for her book on "the art of foreignness," *Foreign Dialogues* (Sydney, Australia: Pluto Press, 1998) with the following introduction: "*Scent, Sound, and Cinema is about the tracks of passion and the languages of love. How do we experience love, loyalty, and betrayal between and within different languages and cultures? How do we translate these experiences? Trinh T. Minh-ha is a writer, filmmaker, and composer whose recent film,* A Tale of Love, *explores the politics of passion.* A Tale of Love *is [partly] set in San Francisco in the 1990s and tracks a Vietnamese-American woman named Kieu who is writing about the impact of the Vietnamese national poem* The Tale of Kieu *in the Vietnamese communities of the diaspora. It resonates and reverberates the experience of cultural otherness, the multiple layers and relationships to love, language, and writing. I talked to Minh-ha about passion, cultural translation, and the fidelities of love. And, the aesthetics and poetics involved in the production of her writing and film texts. This conversation took place through various encounters and modes of communication. We met in Sydney, talked in Melbourne, linked up via the telephone in Sydney and California, December 1996. The conversation traveled through the static on the phone line and the interrupting sound of telephonic beeps. And, the time it took to correspond and rework this interview piece. In this process, I asked Minh-ha about the politics of interviews: how we create the text as we speak, write, and translate through different mediums.*"

Trinh: The interview has a special mystique in the world of documentary making, and I've dealt with this at length in some of my film work. What is again at stake in the politics of interviews is the unavoidable question of truth and information. The news media has had a definite influence on the popularized use of the interview, both as a form of oral witnessing and as a privileged access to personalities. Interviewees' words presented in their immediacy and with their effect of vérité often serve to authenticate the planned message, to lend legitimacy to what remain largely opinions and judgments; or else, to reveal a more private, more direct—if not entirely unmediated—self-image of a public figure (an image in his or her own words).

But most of the time neither the roles of the interviewer and of the recording device, nor the transformative process involved in making the interview accessible are dealt with integrally. The posture of objectivity is still all-pervasive, and the prevailing media strategy of covering "the two sides of the story" is a good example. Such a strategy is not only naive (suggesting that reality, events and ideas can be captured unmediated and reduced to a question of pros and cons), it also denotes a politically and creatively weak stance (as it remains unaware of its own formation and politics in its desire to pass for neutral, unbiased information). Although multivocal in its appearance, the final product as a whole lacks a voice of its own, and ultimately what you have is simply a noncommittal stance, more preoccupied with correct formulas than with social inquiry. The politics of the interviewer are not absent here. They are quite evident in the way the mesh of questions and answers is constituted; but this is usually not engaged with, and hence the work remains caught in the binary machine that governs the programming of information in the media.

This is not to say that the art of staging an interview or of participating in a "public dialogue" is not important. There are many ways to break away from the mass communication mold. I myself have structured the book *Framer Framed*, of filmscripts and a number of interviews on my work, which probably accounts for this more recent tendency among interviewers to open our conversation with a question on the interview itself. Some have, for example, voiced their concern about its legitimizing function in the interpretation of the work at issue. And, of course, it is a well justified concern, because the interview's effect is by nature totally fabricated, and the interviewee is conventionally either a typical layperson, an expert, or else a celebrity. But again, much of how one enters and engages in a conversation, of how an interview unfolds and is received also depends on the kind of space opened up, and on the interviewers' attitude, the way they situate themselves in the event they've initiated.

With the best intentions, interviewers sometimes get caught in their own framing, being too eager to proceed with their list of preformed questions, regardless of what the answers given are and where these are heading. In other words, they rarely commit themselves in their questions, which are often based on answers they have already assumed ahead of time. Hence they are more anxious to carry out the task as planned than to engage in the conversation itself. In the end, even though the voice of knowledge may be deferred to the interviewee, and unless one remains inventive and exerts one's skill to make detours so as not to get caught in mere "answering," as interviewee, one can only speak within a preconceived role and a forced itinerary. Self-explanation and self-image each have their own problem, and it's a problem of translation. As I've suggested in my film *Reassemblage*, the space opened up should not be that of "speaking about," but rather of speaking with or nearby. How can one speak of oneself and one's work in the plural? How can the interview remain a site of multiplicities?

Here I would come back to a definition of the interview that stands out more clearly in the French terms *entrevue* and *entretien*: *entrevue* from the verb *(s')entrevoir*, to see one another, to meet; and *entretien* from the verb *entretenir*, to maintain, prolong, or cultivate. Most relevant is the sense of mutuality and betweenness (*entre* or inter) and the sense of sight and touch—*voir* (*vue*) and *tenir* (*tien*), to see and to hold. In the use of *entrevoir* and *entrevue*, what is often implied is an inkling of something imprecise, partially or suddenly perceived, a sounding of something to be discovered, a foresight, a view forward. While in the use of *entretenir* and *entretien*, what is connoted is the idea of holding together, of nourishing, of maintaining someone in an affective state. When this term is applied, for example, to a woman (*une femme entretenue*)—usually a lover or a prostitute—it refers to a liaison, a relationship that is kept living through both emotional and financial support. These are just a few examples of the range of possibilities of meaning that define the interview and can act on it creatively. We have here a situation in which something happens that is at the same time a seeing and a holding, a sighting, and a sounding, a feel or a view between and forward. Further, this encounter with different thoughts, discourses and events yields what one can call a "third ground"; one on which something comes to pass between the two of us, which is not necessarily something that passed between the interviewer and the interviewee. It's a relationship, let's say, between energies, between languages, or between words, concepts, and concerns.

In this sense, the reading of one's work, or more precisely, my reading of my work has never been that of a single individual. It does not exist *before* the making, hence it's not determined only by my intentions. It's built with both the unpredicted interactions of the different elements in the work among themselves and from the many readings and feedback that viewers have advanced in response to the work. Such a reading is always densely populated by other people's readings, and yet it constitutes a voice of its own because everything holds together with precision when one works with resonance rather than seeks to settle meaning. The notion of translation that interests you is quite relevant here, because through interviews a form of autotranslation is generated, a spectral relationship to the work takes on a life of its own, which while "failing" to do what the "original" does, contributes to the life-as-afterlife of this work.

Just as people read a translated work because they cannot read the original, or they read both original and translation for further insight, they may come to a work first through reading an interview or they may read interviews so as to get a different flavor of the work. It's not only a question of accessibility and interlinearity that is involved here, but also of the life-afterlife cycles that allow a work to travel and live on. The interview has its own place and that's why I guess complex thinkers of our time like Derrida, Deleuze, Foucault, Virilio, Barthes, Cixous, Lispector, and Kristeva all have their interviews published in book form. It is by the translation that their texts literally survive and are kept in circulation.

Z: *The issue of translation is crucial because it is a move from the oral to the written word. So there is a whole network of different conceptions of language, because clearly as you write, as you transcribe and edit you are changing the language. When you read an interview it is highly edited and transformed, and I think that side of it gets lost in terms of the reader. In the sense that an interview is worked over (even though it is meant to capture a "moment" between two or three people), so there is a way in which it is transformed, its original mode alters and it circulates in a different way—to a different audience. Maybe that's what you mean by an afterlife. . . .*
T: What you have just mentioned here—the process of transforming a text, the passage from what is heard to what is read, or else the realization of something that lies between the spoken and the written sign—offers many possibilities when one takes into full consideration the condition and nature of a published conversation. Why, for example, the need to record the event?

Why the printed word rather than the audiotaped word? When the term translation is used in its [Walter] Benjaminian "afterlife" sense, not in the distinction he made between translation and poetry, but in the way he radicalizes its impossible relation to the original, one can talk about many forms of translation that are not only relations between one language and another. The relations between linguistic, extralinguistic, and nonlinguistic events are infinite and each generates a set of problems of their own as one reality passes into another—"lived reality" as distinct from film, dance, or writing reality, for example. So, if the transformation necessitated by the published interview is another form of translation, a mode simply different from the original mode, then the loss you imply is no mere loss.

It's an art of losing without losing. The difficulty is to keep this edge in the *trans*formative process. One cannot, for example, merely point a video camera at a passionate strike and expect the footage obtained to provide the viewers with anything but an impoverished, if not entirely boring experience of the live event. One can only avoid this by working precisely on the translation of this event into the video medium—that is, on what video can specifically offer that allows one to grasp the event differently while recreating it in its full intensity and multisensorial dimension. The same applies to the processes involved in the published interview. If video is commonly used as a mere recording device, interviews are often considered to be a means for the mere retrieval of interviewees' spontaneous words. There is still a widespread tendency to sanctify spontaneity, and media publications abound with this type of interview, which are fine to listen to but do not have much to offer to the reader.

What cannot be taken for granted is the acute difference between speech and the printed text. If you lose the subtlety of body intercommunication and the rich fabric of audiovisual inflection of the live conversation, which the transcribed text misses or cannot retrieve, then what do you offer the reader in its place? Words used to appeal to a listener differ in their impact from those used to sustain the interest of a reader. What appears irritatingly useless, flat, repetitive, redundant, or ridiculous when written down, has a very definite function when spoken aloud. Roland Barthes wrote lucidly on these "scraps of language" and on the trap of scription. But as with Benjamin's translation, if the transcribed text loses in relation to the live event, it also makes the original lose its "sacred" character by making the transcriber and editor aware of its "inaccuracies" (the forced coherence, the quick assumption, the unintelligible reply, the non-articulated argument, the misstatement, the disjunction, the mending, the posing, in brief, the conventionality of Old Spontaneous Me, which I've questioned in *Woman, Native, Other*). As we've seen, an interview involves the sighting and sounding of something imprecise to be discovered. A "bad" translation is then one that remains oblivious to the necessary becoming of the text, to this third ground, where what comes through asserts itself as neither speech nor writing.

For me, one of the most challenging aspects in the passage from word (spoken) to word (written) or from image to word has to do with what I call a certain "residue." When you deal with translation and the critical relation between realities, you are always caught in a gesture that is at once blind and lucid: On one level you can all too clearly show or communicate through the power of the image and the word; on another, you realize acutely that in showing, you actually cover what you try with infinite skill and care to lay hold of. The word only serves

TL

to block out another reality, while the image, even and especially with its photographic authority, constantly veils in exposing. No matter how much you want to give away, something "sits back" and remains, that may not be seen but is not necessarily invisible. It's impossible to put this residue into a form of direct communication, and the power of the image and of the word is not simply to be located in what is visible *or* invisible, intelligible, *or* unintelligible. I've always had to work with this predicament in my films, but it is in the last one, *A Tale of Love*, that such predicament becomes more manifestly a salient feature of the film.

Z: *A Tale of Love is about a kind of translation, although it is not necessarily just about this. But, nonetheless, it has various modes of transformation and translation in relation to the story. How does the notion of residue and image, the different elements and components of that make up the story emerge in the film.*

T: I am reminded here of the distinction the late film critic Serge Daney made between the *visual* and the *image*. Here, the visual refers to seeing what is given as legible, so that one can talk about the visual of a newspaper, for example, even when there's no photos in it. Whereas the *image* refers to an experience of vision that inherently involves *alterity* (or otherness). Everything is overwhelmingly visual around us today, and as Daney suggested, we're heading toward societies that know more and more how to *read* (to decipher or to decode), but less and less how to *see*. He used such a distinction to offer, among others, a complex political analysis of the media's Gulf War, but one can say more generally that working with and on the image has become more and more rare. I find this work more likely to survive in films from Eastern Europe, Japan, the Middle East, or certain other parts of the Third World than I find it in the States, for example.

It's difficult to work in the realm of the image when the widespread mode of production and reception only knows the visual. My experience with a good number of programmers', viewers', and reviewers' reactions to *A Tale of Love* is very telling in this respect. A "critical" or more truthful treatment of love requires that one deals with its banalities and clichés, displacing them rather than hiding or glossing over them. But what tends to go unseen is that which can radically not be said or shown directly: The built-in capacity of certain images to become other than what they seem to be, the *con*-text and *alter*-text that come with the very legible use, in *A Tale of Love*, of certain typical details and events in the film. In other words, the common tendency is to see in exclusive terms, original or copy, loyalty or betrayal, but not in both at the same time. So that to be "critical" often means to point out, from a safe place, to what is wrong in the state of things. Whereas for me, it means mainly to work with freedom. The gesture of pointing outward carries with it that of pointing inward, to oneself, and vice-versa, and hence there's no safe place from which to voice criticism.

The *image* always runs the risk of being reduced to the *visual* in the reception of critical work. Many viewers have had problems, for example, with what they read as "typical," "familiar," "too explicit," "so recognizable," "something we already know," which some locate in the visuals of *A Tale of Love*, and others in its specific dialogues or verbal events. Still other viewers—perhaps we should call them "seers"—immediately *see* what in the images here is given and yet does not give itself *up* to sight. They immediately take in the images' self-other dimension and have managed to verbalize with great subtlety and accuracy what comes with, but is not given as legible in them. Of course, the difficulty with a film categorized as "narrative feature" is that mass media-trained viewers come to it expecting story line, action, dialogues, and actors—areas with which I have worked quite critically. What often goes unseen by these viewers is the multiplicity of languages within the film—such as the languages of lighting, of setting, of color, of music, of movement (not only the camera movement or the movement between images created in editing, but also the movement within the image). These nonverbal components of the image strongly affect viewers, whether they recognize them or not, but what continues conventionally to dominate their viewing/reading of the film are its all-too-legible elements. Obviously, for these viewers, my films have, at least at first sight and hearing, very little to offer.

Since things constantly shift in the realm of the image, where fidelity of representation and of meaning have only a limited role, it is necessary that the relationship between what is seen and what is heard not be made uniform in my films. Although tightly woven in the fabric of the film, the verbal texts are treated as only one among many other events; or let's say as an action, a character, a performance of its own. They have a precise role, but they are not central to the making of meaning, nor are they used to consolidate meaning. On the contrary, by their sparseness (as in my early films) or excess (as in the last three films) they often serve to undermine meaning and to bring about a state of non-sense or of over-sense where contraries mate. Likewise, the image "shows" rather than directs, decorates (as with stereotypes and clichés), or illustrates a message. There is a lot to absorb and nothing to decipher in the images of A Tale of Love, for these don't function to advance any plot nor are they subject to a central story. Usually "image seers" are not only highly responsive to the plastic-musical dimension of this film, they're also sensitive to the tight interactions of its verbal with its nonverbal components.

Z: *I want to pick up on the notion of performance here, the different languages and components that make up the film. There is a line in the film that says, "narrative is a track of scents passed on from lovers to lovers" and that is very interesting in terms of storytelling and modes of narrative; that stories do have these other elements, sensuous components—like a language of the body, a language of rhythm, a language of passion. I think these elements often escape the ways in which we understand narrative—but also how we understand love to a certain extent.*

T: I work mainly in terms of resonance. This whole preoccupation with the sense of smell in A Tale of Love, which is quasi-impossible to render in film, is certainly related to the notion of residue and resonance. What interests me is not the love story—which I differentiate from the story of love—but the state of being in love: a state in which our perception of the world around us radically changes. Love can awaken our senses in an intense and unpredicted manner. It can open the door to an *other* world never experienced before, while literally blinding us to the familiar world of reason, of common logic and of everyday practicalities. The spell of a lover's fragrance, the smell of certain places, certain cities, certain things related to the beloved is so powerful that it can induce a state of trance and of madness quite incomprehensible to those who are not in love. When a forgotten scent hits you, you never know where it leads you,

TL

what it will do to you; and as a character in the film said, "by the time you realize it, it's too late. You're hurled into the dark corridors of buried memories. And you walked around crazed, feeling like a murderer again." Each scent unfolds with it a whole narrative track, whose details emerging wildly, in an apparently random way, allow the narrative to take shape effortlessly. The sense of smell is continually said to be the sense of memory and of imagination.

Odor can attract or repulse just as a story of this kind can spellbind or repel, depending on the state in which one is when one receives it, or more specifically here, on whether the eye/ear looking at the image is one in love, one that sees/hears beyond the screen of the legible. It is through odors that one intimately takes in or rejects the Other, and smell, like residue, resists direct (verbal) communication. Commonly associated with mud and refuse, residue connotes something of no value and no use, to be discarded. But, as mentioned, residue also means deposit, sediment, something that persists in remaining behind. In our modern societies where odors are repressed and everything is deodorized, it is hardly surprising that the sense of smell is devalued and regarded as inferior because it is supposedly subordinated to the emotions. The line you quote was inspired by the poet and ecologist Gary Snider who wrote, "Narrative in the deer world is a track of scents that is passed on from deer to deer." This reminds me of a comment by a Chilean economist when he saw my film *Reassemblage*. Describing the movement of discovery and the unexpected, fleeting character of the images, he said "It's looking like a deer. I feel like a deer looking around." I've had many similar comments from viewers about the ephemeral quality of this film and the freshness of its looks, but his comment is striking in its imagery. For me, what is condensed in this image given in response to other images is the animal sense of sight, sound, and smell all together.

The becoming animal is both regressive and progressive. Smell can betray us, but it is also our most faithful detecting ability. With the devaluation comes the rehabilitation of the "lower senses" (touch, taste, and smell) in the production of knowledge. While Freud links the repression of smell to man's break with the animal in the civilizing process, Nietzsche vindicatively declares: "All my genius is in my nostrils." In addition to the definite role the olfactory continues to play in social (race, class, gender, age) discrimination, there is also a long aesthetic and spiritual tradition associated with it. It is worth mentioning here the controversial reactions I've got from viewers across genders to the sections dealing with perfumes in *A Tale of Love*. Some said the verbal treatment of smell is what works best for them from the script; others were particularly enraptured by the visual setting of the perfume sequences; others yet viscerally hated this very part in the film, a reaction they attributed either to the text or to the actors' performance. There is a general tendency among the latter to scorn the relation between the female and the sense of smell, or between women and intuitive knowledge. Which is understandable. But as I mentioned earlier in relation to love, it's not a question here of censoring, hiding, or excluding in order to present a correct image of women in love. I find it more important to work with clichés to unsettle clichés.

While writing the script of *A Tale of Love*, I deliberately went into women's magazines to learn the rhetoric of perfumes, not only because Juliet, the character in the film who loves through smell, is editor of a women's magazine, but also because fragrance is the area of creativity in which women have excelled. In my reading of the nineteenth-century poem, *The*

Tale of Kieu, from which the film takes its inspiration, the olfactory world consistently merges with the musical world. It is with the link I make between the creation of perfumes and that of love narratives, or more generally, between the creations of sound, scent, and image that today's commercial rhetoric of perfumes is both displayed and displaced in the film. The power of smell to move us beyond the rational is also the power resorted to in spiritual contexts to purify the senses. For example, it is common practice to use perfumes and incense during prayers. Chinese and Japanese incense connoisseurs have a perfect expression for their subtle activity: They do not smell, but rather "listen to incense." In their curative, creative, and spiritual powers, both sound and scent can facilitate access to altered states of consciousness and the passage from the material to the immaterial. Each fragrance has specific resonances, and the ability to "scent out" is the ability to resonate with scents. In saying narrative is a track of scents emitted and transmitted from lover to lover, what is involved is not only the passion—since passion here is first and foremost an effect of cinema, which may reveal itself everywhere without showing itself in one specific location—but also the performance-as-performance of passion, its mise-en-scène, its condensation and vaporization, which constitute the politics and aesthetic of the film.

Scent, sound, and cinema are all experiences of transience. No matter how strong and persistent their impact can be, fragrances are volatile, and sounds do not last. Paul Virilio spoke of cinema and its universe of light-in-motion in the terms of an aesthetic of disappearance. With this peculiar link between sight, sound, and scent, we are here very far from the confines of emotions commonly conveyed by the relation between women, animal, and the sense of smell. So no matter how silly, banal and stereotypical one's love relationship can be, the person one loves always remains unique, and being in love always has the potential to open oneself up to new realms of consciousness. Benjamin wrote about translation as aiming for that single spot where the echo is able to give, in its own language, the reverberation of the original work. Critical film work calls for critical reading, which requires that viewers activate the film the way performers play a musical score. For Barthes, the reduction of reading to a consumption and the inability to set the text going, in collaboration with the writer or maker, account for the "boredom" that many experience in the face of the modern text or of the experimental film. This is where love comes in again, as I've suggested earlier. If one is available to love, one has this capacity to activate things, and one is open to the translatability of the film—a feature inherent in certain works, in their radical ability to yield a multiplicity of readings.

Z: *The love relation that you are signaling between the text and the reader also links to issues about how you love, as you have said elsewhere, you do have to love "the object of your study." And what is important in the film is that it has various love relations running through it. It is about a Vietnamese American woman, her experience of exile, and her rewriting of a tale of love,* The Tale of Kieu *but it also locates the fraughtness of love. I am thinking about this love relation in terms of cultural analysis and feminist theory—where that kind of love relation to others, to cultural others' sometimes signals there isn't a relationship in a way. That is, the relationship between feminist theory and the ability to kind of activate or understand other types of love if you like, or other people's modes of being in the world.*

T: I think of myself and my work as a continuum in which everything is linked and in constant motion. Certain links are more articulated than others because I've thought about them more or I have encountered them more often in audiences' responses. Other links are less evident; they remain in the background, non-talked about. They emerge by accident in the processses of thinking with the work, or when a viewer accurately hits on certain chords and releases them from their unnamed status. This is what I also mean by resonance. A work begins, for example, with a throw of the dice. I would take up the element of chance and dwell on the configuration of the dice until their inherent relations rise to visibility and reveal to me something of our encounter. Listening to how things resonate among themselves has led me into totally unforeseen areas. This is where my work markedly differs, for example, from the work of Chris Marker, whom people often evoke together with Ivens, Kubelka, Godard, and (Johan van der) Keuken when commenting on my films. The voice of Marker's films (rather than his installations) is mainly that of a decipherment. A subjectivity is here centralized and the speaking subject is a masterful decoder, whether this subject expresses itself in the first or the third person pronoun, whether indirectly via a fictional character or via a female interlocutor.

It's difficult to pin down the way resonance works without being immediately reductive. But let's say in *A Tale of Love*, the directions love can take and the threads woven with it are indefinite. Kieu, the Vietnamese-American protagonist of the film, is doing research and writing on the afterlife impact of *The Tale of Kieu* in the Vietnamese diaspora. As you see, she and the Vietnamese protagonist who personifies love in the poem[1] have the same name. This is something I obviously play on in the film. For, in love, loyalty and betrayal painfully come together. One can say the same of translation. Conventionally, loyalty has always been in conflict with freedom. To be loyal is to strive for likeness in the reproduction of meaning, while translation also requires that one frees oneself from the all-importance of meaning to bring about the spirit of the original, as Benjamin said, or to let one's language be powerfully affected by the foreign tongue. I would have had to make a film of six to twelve two-hour episodes to *illustrate* faithfully *The Tale of Kieu*, as most viewers from the Vietnamese communities expect. But, instead, I offer them an open "haiku" of *The Tale*, and "betray" what they want to see in the visual rendering of the poem. By simply conceiving "Kieu" not as a name belonging to an individual, not as a character in a story, but as a *situated multiplicity*, a mirror that reflects other mirrors, I have broken loose from the dualistic relation between translator and originator. One can say that placed in the context of the film's treatment of voyeurism, the work of translation turns out to be the work of a crowd, for it involves all active participants—makers, actors, viewers, tools of creation. This takes on a complex dimension, and the links at work can't all be foreseen, since

---

[1] As Trinh writes elsewhere, the film is loosely inspired by *The Tale of Kieu*, the Vietnamese national poem of love, written in the early nineteenth century (Kieu's story was told in 3,254 verses—the poetry and rhythms were drawn from the songs and proverbs of folk tradition). The poem tells of the misfortunes of Kieu, a martyred woman who sacrificed her "purity" and prostituted herself for the good of the family. Vietnamese people (both in Vietnam and in diaspora) see the poem as a mythical biography of the "motherland," marked by internal turbulence and foreign domination. —MZ

resonances are infinite. As I proceeded with the film, it *was* the material-in-progress and love as a multiplicity that worked on me, not the contrary.

One of the links that remain constant throughout the film is certainly that with feminism. As you know, in the late sixties and in the seventies, the second-wave feminists produced a large body of work critical of love. It was the time when the rhetoric of the "sexual revolution" left women in a double bind as to whether they should seek approval in being "a groovy chick" and lose their individuality in the apparatus of sex privatization, or be called names and give up love as their expression of liberty. Shulamith Firestone, for example, wrote at length on this "political of love" and its unequal power context. She carried on arguments advanced some twenty years earlier by De Beauvoir, reintroducing logic in the bedroom, because, as she sustained in her work, women and love are underpinnings; if one starts looking too closely at them, one threatens the very structure of culture. In a situation of profound devotion and of mutual emotional vulnerability, one is easily caught in this pathetic delirium where "she is he," and as De Beauvoir concisely put it, "It was to find herself, to save herself, that she lost herself in him . . . for her the whole of reality is in the other." But that feminists have questioned women's victimization and self-victimization in love does not mean they are blind to forms of love other than sexual love or romantic love. Both Firestone's and De Beauvoir's general definitions of love in their analyses of power inequality have attested to this.

So, it's very difficult today to make a film on love without bearing in mind what feminists have over the years revealed to be the pivot of women's oppression, the place of women's sexploitation and uncritical identification with emotion and sex appeal. Even if you are not a feminist it's still difficult, because in these post-sexual-revolution times, it's hard not to be blasé about love in its expression and representation. Love is said to be "liquid"; anything goes here, because of its die-hard, all-sentimental connotation. One of the familiar pieces of advice given to young poets by their mentors—and here Rainer Maria Rilke comes to mind—is to avoid writing love poems. Love poems, like love stories, are the most difficult to write because it takes maturity to give something of yourself without falling prey to facile forms. That's partly why, in *A Tale of Love*, instead of going directly at it and killing it; or instead of aiming for a "unique," "unheard of," "exceptional-individual love story," I'd rather work with subtle differences in the play of the common with the uncommon, or better, in the dynamics between the overseen, the unseen and for some, the ultraseen. Being open to translatability from its inception, the film—which comes together in an unachieved way—invites unachieved seeings and readings. These have their own blind spots and sharp edges that remain indefinite, all depending on how each viewer engages in a work with multiple entries and exits. We return here to the notion of multiplicity—which for me is clearly related to the notions of difference and resonance. One can also say here that multiplicity is at the heart of both the feminist struggle and the struggle of people of colour.

Z: *This notion of resonance and multiplicity is interesting in terms of people of colour and migrants. For me, one of the things that resonates this multiplicity in* A Tale of Love *is the generational issues Kieu experiences. Kieu is researching and rewriting* The Tale of Kieu, *but she also has to negotiate different sorts of love relationships (with her aunt, her friends, her photographer).*

This raises important questions for children of migrants whose experiences of love and loyalty are quite complicated. I think (from my own writing and experience) there is a way in which you live between two (or three) languages and cultures, and trying to make meaning out of that involves the constant negotiation between past and present lives and cultures. This produces various forms of love, loyalty, and betrayal across and between different cultures and generations. It produces interesting affects (I take affect to mean feelings or emotions)—the multiple emotions that are experienced like love and hate, pleasure and pain, anger, loss, and betrayal . . .

T: Talking about generational issues, there's more recently been something like a new wave of works focusing on love by mature women. June Jordan in poetry; Valie Export, Yvonne Rainer, Mira Nair in film; Julia Kristeva, Teresa de Lauretis, Kaja Silverman in theory; and the list goes on, not to mention others like Clarice Lispector, Marguerite Duras, Helene Cixous, or Assia Djebar for whom love (and death) has always been at the core of writing. In a different gamut of color markers, Love has returned, and with it, the question of loyalty and freedom. This may be very telling about our times, which are those of the migrant self, of mass refugeeism and of forced immigration. Loyalty is commonly thought of as a form of constraint but, as I've mentioned, loyalty and betrayal go together, even though ethically one can be quite negative, the other quite positive. In order to be loyal one has to betray in certain ways, and in order be free one can only be loyal, not the contrary.

The question of freedom would definitely arise if I were to compare my last film to my previous films. The film world tends to see them in terms of documentary and narrative. I see them more as different attitudes towards freedom. Working with largely "non-staged" material led me to conceiving freedom mainly in terms of instant alertness, and of unpremeditated, unrehearsed gestures, which, when pushed to the limits, are able to inscribe the hesitations, the lapses, the blank spaces, the white flares, the in-betweens of events. Whereas working on *A Tale of Love* required a very different way of conceiving freedom. We are dealing here with a scripted itinerary in which every element of the film has been so very carefully thought through that even the notion of "beauty" is contextualized. The tendency is no longer to "go natural," but to fully work with beauty in its artifices and rituals (nonnaturalistic and nonpsychological writing, setting, lighting, acting, editing, camera movement, score composition). This is so as to make of the meticulous filmic arrangement a "ceremony" of love. A critic called *A Tale of Love* "a sensual bombardment"—a very adequate comment, and yet the film is also made to work on more than one level. In the way the film comes together, the relation between each independent element and the whole is never stabilized, for what is involved is not one, but a multiplicity of centers. It can be odd to experience a rigorously built structure whose rigor does not serve any single interest or central purpose. Because of the different ways in which we understand freedom, viewers' first reactions to the film tend to be wildly contradictory. Quite a few viewers coming out from the screening of the film exclaimed "What a freedom!" while others asked "What's experimental about it?" or more relevantly to our inquiry about loyalty and betrayal, "Why this film? Why can't she just go on doing what she's so good at?"

Z: *I was recently rereading* Woman Native Other. *I read it very closely and the language produced a kind of rhythm for me. This was an intense experience. It was creating, what I would call,* *a revolutionary mode of language. I experienced a freedom and loyalty (freedom not in the liberal sense of the word) and betrayal and deception in the writing and my relationship to it. You have talked about your writing elsewhere, but what is the relation of loyalty and betrayal to the passion of writing and your passion in writing.*

T: The notions of rhythm and of foreignness are relevant to both writing and filmmaking even though the realms of activities involved are very different. I don't quite know yet how I'm going to make the link between rhythm and loyalty and betrayal in writing, but your reintroduction of freedom and passion here may help. I have tried many times elsewhere to articulate this notion of rhythm in my work, but I don't think I've even come close to conveying its importance and complexities in our lives and aesthetic experience. I'll give it another try here. Rhythm relegated to the realms of music and poetry is often thought of as a mere arty device, bound to notions of meter, measure, pattern and symmetry; while the sense of rhythm is either reduced to a technical musical ability or mystified as a godsend, that is, a gift one is either naturally endowed with or not at all. For me, such a narrow understanding of rhythm is indicative of the degree to which we revel in ignorance when it comes to non-verbal communication. I would say that rhythm is what basically determines the "quality" of social relationships and of artistic manifestations. What makes a work "inspiring" is not the idea, the vision, the information, the insight, or the craft per se. It is how all these unexpectedly click in, come apart, meet halfway, and so on; in other words, how they do and undo one another in their diversified movements, forming a strong assemblage of *No Thing*, rather than of *nothing*. This is rhythm.

The description you gave of your aesthetic experience (by which I mean a mode of perception) in reading *Woman Native Other* touches very keenly on another basic aspect of what rhythm can do. Rhythm finds resonance in our whole organism; it cannot be consigned to the ear, the hand, the foot or even the eye. Its experience is an experience of both the mind and the body. Its stimulating effect excites one to action; it arouses one's ability to connect, proliferate, and enrich; and it takes one continuously from one association to another. In that sense, rhythm invites the reader's or viewer's collaboration with the writer or filmmaker in bringing about the full resonance of the work. I've often heard from both my enthusiastic and recalcitrant audiences/readers about the recurrent aftermath effects of my works, whose images keep on coming back vividly and with precision, marking them deeply, or staying on with them for weeks, as in the case of the films. For me, this is clearly the work of rhythm. The way one marks the social or artistic moment makes all the difference. One is invited through rhythm to perceive by grouping (impressions and intervals) with precision in time, tonality and intensity; or else, to expand one's attention so as to grasp or to handle a vast amount of materials while engaging in the trajectory of a work.

Rhythm helps both to focus and to disperse without the fear of losing one or the other. But for me, whether something works or not in my films and books would also largely depend on the effortlessness of the rhythm. The grouping, spreading and stressing of relations and intervals have to take shape quite effortlessly; that is, they need not be conspicuous or entirely conscious. I'm not talking here about the fluidity of "phrasing," of interrupting and of assembling; in other words, about the work of editing while creating. Also, I'm not talking about the specific rhythm created with the movements between and within the images, or between image and

sound, for example. All these form the more visible part of an extensive praxis of rhythm. I'm implying an indefinite amount of possible relationships that happen on many levels at once. Rather than having one centralized or hierarchized relationship to which everything else is subordinated, we have here a net of relationships, whose intensities are accented with precision and subtlety mainly to invite other markings and unmarkings. The ability to achieve this effortlessly comes with the love and passion that one has for the "raw" material, the matrix from which things come together or apart, take shape, and dissolve largely on their own accord.

Ultimately, what comes first and foremost with the sense of rhythm is the feeling of freedom. With rhythm, one is free of meter and steady measure; free to play with a recurrent beat, to miss it, or to fill in the gap with one's own beat; free to follow, to leave off or to meander along a trajectory; and free to take in the periodicity of a process in countlessly different ways. Loyalty to a marking and betrayal of this very marking are both necessary, artistically as well as culturally and politically speaking. Rhythm as a determinant of the intricacy and beauty of relationships leads us back to love and passion, with its loyalties and dis-loyalties. You have chosen to focus on the passion in writing and the relationship between writer and writing. Freedom here would also refer to the difference between and within; to the element of foreignness; or to the third ground mentioned earlier. Again, is the encounter between interviewer and interviewee an encounter of languages? of cultures? or of rhythms? Fidelity to one's vocation means that somewhere along the line, at one moment or another, one is bound to break with many conformities. For Maurice Blanchot, the essence of infidelity lies in its "unlimited power of dispersion." It was in the terms of a fidelity to this power and an infidelity to herself that he linked Virginia Woolf's insecurity and agony as a writer to her talent, her passions and her chosen death.

Passion can be a driving force for writing; but in writing, passion with its illogical blindness and lucidity becomes legible and intelligible. I've already written at length on the difficult relation of woman to language, that is to a social contract, when, for her, to align a trace on the page is to recognize the trace of His traces. To be a writer and a feminist (among other things) is to assume one's marginality and to become a foreigner to one's own language, community, and identity. Writing, as Kristeva has affirmed, "is impossible without some kind of exile." This is why, for me, to make a film on love is no doubt to betray (one's) love. One can only fulfill the task by stubbornly turning around Love, looking as a foreigner at its surfaces, and refusing, as I wrote in Woman Native, Other, to perforate meaning—an act as crippled as that of ripping open the mother's womb to verify the sex of an unborn child. A Tale of Love has no use for psychological realism or for perspective and depth of field. Its images are insistently frontal and "realistically" two-dimensional; and the actors are not so much characters as they are signs, bodies, voices; in short, multiplicities. The illusion of three-dimensionality in a two-dimensional medium being rejected, what is finally projected on the screen is unequivocally the surfaces of passion.

Production of A Tale of Love. Upper: Trinh T. Minha-ha at sound mixing studio. Lower left: Trinh T. Minh-ha and Tracey Thompson. Lower right: Jean-Paul Bourdier and Lana Bernberg.

I feel great affinity with Marguerite Duras' remark that after the premiere of her film *India Song*, she had the impression of being dispossessed, not only of a given area, a place, her habitat, but even of her identity. In making the film she realized she had killed Anne-Marie Stretter, the protagonist of her film and book. Stretter was also the woman whom she had known from her time in Vietnam and whose power of death had obsessed her to the point that it was what kept her writing moving until the release of *India Song*. She had to kill Stretter for the film to materialize; it was her utmost gift to this film, whose story is also that of a *dead* woman. Both betrayal and loyalty are here poignantly at work. The question of dispossession and of foreignness leads me back to your question on migrants and immigrants, which is an area also dealt with in *A Tale of Love*, as you've pointed out. It is through the politics of denationalizing the refugee and the emigré, that a person-who-leaves becomes normalized, being systematically compelled to undergo the process of giving up their home, their country, their language, their identity, their proper name. In order to be accepted, one has to abandon one's unwanted self. In order to belong anew, one has to take the oath of loyalty, which entails dis-loyalty to one's home nation and identity. Hardly have the newcomers reached the host territory that they're made to experience the mutilation of their name which, if not entirely changed, can only survive in fragments—shortened, mispelled, mispronounced, or replaced by an equivalent. In this denationalization of the foreigner, we can better grasp the complexity of loyalty and betrayal in relation to love, to freedom, to one's own subjectivity. . . .

Z: *This is what interests me, the ways in which one's subjectivity moves through different levels of love, loyalty, and betrayal. And, that you can't always reconcile these relations, because you are forced into a false sense of loyalty and fidelity when you enter into another language, nation, culture.* . . .

T: Even if you stay in the same place all your life and speak the same language, you cannot avoid the processes of change. The importance of a language's growth and renewal has been a well debated issue in translation. Words take on a new life, expand, shift, suspend, become trite, decline, and die within a language. But perhaps such a maturing process becomes all the more destabilizing when it intermingles with processes of hybridization and of deterritorialization, as in the case of migrants, marginals, and women. To unsettle what tends to be naturalized, to return to emotion without simply reviving the old discourse of passion and love, or to write differently, one needs to fare—whether in one's own language or in the adopted language—as a nomad and a foreigner. For example, in *A Tale of Love*, you know going through the film that there's hardly any "tale" in the conventional sense of the term. "Tale" as used in the title of the nineteenth century poem (*The Tale of Kieu*) means something quite different from *Tale* as used in the title of my film, which situates itself at the end of the twentieth century. For me, rather than connoting a narrative of legendary events enchantingly composed for amusement, *A Tale of Love* carries the term in its modern connotation, implying a series of fictitiously related events or a fabricated story. Rather than being fabulous, the tale has grown to be a fabulation. The emphasis is on the making and on the fabricated nature of the work; and since in this case, a relationship is drawn between Tale and Love, what is also evoked is the problematic nature of both terms.

Z: *I am thinking about this movement from within language, that being foreign to a language comes from the inside, as well as from the outside. I find this interesting in terms of how I translate myself between different languages (Greek and English) and how I move between them with some difficulty (some times I lack the rhythm in languages, I feel "tone" deaf to the musicality of words and the rhythms they produce). To enable yourself this freedom—to see yourself as foreign to language from the inside and the outside is liberating. The notion of fabulation and the nation that you raise, how fiction operates in relation to language opens up another relation to love and freedom. And, maybe, the way we make meaning in everyday existence is partly through stories and fiction—and this allows for a freedom and movement in language.*

T: I remember how I've once provoked a violent reaction from an anthropologist in an informal gathering by talking of the nation in terms of fiction. Such a reaction is after all very common among those whose rationality and discourse on the modern state still hold on desperately to the fact-versus-fiction dichotomy. But as respected scientists around the world have been repeating, science cannot do without poetry. The idea of the nation as a homogeneous and anonymous whole is quite obsolete, as the current political situation in the world has amply confirmed. The dictum "many voices, one people," which was meant to convey the cohesion of the "many *as* one" can only be used today to convey the heterogeneity of the "many *in* one." The totalitarian discourse, pedagogy, and perfomance of nationalism may still have a strategical value in certain specific contexts and political languages, but grand narratives have lost their impact as they continue to be contested by storytelling in the margins. Hence, when it comes to the political consciousness of women, refugees and émigrés, or of the diasporas of color, recognizing the notions of nation, country, or community as being above all a fiction, a narration, and a fabulation (that is, a product of language) is emphasizing the constructed nature of cultural authority. It is a way of questioning established power relationships and of giving agency to the oppressed. What is naturalized can be denaturalized. And since stories are made, they can be unmade and remade.

This movement of multiple grafting and "fasting" in language, of turning an oppressive expression against itself, of deflecting words from their homely meaning, or of mistrusting them as one mistrusts an "alien" is certainly nothing new among marginalized groups. In the impossibility of speaking or writing otherwise, you're bound to create a language within a language or to pollute, contaminate, and "im-purify" the dominant language. Jean Genet's obsession with betrayal has largely to do with a sense of not belonging (being "different" from his peers, as a thinker, a poet, an aesthete, and a homosexual). He went as far as to make this cruel but astute statement: "Treachery is beautiful if it makes us sing." As in my writing, I've been speaking of myself all along here, without speaking only of myself. The translator, in Barbara Johnson's term, is a faithful bigamist whose loyalties are split between a native and a foreign language. I feel more like a polyandrist, being torn between the use of Vietnamese, French, and English, while loving also Spanish and German—two languages that I don't speak fluently, but which oddly enough, I often use and confuse in my dreams. I've always been fascinated by the physical and musical impact of languages. For example, I remember little of Wolof, which I've learnt from the years I lived in Senegal, but its inflection and modulation strongly remain with me—the way people nonchalantly suspend the end of their sentences or use sharp onomatopeias to express a range of feelings.

Needless to say, a body is a resonating tool and individuals are vibrating mechanisms. You certainly "feel someone's vibes," just as you respond to the deep resonance of a voice. It is through spoken languages that you hear the music of a person and a people. Our language and music are our identity. The issue of whether to nationalize a native language or to continue to use the colonizer's language remains an important issue in many contexts of the Third World and the diaspora—one that concerned writers have debated at length in their works. To be trilingual, for example, means to be triply faithful *and* unfaithful to the languages that define oneself and one's activity. The place of identity being a place of radical multiplicity, as I've suggested elsewhere, the question is no longer: *Who* am I? or *What* language should I abide by? But *Which* self? *Which* language? *When, where* and *how* am I? Foreignness is both a space of confinement and a space of non-conformity. Again, it is very difficult to be a stranger, but it is even more so to stop being one.

"What the voyeur is looking for and finds is a shadow behind the curtain."

Dialogue between voyeur and voyeur after a screening of
A Tale of Love:

—*I don't like it, the man and his voyeurism. I don't like the role. It's too evident.*
—*His or hers?*
—*Well, his of course. I mean the photographer.*
—*She's a woman.*
—*I don't understand . . . I mean, the man who photographs that pin-up on the motocycle. What's his name already?*
—*The photographer for the film is a woman. Two women and a man.*
—*What do you mean, two women? They are both models. He's the man, the photographer.*
—*Are you so sure the photographer is a man? It may appear so ultimately. But who's he? The photographer in the film, Alikan, who is a man, or the photographers of the film— the director who is a woman, the codirector who is a man and the director of photography who is a woman, not to mention all the women camera assistants. And what about you? I'm Alikan. We are Alikan.*
—*Oooh! Isn't that fascinating . . . I hated Alikan.*

"When we were in love I didn't know that love happened much more precisely when there was not what we then called love. The neuter of love, that is what we were experiencing, and what we rejected . . . and we called that nothing an interval"
                                                                    —*Clarice Lispector*

INDEX